EMERGENCY PROCEDURES

Taken from:

Understanding Terrorism and Managing the Consequences
by Paul M. Maniscalco and Hank T. Christen

Mass Casualty and High-Impact Incidents: An Operations Guide
by Hank Christen and Paul M. Maniscalco

PEARSON
Custom
Publishing

PEARSON
Prentice
Hall

PEARSON CUSTOM PUBLISHING
75 Arlington Street, Suite 300, Boston, MA 02116
A Pearson Education Company

Contents

Part I

Understanding Terrorism and Managing the Consequences

1
Terrorism: Meeting the Challenge

James P. Denney
Paul M. Maniscalco
Hank T. Christen
Frank J. Cilluffo

Source: Courtesy AP/Wide World Photos

Chapter Objectives

After reading this chapter, you will be able to accomplish the following objectives:

1. Understand the critical concept of local preparedness for terrorism/tactical violence response.
2. Have an overview of the federal agencies in the national response spectrum.
3. Recognize the changing history and threat evolution of terrorism.
4. Discuss the capabilities and limitations of local response systems.
5. Understand the risk to responders in the modern terrorism environment.
6. Recognize the differences between advanced trauma life support protocols and casualty care in the urban combat environment.
7. Outline the key concepts in a mass fatality management plan.

Organized Terrorism

In the past, what was referred to as an "international terrorist network" was attributed to the Tricontinental Congress held in Havana, Cuba, in January 1966. At that congress, 500 delegates proposed close cooperation among socialist countries and national liberation movements in order to forge a global strategy to counter "American imperialism."

Meetings among terrorist organizations increased in the years that followed. Examples of networking include the American Black Panther leaders who toured North Korea, Vietnam, and China. In China, they had an opportunity to meet with Shirley Graham, wife of W.E.B. Du Bois, who was visiting with Zhou Enlai.[1] The network advanced terrorism on global, national, and regional levels by providing economic support, training, specialty personnel, and advanced weaponry. For example, in 1978 Argentine terrorists received Soviet-made rockets from Palestinian terrorists and the Baader-Meinhof group supplied three sets of American night vision binoculars to the IRA and American-made hand grenades to the Japanese Red Army. Terrorist training camps sprang up in Cuba, Algeria, Iraq, Jordan, Lebanon, Libya, and South Yemen, while Syria provided sites for advanced training.

Acts of terrorism had prompted the Tokyo and Montreal conventions of 1963 and 1971 on hijacking and sabotage of civilian aircraft. This was followed by the 1973 convention on crimes against diplomats, and the 1979 convention on hostage taking sponsored by The Hague. These conventions established categories of international crimes that are punishable by any state regardless of the nationality of the criminal, victim, or the location of the offense.

Following President Reagan's ordering of U.S. military forces to attack "terrorist-related" targets in Libya in 1986, seven Western industrial democracies pledged themselves to take joint action against terrorism. Those nations include the United States, Germany, Great Britain, Italy, Canada, France, and Japan. These nations agreed to deny terrorist suspects entry into their countries, to bring about better cooperation between police and security forces in their countries, to place restrictions on diplomatic missions suspected of being involved in terrorism, and to cooperate in a number of other ways.

The Cold War Ends, Threat Shifting Begins

The breakup of the former Soviet Union and its subsequent economic collapse significantly altered the global security landscape. At the time of the breakup, the Soviet Union was a superpower with well-developed nuclear, chemical, and biological warfare capabilities.[2] Unfortunately, a newer, more sinister threat has begun to emerge from the former Soviet Union, a thriving international black market in arms and weapons technology.

The economic collapse of the Soviet Union is manifesting in the nations' inability to meet their fiscal obligations, including military and other payrolls. As a result, Russia is suffering a tumultuous period with an ever present threat of coup d'état and organized crime emerging as a significant influencing factor within their domestic and international affairs.

With available weapons ranging from "suitcase" nuclear devices to submarines and MIGs to missiles, the former controlled threat has been transformed into an uncontrolled threat market strongly influenced by the Russian Mafia, a market where unpaid government employees have already attempted to sell limited amounts of fissionable material and other articles or substances that are of value to terrorist organizations.

In addition to the black market in weapons, there also exists a potential for weapon thefts, including those weapons stored at poorly guarded chemical and biological storage facilities located throughout the former Soviet Union and its satellite nations.

A New Threat Emerges

The Middle East region has emerged as the primary contributor of personnel, funding, training, and arms for the current terrorist movement. Unlike the Marxist-Leninist of the 1960s and 1970s, who were motivated by political and social conditions,[3] today's international terrorism is an amalgam consisting of anarchist-nihilist and Middle Eastern religious-based fundamentalists who despise American hegemony and the resulting influence on world policy. Bent specifically on the destruction of American values, influence, and economy, they have targeted U.S. interest worldwide.[4]

Globalization

Globalization[5] is changing the context in which terrorists operate. A transnational cast of characters that, in most cases, cannot be directly controlled by governments, either individually or collectively, increasingly affects even so-called domestic terrorism. Information technology has effectively removed the ability of countries to isolate themselves. Information and communication control is difficult, if not impossible, to achieve because the information revolution has resulted in a democratic access to technology. Two important results are that the terrorists' prospect base has expanded exponentially and free speech and civil liberty have been given an inexpensive international medium with which to voice discontent.

The notional concept of a centrally controlled international terrorist network, previously investigated during the 1960s and 1970s, was deemed to be unlikely due to conflicting ideologies, motivating factors, funding, and arming and training among global practitioners. However, networks are now quite possible with the advent of public access to the Internet, the ability to transfer funds and conduct banking electronically, the international arms market, encrypted digital communication technology, and the emergence of "state-less" terrorism. An important result is that instant global communication between offensive action cells and their controllers are now possible. Controllers now have global reach and can run multiple independent cells from a single location with no interaction between the cells. They can also contract terrorism services utilizing mercenaries composed of local indigenous practitioners in a given target community.

Technology has also resulted in a reduced requirement for infrastructure, security, and detection avoidance and has resulted in an asymmetry between cause and effect. The complexity of weapons acquisition, production, transportation, lethality, and delivery platform has been diminished.

Critical Factor: The historical, organizational, operational, and behavioral complexities posed by terrorist organizations are numerous. Although the previous section was designed to provide minimal clarity and foundation for the background material, it is only a snowflake on the tip of an iceberg. We encourage continued acquaintance with these issues by conducting in-depth research via any of the numerous comprehensive texts that were developed to address these topics.

FIGURE 1-1   Walt Disney helped design this gas mask for American children during WWII. *Source:* Courtesy Soldier Biological Chemical Command (SBCCOM)

Preparing for Threats Involving Weapons of Mass Destruction

The 1993 bombing of the New York City World Trade Center and the 1995 bombing of the Alfred P. Murrah Federal Building in Oklahoma City clearly illustrated America's vulnerability to terrorism—not only abroad, but to the homeland as well. These acts demonstrate the willingness and ability of determined terrorists to carry out attacks against high-impact targets. The March 1995 sarin gas incident in the Tokyo subway demonstrated their willingness to kill several thousand in a single event.

Twenty-first century threat evolution will require public safety and emergency service organizations to reevaluate their priorities and consider their ability to address multiple new tasks.[6] These tasks include support for new and emerging technologies; the increasing significance of resource linking and specialization; and a better understanding of issues such as the threat environment including terrorism, drugs, gangs, and crime. These changes, coupled with severe budgetary pressures to reduce costs and find more efficient ways to carry out their responsibilities, force these organizations to exercise greater care in matching available resources to priorities and to integrate political power with economic requirements.

To meet these challenges effectively, emergency service organizations must address flaws in their procedures for allocating personnel and financial resources to meet developing priorities and objectives, including training problems, staffing, and the inadequate integration of multifunction components. Unfortunately, these tasks will be made more difficult by past management reforms such as decentralization and the devolution of decision making to lower level administrative units that have resulted in the development of new multilevel policy systems.

Emergency Medical Services

Pre-hospital health care no longer consists of a simple emergency transportation service. Since the early 1970s, new levels of training have added to what was basically a first aid and transportation system. It is now known as the emergency medical service (EMS) system. The EMS system provides a sequential process that includes patient problem recognition, system access, basic and advanced intervention by first responders and bystanders, and transportation to the hospital, if necessary, by ambulance. The advent of this system completed the public safety management triad of law enforcement and crime prevention, fire prevention and suppression, and emergency medical care and transportation.

Pre-hospital health care has changed significantly with the advent of specialized emergency medical technician (EMT) and EMT-paramedic (EMT-P) training. Capabilities now include responding to the public need with mobile intensive care units, and providing specialized advance life-support measures when necessary.

Public safety EMS is available nationwide and is provided by private and public agencies. The management and provision of the service provided by them represents a sizable investment in training, human resources, supplies, and equipment. The ability to utilize various system delivery models has made it possible for agencies and communities of all sizes to participate in this vital public service.

Complex Organizational Capability

In the fire service, distribution of the workload is not characterized solely by volume nor is it completely configuration dependent. In order for the fire service to maintain its robust capability, it vertically integrates multiple competencies and each individual resource is configured for multitasking. Within the fire service, where consequence management is the fundamental imperative, "high-performance" is measured by organizational effectiveness in the areas of preparedness levels, community loss prevention and reduction, and decreased mortality and morbidity.[7]

Through integrated stability, the American fire service provides both high reliability and high trust to its constituency. High reliability organizations are complex, and complexity mitigates risk. High reliability organizations use organizational structure to adapt and then mitigate events through processes such as risk awareness, decision migration, and process auditing.

As a result of budget corrections, operational adjustments, and technological advances that began in the early 1990s, the twenty-first century American fire service will emerge as a complex, precision force that possesses the nation's dominant body of knowledge regarding emergency service consequence management.

Complex Interface Development

Interface complexities involving multiple interdependent agencies, external resources, and federal assets can be mitigated through the implementation of a standard, multipurpose event management system that conforms to the scope and type of event and the capabilities of responding agencies. Although variations of this event management system exist, it has not yet been fully implemented within the inclusive public safety-emergency service amalgam.

UNREALISTIC EXPECTATION

Notional concepts, including the all-hazards capability, are unrealistic, unproven, and dangerous. The assumption that a local emergency resource is capable of managing an event equivalent to that found in military warfare could potentially result in the loss of significant operational assets and personnel and place the community at catastrophic risk.

Contemporary training is invariably conducted in daylight, in good weather, and consistently results in a positive outcome. The ability to survive a given operation is not addressed and casualties, if any, are attributed to the civilian population at risk. Training must now include an ability-to-survive-operation (ATSO) component and measures to implement when conventional practices fail.

Threat Issues

Since 1992, direct physical threats aimed at America's EMS, police, and fire responders have begun to emerge with increasing frequency. These threats specifically target first responders and public safety personnel. These tactics appear similar to those espoused in *The Minimanual of the Urban Guerrilla*, written by Carlos Marighella in 1969, which states in part:

> *Thus, the armed struggle of the urban guerrilla points towards two essential objectives:*
>
> 1. *The physical elimination of the leaders and assistants of the armed forces and of the police;*
> 2. *The expropriation of government resources and the wealth belonging to the rich businessmen, the large landowners and the imperialists, with small expropriations used for the sustenance of the individual guerrillas and large ones for the maintenance of the revolutionary organization itself.*
>
> *It is clear that the armed struggle of the urban guerrilla also has other objectives. But here we are referring to the two basic objectives, above all expropriation. It is necessary for every urban guerrilla to always keep in mind that he can only maintain his existence if he is able to kill the police and those dedicated to repression, and if he is determined—truly determined—to expropriate the wealth of the rich businessmen, landowners and imperialists.*

The threats are tactical violence[8] and 911 target acquisition.[9] These threats have four applications:

1. To control the criminal environment
2. To divert law enforcement attention
3. To kill or injure law enforcement personnel
4. To compel law enforcement-assisted suicide

Tactical Violence

Since the 1992 Los Angeles civil disturbance, a disturbing phenomenon that directly affects emergency service providers has surfaced. The phenomenon has been identified as tactical violence.

Tactical violence is primarily employed by criminals. It is defined as the predetermined use of maximum violence in order to achieve one's criminal goals, regardless of victim cooperation, level of environmental threat to the perpetrator, or the need to evade law enforcement or capture. This method also usually results in physical or psychological injury or death to the victim. The rationale for employing tactical violence is predatory control of the immediate criminal environment through the creation of chaos and the infliction of terror, trauma, and death on presenting targets.

911 Target Acquisition

One tactic utilized by the criminal and extremist elements (including but not limited to militias, white supremacists, environmentalists, animal rights activists, and anti-abortionists) is 911 target acquisition. This tactic has been employed for the following purposes:[10]

- to divert public safety resources prior to, during, or after the commission of criminal acts
- to draw resources into an ambush situation
- to draw resources into environments laced with improvised explosive antipersonnel devices
- to compel law enforcement-assisted suicide

Although these threats primarily target law enforcement organizations (crisis managers), fire and EMS first responders (consequence managers) have the highest exposure by virtue of their response configuration and resource staffing levels.[11] Recovering from these events can take up to one year, during which time the community's vulnerability to all hazards is significantly increased.

Covert Intimidation

Local and federal law enforcement agencies are not the same as military units and rely to some extent on the intimidation factor. The primary goal of law enforcement is crime prevention/control. There are many subtle intimidation strategies incorporated into this function that have a psychological impact on the community, including vehicle color schemes and emergency lighting configuration, uniform design and color, the visible wearing of side arms, and officer bearing and demeanor.

Overt Intimidation

Law enforcement special teams include special weapons and tactics (SWAT) and hostage response team (HRT). These units are semi-militarized and affect quasi-military status through the wearing of military-like/special operations/commando garb. They carry special weaponry and devices not seen in routine law enforcement operations. Their presence at an incident is an implied threat to targeted perpetrators and demonstrates the capacity to employ overwhelming force and special aggressive tactics if necessary.

Overt intimidation tactics have been adopted in other areas as well, such as the serving of high-risk warrants or drug raids. It is common to see various law enforcement agencies entering a suspect dwelling en masse creating confusion, shouting commands, and displaying drawn weapons. Although intimidation may play a roll in deterring terrorist activity, it will not be a factor once crisis management transitions into consequence management.

Outcome Training

Local law enforcement is not trained to participate against sustained armed resistance with an opposing force without external support.

In all cases, law enforcement personnel are trained in a manner that results in a positive outcome for them on any given incident. Although vulnerability, danger, and personal risk are discussed, it is presented in general terms suggesting that, although they exist, it is unlikely that they will occur to a particular individual if training is followed.

Special aggressor teams such as SWAT and HRT are trained to conduct assaults if necessary in order to affect closure of a particular incident. However, this training implies that an assault is both inclusive and conclusive relative to a given criminal problem. This means inclusive of all threats and conclusive once the threat is neutralized. An example is to gain entry and subdue/arrest/kill perpetrators and/or rescue hostages.

Unlike the military, law enforcement agencies are not prepared to conduct an assault in the face of withering automatic weapons fire, rocket-propelled grenades (RPGs), hand grenades, claymores, mortars, or other similar type weaponry. This is especially true if they incur substantial casualties among their personnel. They must rely instead on special teams for this type of activity (England discovered this during an IRA assault against Parliament, as well as the Los Angeles police department during the North Hollywood bank robbery). Nor are law enforcement agencies, whose primary objective is the safety of its personnel, prepared to conduct operations against a sustained, widespread, or diffuse hostile faction operating from several venues simultaneously. These groups have no acceptable loss provisions.

Acts of terrorism perpetrated against society present many problems to those charged with crisis and consequence management response. An act of terrorism is similar to other man-made disasters in that the main characteristic is sudden onset and the resultant effect is significant human injury and/or death. Because of the nature of the incident, in many cases, there is no opportunity for crisis management or intervention.

These incidents, by their nature, are not telegraphed in advance to the authorities and therefore, the appropriate response may consist solely of consequence management and criminal investigation. To the consequence manager, these responses may represent the greatest challenge that can be faced by an emergency agency.

To begin with, the physical impact of a "conventional" terrorist incident is characterized by rapid onset. Unlike a common conventional response, where initial units are dispatched and the event accelerates or expands based on the observation and assessment of first arriving companies, conventional terrorist incidents require an immediate maximal response of appropriate resources in order to optimize the survivability of victims.

This may indicate that a new standard or ad hoc response configuration is necessary for terrorism incidents—one that combines emergency medical care providers, hazardous materials management, and search and rescue capability with conventional resources on the initial dispatch to specific types of incidents.

Federal Asset, First Responder Integration

The Marine Corps Chemical Biological Incident Response Force (CBIRF) responds to incidents involving weapons of mass destruction (WMD) in support of local responders. Their mission is to deploy domestically or overseas to provide force protection and/or mitigation and to assist federal, state, and local responders in developing training programs to manage the consequences of a WMD event.[12]

The National Guard originally commissioned 10 WMD civil support teams (CST),[13] formerly known as rapid assessment and initial detection teams (RAID Teams),[14] consisting of 22 full-time members of the Army and Air National Guard. At the direction of the U.S. Congress, the Department of Defense commissioned an additional 17 teams. With this addition, the total number of states with WMD-CST capabilities is 27. The teams are stationed in Alaska, Arizona, Arkansas, California (two CSTs), Colorado, Florida, Georgia, Hawaii, Idaho, Illinois, Iowa, Kentucky, Louisiana, Maine, Massachusetts, Minnesota, Missouri, New Mexico, New York, Ohio, Oklahoma, Pennsylvania, South Carolina, Texas, Virginia, and Washington. The teams will deploy, on request or based upon mutual aid agreements, to assist local responders in determining the nature of an attack, provide medical and technical advice, and prepare the way for identification and the arrival of follow-on federal response assets.

Both of these response components will integrate with local responders through implementation of the incident management system. With the establishment of a unified command, a fully capable civil-federal management team will oversee management and operations of combined assets in weapons of mass destruction and other events impacting communities in the United States.

Although these external assets along with other federal agencies (other divisions of the Department of Defense, Department of Health and Human Services, Centers for Disease Control, Federal Emergency Management Agency, and Public Health Service) will respond to assist the primary impact, the response to the aftermath of an event remains the responsibility of local communities. It is critical that this facet is not lost in the planning process due to the reliance on federal response and capacity. Managers, chief officers, planners, and elected officials must remain cognizant of the critical factor that the arrival of these assets are time and distance limited. In many cases, depending on the proximity of federal resource stationing and/or the availability of aircraft with appropriate lift capacity, it can be many hours or perhaps days prior to arrival and full operational activity.

Physical Constraints

It is not unusual for terrorist incidents to involve structural collapse, multiple casualties, fire, and chemical release. Is there a difference between a terrorist act and a conventional incident? Aside from the possible psychological factors, not to the consequence manager, who must implement operations based on the present state of the event rather than the precipitating factors. Therefore, attribution is not a consequence priority. Regardless of motivation, both function as casualty generators that result in short-term resource commitment on a large scale. Both have the potential to cause collateral injury to responders and, by their nature, generally do not afford an opportunity for crisis management or intervention prior to the event.

However, because terrorism is a deliberate act, these incidents may present unique hazards to response personnel. For example, it would not be unusual for terrorists to plan secondary events that target emergency responders; events that can be triggered once emergency operations begin and responders are most vulnerable to attack. Therefore, although the results of a terrorist act may not be different than a conventional incident, the approach to them must be.

Aggressive response to these incidents must be curtailed. Courage, valor, honor, and integrity are not issues in these instances. Any response to suspected terrorist acts must be moderated and coupled with careful consideration of any potential secondary threats to responders and the general public.

Political Constraints

Terrorism is both a federal and a state crime. However, all incidents are manifested locally and initial reaction to them will be provided by local crisis and consequence organizations. As these incidents expand, they will involve multiple organizations. Therefore, both at the planning and response level, local crisis and consequence managers must interact with external entities with, in some cases, broader authority over the incident and in other cases, with near equal power but radically different missions, perceptions and value systems. They must also cooperate with political crisis managers and co-response organizations from within a unified command structure.

Political, strategic, operational, and tactical direction is necessary in every case of joint or combined force operations. Political direction will set

FIGURE 1-2 2000 National Commission on Terrorism Report. *Source:* Courtesy National Commission on Terrorism

political objectives, define basic strategy to achieve these objectives, and provide basic guidance for operations. Strategic direction will define desired operational target conditions and sequencing. Operational direction will coordinate the efforts of multiple organizations to achieve a successful outcome. Tactical direction will issue orders to the front-end operators actually engaged in problem resolution.

These unusual circumstances may result in the consequence manager's inability to manage the incident effectively, particularly if the responding organizations do not have a familiar, working relationship. It is therefore imperative that all responsible organizations plan, organize, and conduct training within a single incident management system/incident command system (IMS/ICS) and that individual organizational roles and responsibilities be clearly defined and agreed upon prior to an event and preferably during a comprehensive planning process.

Ethical Constraints

In unconventional terrorist incidents involving WMDs such as chemical, biological, or radiological agents, local agency limitations may preclude response into an impacted area. Therefore, the interval to intervention time will increase. This will be one of the more difficult concepts for emergency managers to instill in their personnel.

However, the current response capability of specialized federal resources is limited by geographic/regional time constraints and may not be available for the better part of a day. Additionally, the medical community currently has no capability to manage mass care for local populations.

Under these circumstances, the function of emergency response organizations may be to limit environmental expansion of the incident if possible, protect the unaffected population through evacuation, and establish shelters or safe havens capable of providing for basic human needs.

Because of potential delays in access to unconventional incident sites involving WMD, the critical interval to intervention time may be protracted. Therefore, the survivability potential for victims will diminish. Prolonged waiting times will increase mortality and the consequence manager may have to consider the implementation of disaster mortuary plans a priority once the site becomes accessible.

Unconventional incidents involving WMDs are likely to convert from EMS/fire/rescue incidents to body recovery, identification, and disposal operations in cooperation with criminal investigative organizations. This final fact, as observed in the Oklahoma City bombing, will have a tremendous psychological impact on emergency response personnel who are neither trained nor experienced in mass fatality management.

Evolution and Application of the IMS to Terrorism, Tactical Violence, and Civil-Military Coordination

The IMS began as a fire-fighting system for managing California wildfires. The system has now expanded into an all-hazard (all-risk) system and is employed at routine emergencies as well as natural disasters, technological disasters, and mass casualty incidents.

The IMS is designed to manage operations and coordinate resources. It is a functionally based system structured on the principles of common terminology, resource allocation, support functions, span of control, and chain of command. The IMS structure is based on a management staff that directs and supports four major sections. The management staff consists of an incident manager, a liaison officer, safety officer, and public information officer. The four sections are operations, logistics, planning, and administration.

The IMS is very similar to the military organization of NATO countries. The military staff positions of intelligence, logistics, and plans/operations closely parallel the four civilian IMS sections. The civilian system also utilizes a liaison officer and the concept of unified command to integrate with a military counterpart. This is an effective boilerplate for military support to civil authorities (MSCA) and coordination during a terrorism/tactical violence incident.

The mass casualty aspect of IMS makes it effective for managing terrorism/tactical violence incidents. For mass casualties, a medical branch is assigned to the operations section, and manages a triage unit, treatment unit, and a transportation unit. The system stresses early triage and transport of critical patients, and scene safety for the rescuers.

In the terrorism/tactical violence arena, the common weapons are still automatic weapons and improvised explosive devices (IED). A chemical attack is managed by an extension of the hazardous material IMS, with emphasis on detection, personal protective equipment, and patient decontamination. A biological attack has a delayed onset, and presents special problems relating to recognition, pathogen identification, treatment protocols, and personal protection.

Hospital Emergency Incident Command System

The Hospital Emergency Incident Command System (HEICS)[15] is a management tool modeled after the ICS. The core of the HEICS is comprised of two main elements: (1) an organizational chart with a clearly delineated chain of command and position function titles indicating scope of responsibility, and (2) a prioritized job action sheet (job description) that assists the designated individual in focusing upon their assignment.

The benefits of a medical facility using HEICS will be seen not only in a more organized response, but also in the ability of that institution to relate to other health care entities and public/private organizations in the event of an emergency incident. The value of the common communication language in HEICS will become apparent when mutual aid is requested of or for that facility.

The California Earthquake Preparedness Guidelines for Hospitals served as a cornerstone in the development of the HEICS. The HEICS has attempted to embody those same characteristics that make the ICS so appealing. Those attributes include the following:

1. Responsibility-oriented chain of command
2. Wide acceptance through commonality of mission and language
3. Applicability to varying types and magnitudes of emergency events
4. Expeditious transfer of resources within a system or between facilities
5. Flexibility in implementation of individual sections or branches of the HEICS
6. Minimal disruption to existing hospital departments

The HEICS includes an organizational chart showing a chain of command, which incorporates four sections under the overall leadership of an emergency incident commander (IC). Each of the four sections: Logistics,

Planning, Finance, and Operations, has a chief appointed by the IC responsible for the section. The chiefs in turn designate officers to subfunctions, with managers and coordinators filling other crucial roles.

Each of the 36 roles has prioritized job action sheets describing the important assignments of each person. Each job action sheet also includes a mission statement to define the position responsibility. The end product is a management system with personnel who know what they should do, when they should do it, and who to report it to during a time of emergency.

FEMA First Responder Nuclear, Biological, and Chemical Awareness Training

As a result of the changing nature of global politics and the increasing threat of terrorism, new information, training, and technology have begun to emerge. The ability of first responders to recognize and manage acts of terrorism has become essential. The First Responder Terrorism Program is an integral component of national preparedness. It is an introductory class developed for, and directed to, emergency service first responders, specifically fire, hazardous materials, and EMS providers. The secondary audience for this program would include members of law enforcement, emergency management, military, disaster response organizations, public health, and public works.

Metropolitan Medical Response System (MMRS)

Most nuclear, biological, and chemical events will present a relatively limited opportunity for the successful rescue of viable victims (usually no more than 3 hours). However, the more expeditious and aggressive the actions taken in the initial stages of the event, the more victims will be recovered that can be decontaminated, treated, and transported to medical facilities.

The MMRS was developed to provide support for, and to provide assistance to, local jurisdiction first responders in nuclear, biological, or chemical (NBC) terrorist incidents.[16] The MMRS has a strong emergency medical care focus and has the capability to provide rapid and comprehensive medical intervention to casualties of NBC events.

MMRS development was based upon providing a coordinated response to NBC incidents in a metropolitan environment. Special emphasis is placed on the ability to identify the specific agent involved and provide the earliest possible correct medical intervention for victims of these situations.

The MMRS is a specially trained and locally available NBC incident response team. These teams consist of 43 persons comprising five major functional elements: medical information and research, field medical operations, hospital operations, law enforcement, and logistics.

The MMRS is organized, staffed, and equipped to provide the best possible pre-hospital and emergency medical care throughout the course of an incident, and especially while on the scene. Medical personnel are responsible for providing the earliest possible medical intervention for the responders and civilian victims of NBC incidents through early identification of the agent type and proper administration of the appropriate antidote(s) and other pharmaceuticals as necessary.

It is not the intent of the field medical operations unit or hospital operations unit to be freestanding medical resources at the incident. However, they are part of the first line of intervention in a chain that stretches from the field to the local hospital medical system. It may be necessary for the hospital operations unit to contact local hospitals by telephone to give advice on decontamination procedures for convergent victims, for agent treatment protocols, and other information as requested by medical facilities.

Casualty Care in the Combat Environment

Unlike the military, civil first responders are not trained with consideration for the ability to survive a given operation. Civil mission priority does not prospectively accept personnel losses, and no first responder organization includes an acceptable loss ratio as part of their mission goal or planning efforts.

First responders are currently trained to manage trauma based on the principles of trauma care taught in the advanced trauma life support (ATLS) course, a standardized approach to trauma care. However, there are issues inherent in the ATLS training program relative to its appropriateness and application in the combat environment:

- It assumes hospital diagnostics and therapeutics can be accessed rapidly.
- It does not presuppose delayed transportation.
- It has no tactical context.

ATLS does not take into consideration the issues of care under fire, in complete darkness, various environmental factors, and delays to definitive care or command decisions.[17]

Tactical care objectives include turning casualties into patients, preventing additional casualties, and preventing response personnel from becoming casualties. Under these circumstances, basic protocols should be considered a starting point; ad hoc protocol modification may have to occur in response to a specific situation. In tactical situations, medics must be prepared and permitted to adapt and improvise within their scope of practice as conditions dictate.

The following new terminology and definitions appropriate to tactical field care (TFC) must be added to the ATLS program and incorporated into training in order to reflect the care rendered in the tactical environment:

I. Care Under Fire
   A. The care rendered by a medic at the scene of an injury, in a hostile environment, while at risk.
   B. Available medical equipment and supplies are limited to that which is carried by the individual medic.
   C. Aseptic technique is not a consideration.
   D. Control of hemorrhage is the top priority because exsanguination from extremity wounds is the number one cause of preventable death in the combat environment.
   E. Patient extraction is delayed due to the threat potential.

II. Tactical Field Care
   A. The care rendered by a medic at the scene of an injury, in a hostile environment, when not at risk.
   B. Available medical equipment and supplies are limited to that which is carried in the field.
   C. There is more time to render care.
   D. Care is rendered under non-sterile conditions.
   E. Patient extraction is possible.

Mass Fatality Management

When planning for nuclear, biological, chemical, or other acts of terrorism, the plan must include provisions for the management of mass fatalities. Evolving terrorist capabilities, coupled with the availability of WMDs, lead to consideration of the potential for mass fatalities. Many chemical agents result in fatal injuries to those exposed within a short period of time. In a similar manner, large improvised explosive devices placed strategically within a high-rise building, apartment, or other large public gathering can result in hundreds, if not thousands of deaths. Unlike the military, civil authority rarely finds itself in the position of managing, processing, and disposing of contaminated human remains.

A mass fatality management plan that provides organization, mobilization, and coordination of all provider agencies for emergency mortuary services is an imperative. It is important to delineate the authority, responsibility, functions, and operations of providers by agreement prior to an event of magnitude.[18]

Mass fatality plans should be regional and come under the auspices and management of the local coroner or medical examiner. The operational concept of the mass fatality management system is exclusive of cultural, religious, and ethnic beliefs and practices but may be modified as conditions permit. It is a utility system based on three levels of response:

- **Level I**—A minor to moderate incident wherein local resources appear to be adequate and available. A local emergency may or may not be proclaimed and fatalities may range from 50 to 100.
- **Level II**—A moderate to severe incident wherein local resources are not adequate and assistance is requested from other jurisdictions or regions. A local emergency declaration is imminent. Fatalities may exceed 100.
- **Level III**—A major incident wherein resources in or near the impacted area are overwhelmed and extensive state and/or federal resources are required. A local and state emergency will be proclaimed and a principal declaration of an emergency or major disaster will be requested. Fatalities may range in the thousands.

Mass Casualty Target Management

Many population centers include high-rise building complexes that commonly have transient censuses exceeding 10,000 people. The complexities involved in planning a response to these edifices can be a daunting task. These buildings exist globally and because of their accessibility represent attractive targets to terrorists.

For example, the New York City World Trade Center represented a target of colossal proportions, and an unprecedented opportunity to strike at the symbol of Western international commerce. In a single act of terrorism in 1993, over one hundred and fifty thousand individuals were placed at risk when an improvised explosive device detonated in a subterranean complex.

Fortunately, high reliability organizations such as EMS, fire, and law enforcement agencies use organizational structure to adapt to, and then mitigate the uncommon yet catastrophic event. This emergency was mitigated by a diverse public safety system, a convergent volunteer effort, and a systematic approach to disaster service operations. The adherence to an IMS provided the impetus for a unified command structure and an unprecedented level of cooperation between local and regional resources and state and federal assets. Through the application of this management process, a catastrophe was averted.

Mitigation of Individual Performance Degradation in Real Time as a Terrorist Event Evolves

Domestic NBC terrorist events are rare and catastrophic events. The unknowns are when and where these events will occur. The type and material used is also an unknown.

The basis of system function is performance of the individual, yet how citizens and first responders will perform is unknown. Algorithms developed to assist in responding are based on a reductionist approach that most problems can be identified, separated from the larger response, and prepared for. Algorithms for response are best guesses in a totally unknown arena where human and environmental pathology merge.

Latent system error, human performance error due to slips and mistakes, and normal human physiology interfere with well-planned algorithms, policies, and procedures. Organizational structure and decision-making methods for emergency events that can mitigate performance degradation already exist. Use of high reliability organizational techniques and decision-making methodology adapted from the military can mitigate NBC terrorist events in real time as the event evolves.

Latent error occurs when the system sets up the error, but the individual commits the act. On later review a long train of events tied together by ineffective policies and procedures can be identified as the actual cause of the error. Though latent error can sometimes be identified or prevented by review of the system as a whole, the more deeply enmeshed latent errors cannot. They will appear only when the system is strained under the conditions of a catastrophe. The perceptions and actions of the individual can identify and mitigate latent error early in the period of disorder or dysfunction.

It has been pointed out that error is a part of human performance, despite a commonly held view that error cannot exist without negligence. Some consider complications as errors when they are actually expected but unwanted results of interventions. Errors can be unconscious slips or conscious mistakes. Slips are rule-based or skill-based errors that can easily occur when an event evolves in unexpected ways or human performance cannot or does not match environmental demands. Mistakes are more complex, knowledge-based errors where the decision-making process is at fault. Interference with effective decision making comes from a number of heuristics and biases such as representativeness, availability, confirmation bias, reversion under stress, or coning of attention.

Fear, as fight or flight, is a well-known, expected, and natural physiologic response to life threats. Less well known is how these responses will present themselves during the threat. Fight manifests itself as anger, particularly when focused on an individual or tool. It is made plausible by the presentation that an individual's performance is inadequate causing the anger when, in actuality, it is the angry individual's response that leads to performance decrements. Flight manifests as avoidance and is made plausible by redirection of attention to a seemingly more important but safer task. Freeze is an often-unrecognized fear response mediated by cortisol and leads to confusion, inaction, or even paralysis (as in paralysis by analysis).

Decision-making techniques modified from the military, such as the closed-loop decision cycles, allow individuals to learn what works through action. They permit response when the nature of the threat is fuzzy and ill defined or ill identified. In fact, closed-loop cycles allow identification of the structure of the threat and success of the response. They provide a margin of safety by self-monitoring responses to actions for early warning of dangers created by actions of the response team. They are rapid and adaptable to those situations where unintended or unexpected outcomes occur.

Roberts and Libuser's high reliability theory, also developed from military studies, states that complexity will mitigate rare but catastrophic events. This apparent paradox occurs because disasters and terrorist events are nonlinear systems. Linear, reductionist approaches such as response algorithms and prearranged incident command systems do not apply. High reliability organizations can learn and have a culture of both safety and reliability. They allow decision migration and diminish authority gradients that will permit the necessary free flow of information during the terrorist event. They allow effective action before implementation of algorithms, policies, and procedures can be instituted in a rapidly evolving terrorist threat. These organizations will respond to a catastrophic event in the same manner they respond to routine events.

CHAPTER QUESTIONS

1. List and discuss at least three major response agencies at the local level. What are the limitations of these agencies in terrorism response?
2. Discuss the evolving threats of 911 target acquisition and tactical violence.
3. What are the basic functions of the following special units?
   - U.S. Marine Corps Chemical Biological Incident Response Force (CBIRF)
   - National Guard Civilian Support Teams (CST)
   - Metropolitan Medical Response System (MMRS)
4. Discuss how mass casualty care in the combat environment differs from standard advanced trauma life support protocols.
5. Outline the major elements in a mass fatality management plan.

NOTES

[1]Rittenberg, Sidney, and Amanda Bennet (1993). *The Man Who Stayed Behind.* New York: Simon & Schuster.

[2]Sudoplatov, Pavel, and Anatoli P. Sudoplatov (1994). *Special Tasks.* New York: Little, Brown and Company.

[3]Ibid.

[4]Watson, Francis M. (1976). *Political Terrorism: The Threat and the Response.* Fairfield, CT: Robert B. Luce Co.

[5]bin-Laden, Osama, "Fatwa" *Al-Quds Al-Arabi News,* London, 1998.

[6]Strategic Management and Policy-Making, Globalisation: What Challenges and Opportunities for Government, Internet, September 1997.

[7]Office of the Inspector General, U.S. Department of State: Major Management Challenges, 1997.

[8]Denney, James, and Donald Lee (1997). *Millennium Issues Confronting the Fire Service.* Los Angeles: The MJS Group.

[9]Denney, James, and Donald Lee, "The Emergence and Employment of Tactical Ultra-Violence." Internet; ERRI. http://www.emergency.com/stratvio.htm, 1997.

[10]Denney, James, "Emerging First Responder Threats: 911 Target Acquisition." Internet; ERRI. http://www.emergency.com/911target.htm, 1998.

[11]Malone, Major Mike. "Chemical Biological Incident Response Force." USMC-ASPD, 1998.

[12]Cohen, William S. "National Guard Rapid Assessment Elements." Washington, D.C.: Armed Forces News Service, October 1998.

[13]Asst. Secretary of Defense, Weapons of Mass Destruction Response Team Locations Announced, Washington, D.C.: Armed Forces News Service, No. 512-98, October 1998.

[14]Hospital Emergency Incident Command System, Orange County Health Care Agency, Emergency Medical Services, 1991 DHHS Orange County, California.

[15]U.S. Public Health Service (1997). *Metropolitan Medical Strike Teams: Field Operations Guide,* 1997.

[16]Butler, Frank, M.D. (1996). *Combat Casualty Care.* Department of Defense briefing.

[17]Department of Coroner. Emergency Mortuary Response Plan: County of Los Angeles, Los Angeles County Department of Health Services, Los Angeles, 1993.

[18]Minihan, Lt. General Kenneth (1998). *Information System Security.* Washington, D.C.: National Security Agency.

2
The Basics
of the Incident
Management System

Paul M. Maniscalco
Hank T. Christen

Source: Courtesy P. Maniscalco

Chapter Objectives

After reading this chapter, you will be able to accomplish the following objectives:

1. Have an awareness of the history of the incident management system.
2. Define crisis management and consequence management and recognize the distinction between the two terms.
3. Diagram the basic structure of the EMS incident management system (EMS/IMS), fire IMS, and law enforcement IMS.
4. Recognize the importance of prescribing who should be in charge (lead agency).
5. Understand unified management (command).
6. Understand the importance of Emergency Management in supporting IMS.
7. Recognize the application of IMS as a planning tool.
8. Understand the use of IMS for integration with military units.

The History and Development of IMS (ICS)

In the 1970s, after a disastrous wildfire season, California fire managers recognized the need for change. In incident after incident, the same problem emerged: lack of interagency coordination. Specific problems were:

1. Uncommon radio codes—people could not talk to each other.
2. No command system—each agency operated on the personality of its leaders; in some cases, it depended on who was working that day.
3. No common terminology—when agencies did talk, they often misunderstood each other.
4. No method of effectively assigning resources—logistics depended on who got lucky.
5. No clear definition of functions, and how each function related to other elements.

Fortunately, a group of downsized Boeing engineers was assigned to develop the modern ICS. Using a system approach learned from the defense and aerospace industries, they implemented an ingenious management boilerplate that effectively integrated the myriad of agencies needed to combat a wildfire. In the 1980s, other emergency response disciplines recognized the universality of the system. ICS could literally be applied to any type of problem. In the 1990s, minor changes in terminology resulted in the system becoming a management system and referred to as the incident management system (IMS). Please note that throughout this text we use the terms *incident management system (IMS)* and *incident manager*. The terms *incident command system (ICS)* and *incident commander (IC)* are also frequently used and are acceptable terms.

Today the U.S. Coast Guard uses IMS for spill control operations, and law enforcement uses the system in tactical operations. EMS uses the EMS incident management system on mass casualty incidents. These response agencies have learned that IMS is a solution for effective coordination and liaison with their military counterparts in terrorism/tactical violence incidents.

Crisis Management/Consequence Management

Two new terms that have emerged from the federal level in terrorism response are the concepts of crisis management and consequence management.

Crisis management involves measures to identify, acquire, and plan the use of resources needed to anticipate, prevent, and/or resolve a terrorist threat or incident.

Consequence management involves measures to alleviate the damage, loss, hardship, or suffering caused by emergencies. Consequence management includes measures to protect public health and safety, restore essential government services, and provide emergency relief to affected governments, businesses, and individuals.

Crisis management is an important element and is under the direction of the FBI. Intelligence information (called "intel") from the FBI is sometimes shared with local law enforcement agencies, but rarely reaches EMS, fire, or emergency management agencies. Intel on potential terrorists is frequently classified information. This is understandable, as intel agencies must be careful about compromising sources. However, it is practical that managers of response agencies have a secret clearance and receive crisis management information on a need-to-know basis. This intel is not compromised if the source and detail are kept confidential from operations personnel. Managers can order protective actions without sharing the facts.

Consequence management is the action-oriented response that we are used to. On a bad day, when crisis efforts fail, we get the 911 call that drives us quickly into the consequence mode. The consequence mode is synonymous with incident management since consequence operations must have a system or game plan. Without IMS, consequence management is nothing more than well-meaning chaos. Our customers (the victims) deserve something better. In the next section, we will examine the basic IMS structure that allows us to leap into the consequence world and somehow come out alive.

The Basic Structure of the IMS

The system begins with someone running the show (more about that later). That special person is the incident manager (commander) and has a support staff on large and complex incidents. The management staff consists of a safety officer (always critical), a liaison officer (nice to have), and a public information officer (always important).

The heart and soul of the IMS are the four sections of operations, logistics, planning, and administration. Any event requires these four basic functions. These functions also apply to nonemergency activities. You could manage a business, run a nuclear submarine, or raise a family using the principles of IMS.

Operations cover the most obvious aspects of a terrorism/tactical violence response, including visible, dynamic, tactical hands-on functions. Operations is where the "rubber meets the road," where people get their hands dirty, and involves mass casualty EMS response, fire/rescue activities, public health operations, tactical law enforcement, and hazardous materials actions. If things go right, operations people get medals; if things go wrong, operations people get killed.

If operations types are the stars of the show (and rightfully so), then the logistics types are the unsung heroes. Nobody appreciates logistics (read support) until they run out of things. Operations units become dead in the water when they have no equipment, supplies, fuel, or communications. We all take our radios for granted until they go dead.

By nature, terrorism and tactical violence events consume resources. Throughout history military experience has shown that for every soldier, there are multiple support personnel. The same is true for consequence responders. To accomplish this support, the logistics section is divided into a support branch and a service branch. The service branch consists of a communications unit and a food unit. The support branch consists of a supply unit, a facilities unit, and a ground support unit.

In an average response, needed resources are available. In complex and protracted events, the logistics needs grow exponentially. Radio networks fail or require expansion and vehicles run out of fuel. EMS needs medical supplies, and everyone needs lights when it gets dark. The event requires more people and the people need to eat.

Along with resources, operations needs ideas; that is where the planning section enters the picture. The purpose of the planning section is to coordinate with the incident manager and other section chiefs in the development of an incident action plan (IAP). The IAP is a flexible plan that must respond to the dynamics of the incident, and is literally planning "on the fly" by reacting to rapidly changing information. Planning involves gathering data, assembling it into meaningful information, displaying the information in an easily readable form, and finally using the information to make decisions. If this sounds difficult, you get the point.

To accomplish these varied tasks, the planning section utilizes a resource status unit, a situation status unit, a documentation unit, and technical specialists. Early in the game, the incident manager better hit the bricks with a quick and dirty plan. As the incident increases in duration or complexity, gathering data and assembling it into key bits of information are necessary. Hence, the needs for a planning section. There is an old aviation expression that says, "never run out of air speed, altitude, and ideas at the same time." In our business, the planning section provides us with the ideas.

The administration section was designed as an element of the wild-fire command system and for prolonged deployments. In terrorism and tactical violence incidents, administration units such as finance, time keeping, and worker's compensation are in place, but will not be discussed in this text.

Important aspects of the IMS that bear emphasis are:

1. IMS identifies key functions; it is not based on rank or hierarchy.
2. IMS delineates a relationship between four key sections: operations, logistics, planning, and administration.
3. IMS specifies a chain of command and a workable span of control (a leader does not supervise more than three to five subordinate units). The system emphasizes support (logistics) and decision making (planning) as elements complimentary to operations.
4. IMS applies to any agency or incident, event, or disaster. (It works on everything!)
5. IMS is a system of common terminology. (We can talk and understand each other.)
6. IMS is flexible, and is expanded or contracted depending on the demands of the incident.

The EMS Incident Management System

The primary objective of a terrorism/tactical violence incident is to create casualties and fatalities. The death and mayhem demonstrate a cause or help the perpetrators accomplish an immediate goal. For this reason, EMS operations (mass casualty operations) are critical objectives of the first response forces.

Emergency medical operations become a branch in the operations section called the EMS branch. The three functions of the EMS branch are triage, treatment, and transport. These functions are performed by one or two units in a minor incident or expanded to fully staffed sectors in a major disaster.

For example, consider a mass shooting with one fatality and two critical patients. Two units and a supervisor can handle the incident. The supervisor becomes the EMS branch director and coordinates his or her units with other IMS elements. The two units triage the patients, provide stabilization and treatment, and transport to an appropriate facility. In this case, the treatment is minimal; the "load-and-go" mode is in order.

If the same mass shooting resulted in fifteen casualties, the EMS/IMS must be expanded. There is still an EMS branch director, but the elements of triage, treatment, and transport become full sectors. Triage personnel under a sector supervisor triage and tag patients. Several units must be committed to patient treatment. Transport will also require several units (ground and/or air ambulances). The transport sector will have to coordinate with medical control to determine which medical facilities will be appropriate to receive patients.

All of the EMS functions just described do not operate in a vacuum. Simultaneously, a fire rescue branch and law enforcement branch will be working full tilt. Other types of events may require a hazardous materials branch, public health branch, or a public works branch.

Other sections such as logistics and planning are established if needed. Logistics is a busy player as the operational heroes begin to "suck up" supplies, equipment, and communications.[1]

FIGURE 2-1   Use of command vests allows sector officers to be readily identifiable. *Source:* Courtesy P. Maniscalco

Fire Incident Management Systems

The fire incident management system uses the same structure (boilerplate) as the EMS/IMS. There is the same management staff, with logistics and planning sections, fire/rescue, hazardous materials, and mass casualty (EMS/IMS). The wildland fire IMS is branched into ground operations and air operations. A wildland incident management team (IMT or sometimes called an overhead team) can easily restructure for a terrorism incident by utilizing the urban fire structure of fire/rescue, hazardous materials (haz mat), and mass casualty (EMS/IMS). The point is that both systems have the tools and flexibility to respond to the demands of a terrorism event.

The fire/rescue branch provides search, rescue, and fire fighting operations after law enforcement and haz mat personnel clear the area. The fire/rescue branch may need an urban search and rescue team(s) if the incident involves a structural collapse such as Oklahoma City. The fire/rescue branch also closely supports the haz mat branch and the EMS branch. In the haz mat scenario, fire/rescue assists in decontamination operations and provides the management structure for haz mat operations. In a terrorism mass casualty incident, fire/rescue assists in triage, basic medical care, and movement of patients to treatment areas (i.e., the Olympics bombing in Atlanta).

The haz mat branch is responsible for donning chemical personal protective equipment (PPE) and entering a chemical/biological/radiological hot zone (example: the sarin gas attack in Tokyo.) The haz mat branch also performs decontamination (decon). Decon expands to major proportions when there are large numbers of contaminated victims (more on decon in Chapter 6).

In a biological incident, the public health branch would be the lead operations branch. This branch is closely supported by a medical surveillance system, technical advisors (especially epidemiologists), and a medical laboratory system.

A major terrorism incident will require a large commitment of fire resources for a long duration. Operations of this nature place very high demands on logistics and planning sections. On the logistics side, there is a need for fuel, ground support, supplies, communications, food and water, auxiliary power, and personnel. On the planning side, incident action plan development, planning briefings, resource tracking, status boards, and technical specialists are needed.

Law Enforcement Incident Management

A senior law enforcement official once remarked to us, "Law enforcement is involved before the incident, during the incident, and after the incident; long after EMS and fire units have ceased operations." His statement is accurate, for law enforcement (local, state, or federal) is involved in crisis management, consequence management response, and finally long-term investigations and legal proceedings that may last for several years. Law enforcement crisis management and criminal investigation are beyond the scope of this text; however, it is important to elaborate on consequence response by law enforcement agencies.

In recent years, the law enforcement community has begun to adapt the tools of incident management for major tactical deployments. In the law enforcement incident management system (LEIMS) the principles of planning and support still apply. As in other systems, the major differences occur in the operations sections.

The LEIMS divides operations into groups or divisions that can include units, strike teams, or tactical teams. The primary mission groups are special emergency response teams (SERT, also called SWAT), hostage negotiation, bomb disposal, evacuation, air operations, traffic control, and perimeter security. Major terrorism incidents require most of these mission groups to work in liaison with fire and EMS operations. In major scenarios the FBI will establish a Joint Operations Center (JOC) that coordinates federal agencies above the local incident management level and provides appropriate intelligence information to the local incident management overhead team.

The logistics support of law enforcement IMS is similar to the EMS and fire models. Law enforcement requires an additional unit in the planning section called an intel unit. The purpose of the intel unit is to present crisis management intel to law enforcement operations commanders, and gather real-time intel about the incident or the perpetrators as the terrorist scenario progresses.

Who Is in Charge?

If an event meets the federal definition of terrorism, federal agencies will have jurisdiction. In accordance with Presidential Decision Directive 39 (PDD 39) the FBI (Department of Justice) has jurisdiction in crisis management and criminal investigation and FEMA coordinates consequence management. The key word here is *coordinate*, for FEMA does not have a response capability. FEMA can only coordinate federal teams with local teams. Even if everything goes perfectly, it will be many hours or longer before federal support is available.

The local community must be able to establish scene management immediately and maintain command throughout the incident. The critical step is to determine who is in charge. In most local governments the responsibility for scene management in terrorism/tactical violence events rests with the ranking law enforcement official. However, terrorism/tactical violence incidents are complex and require a number of agencies. As previously explained, the incident will involve a large EMS and fire/rescue commitment with the appropriate command responsibilities.

There are two solutions. The first solution is a single agency incident manager, such as a sheriff or police chief, with EMS and fire/rescue operating at branch levels. The second solution is unified management (unified command). A unified management team is utilized when multiple agencies have jurisdiction in a complex incident. Consider a bombing with a building collapse and mass casualties; clearly, there are major EMS, fire/rescue, and law enforcement operations that must effectively coordinate. In this case, a command post with a joint EMS/fire/law enforcement management team is the solution.

Unified management requires that all managers be located in the same area (a command vehicle or an emergency operations center) and share information. The planning section makes this happen by effective status display and comprehensive interagency action plans. Separate command posts for each major agency never work. Each agency tends to freelance and coordination does not happen.

Unified command does not begin in the heat of battle. It starts with effective planning well before a terrorism incident. The responsibility of each agency must be specifically defined and written. Emergency management facilitates the formal development of unified management through the local comprehensive emergency management plan.

In many ways, the informal development of unified management is more significant than the formal process. Managers must get to know each other. As Phoenix Fire Chief Alan Brunacini says, "Unified command begins at lunch." He means that various agency managers initiate mutual support by breaking bread and sharing coffee. A community disaster committee is an excellent vehicle to schedule quarterly meetings where mutual incident management issues are discussed and agency heads get to know each other. In summary, managers cannot meet each other for the first time in a major incident, and expect to coordinate effectively.

Logistics

Throughout this chapter, we have emphasized that terrorism and tactical violence incidents consume resources quickly. Unfortunately, no IMS system can deliver resources, equipment, and supplies that are not immediately available.

Terrorism/tactical violence requires a push logistics system. In push logistics, equipment and supplies are estimated and stored in caches that can

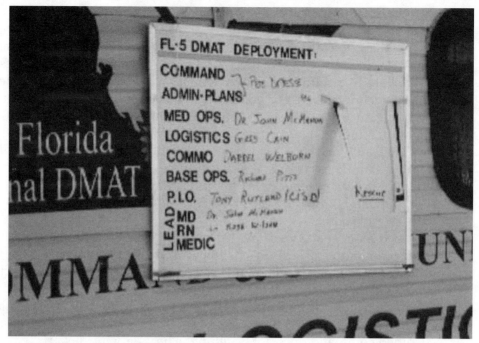

FIGURE 2-2   Command Board. *Source:* Courtesy J. McMahon, M.D.

be quickly "pushed" to the scene. (Note: Pull logistics involves the ordering of equipment and supplies after their need is determined. Pull logistics is a necessary evil in long duration events, but totally ineffective in the early minutes/hours of a fast developing terrorism incident.)

The first step in push logistics is to determine supplies and equipment that will be needed immediately. There is no all-inclusive list; as future events occur, the list will grow based on lessons learned. A generalized list is:

1. PPE—protective suits and respiratory equipment for all response personnel, bulletproof vests for law enforcement.
2. Decon equipment—Tyvek suits for patients, red bags, cleaning equipment, privacy shelters, run-off control materials, and decon showers.
3. Medications—drugs such as atropine and antidotes.
4. Morgue materials—body bags, collection bags, and tags.
5. Medical supplies—oxygen, IVs, airway adjuncts, basic life support (BLS) trauma supplies, and disposable litters.
6. Crime scene supplies—evidence bags, film, tags, forms, perimeter control.
7. Detection equipment—air-sampling equipment, detection kits, radiological detection.

The primary cost of push logistics is the equipment and supplies. The secondary cost is the storage and maintenance. Some supplies such as medications must be rotated from storage to line service before expiration occurs.

The Safety Template

Safety is one aspect of the IMS that may not be fully appreciated. The most important duty of the incident manager is safety. The guideline for establishing a safety officer is simple: As soon as the incident manager cannot directly supervise all the safety aspects of an incident, the safety function should be assigned to a safety officer. This means appointing a safety officer early in the process. Few terrorism incidents are small enough to allow one person to be the incident manager and still maintain a grip on safety.

The safety officer has the authority to temporarily suspend any plan, procedure, or tactical operation that is unsafe to his or her people or customers. In addition, we need to make sure the terrorists are not harmed because the law enforcement people will badly want to talk to them later.

Safety becomes more important when you consider that the intent of terrorist events is to create a harmful scenario and hurt people. In some incidents, the sole objective of the terrorist is to hurt us, the emergency personnel. Examples abound including:

1. A secondary explosive device designed to detonate after first responders arrive at the scene.
2. A biological/chemical/radiological hot zone.
3. Armed terrorists still on the scene when early responders arrive.
4. Unstable structures that are partially collapsed.
5. An incident where emergency responders are intentionally harmed as a diversion for a crime or another terrorism incident.

Complex incidents require a safety group with several safety personnel under the command of a safety officer. These incidents create high safety demands because they are geographically dispersed and involve several diverse tactical operations. As an example, a subway chemical attack could affect several teams at two or three different stations. During the event, diverse operations would include safety issues such as law enforcement weapons safety, fire zones, and perimeter security; chemical hot zone entry, suit selection, and decon safety; and chemical safety for medical teams. In the Oklahoma City bombing there were dozens of areas with mass casualties, each having site-specific safety requirements.

On a long-duration incident, the safety officer closely coordinates with the incident manager, the planning section, and various operations branches. As incident action plans are developed and evolve, they are

FIGURE 2-3 In many instances face-to-face briefings at the scenes of major incidents are the most effective means of communication. *Source:* Courtesy L. Tan

evaluated for safety. The best place to stop unsafe ideas is in the planning stage before aggressive operations officers get creative and start to do dangerous things. Every incident action plan needs a safety officer's signature, and every incident manager's briefing must include a safety briefing.

Special teams have their own safety officers who provide relief for the scene safety officer. SWAT urban search and rescue teams and haz mat teams are all required to have safety officers. EMS must have an infection control officer (not an on-scene position). These team-specific safety officers share the workload and responsibility of incident safety.

A terrorism/tactical violence response means throwing our people into the most dangerous acreage on earth. The death, injury, or hostage taking of a responder greatly inhibits a successful outcome. We have to protect ourselves in order to protect others.

The Functions of Emergency Management

Throughout this chapter, emphasis has been on the importance of planning and logistics complementing operations. Many organizations have fine-tuned their operations because they get a lot of practice with routine events.

Likewise, their logistics and planning efforts are designed to support normal operations. For major terrorism/tactical violence events, logistics and planning may fall short because of lack of expertise. This is where an effective emergency management agency provides optimal support.

By definition, emergency management is a planning and support agency. Emergency management serves to coordinate response agencies, but does not directly provide response units or personnel. Emergency management is well suited for the planning role for two reasons. First, emergency management does not have a "turf protection" mind-set; the emergency response turf is owned by other agencies, namely EMS, fire, and law enforcement. Secondly, emergency management is often responsible for a county or region transcending many agencies. This places the emergency management agency in a good coordination and planning position.

An important emergency management function is training. Most agencies provide their own basic and recertification training. New issues are always on the horizon that require advanced training, beyond the scope of the response agency. These include terrorism response subjects like incident management, mass casualty operations, crime scene preservation, and chemical/biological response procedures. In many cases, emergency management can secure state and federal funding for countywide or regional training seminars. There are also new training technologies such as distance learning and virtual universities that emergency management can facilitate.

Disaster exercises closely complement a training program. Exercises allow emergency response agencies to test capabilities not frequently tested in day-to-day operations. Terrorism/tactical violence incidents certainly fall into this category. At least twice per year (quarterly is even better) response agencies should conduct joint exercises. Each exercise should test one or two functions of the interagency response system and include realistic scenarios. For example, key components include communications, logistics, unified management, mass casualty operations, medical surveillance (public health level) decontamination, operational readiness, air operations, mutual aid, medical transport, and media relations. Scenarios should include at least one terrorism/tactical violence event per year. Probable scenarios can be a workplace mass shooting, a chemical attack, an infectious disease outbreak from a biological weapon, or a bombing with a secondary device.

Emergency managers require certification in exercise planning, and are the pivotal people in exercise design and implementation. In fact, the disaster committee previously discussed is an excellent vehicle to promote exercise coordination. As an overview, there are several steps for effective exercise planning:

1. Determine critical components of the IMS to be tested, such as personnel recall and push logistics.

2. Create a realistic scenario, such as a pipe bomb incident or a mass shooting.
3. Coordinate the players through the disaster committee.
4. Use the IMS model to organize the exercises. The actual exercise must require operations, logistics, planning, and administration.
5. Establish an exercise controller and evaluators who are non-players and unbiased.
6. Adequately fund the exercise. Be realistic about overtime and supply costs.
7. Insist that safety is the key factor in the exercise. (People have been killed in exercises.)
8. Document the exercise; record it, videotape it, take pictures, and write about it.
9. Summarize the exercise results in a lessons-learned format.
10. Hold an after-exercise briefing. Candidly and tactfully point out shortcomings, and stress all the positive results.
11. Most importantly, establish realistic and measurable goals for implementing changes.

The last aspect of emergency management we will discuss is the emergency operations center (EOC) operation. EOC terminology is now evolving into the multiagency coordination center, or MACC. The EOC and MACC concepts have been tested over time in natural and technological disaster scenarios, including hurricanes, earthquakes, industrial explosions/fires, winter storms, airplane crashes, and many other disasters. Terrorism events such as the Oklahoma City bombing, the Olympics bombing, and the sarin gas attack in Tokyo are all examples of the effective use of an EOC or MACC in a terrorism incident.

In most communities, the emergency manager is the commander of the EOC/MACC during emergency operations. There are no specific guidelines to determine when an EOC/MACC should be fully or partially activated. A good rule is that the EOC/MACC is needed whenever the scope of an incident requires support and coordination that cannot be achieved at an on-scene command post. This is often the case when an incident is widespread or regional or there are multiple incidents in progress.

The EOC/MACC is structured like the IMS. All emergency support functions in the EOC are grouped under operations, logistics, planning, and administration. This system provides effective coordination and information flow from IMS elements on the scene with IMS elements at the EOC/MACC.

In summary, make sure emergency management is a major player in your community IMS. Emergency management performs diverse critical functions like planning, logistics, funding, interagency coordination, and liaison with state/federal agencies, training, exercise design, and EOC/MACC operations.

Military Coordination

The IMS is a model system for liaison with military special teams or national guard units. This is because IMS is based on the same principles as military command and control systems. Military organizations and special units have staff officers who are assigned command functions. The functions are identified as follows: (s-staff)

- S-1—administration
- S-2—intelligence
- S-3—plans/operations
- S-4—supplies/logistics

As an example, a military commander would refer a logistics issue to his or her S-4.

At the section level, the military system is almost identical to the civilian IMS. The difference is in terminology. If military officers fully understand the civilian terminology they can easily adapt to our system of operations. Likewise, by understanding military command/control terminology, we can integrate military units into the IMS.

The authors have heard numerous military officers ask, "How can I integrate with civilians? We are not used to going somewhere and not being in charge." The answer is IMS unified management (command), and branching. In unified management, the military commander becomes part of the management team along with the civilians. This ensures that the military commander is privy to all issues, communications, plans, etc. This system keeps civilian leaders in liaison with the military effort.

At the operations level, the military units are assigned to work with an existing branch or assigned as a separate branch. Support functions are carried out by the military staff or integrated with the civilian counterpart if practical. For example, military units have special communications and logistics plans that are executed internally. On the other hand, the civilian logistics section can furnish supplies, equipment, and facilities available at the local level.

Consider a hypothetical scenario of a chemical attack in a downtown urban area with mass patient contamination. The local first responders are on the scene for 10 hours when a military chem-bio team arrives. Patients have been decontaminated and transported, leaving a chemical hot zone. The military mission is to decontaminate buildings, equipment, and vehicles along with setting up decon sites for civilian teams.

Using IMS to integrate with the military command/control system, the following steps are taken:

1. The military commander integrates with the unified management team.

2. The military team is assigned to the haz mat branch.
3. The military team provides its own administration and planning (S-1 and S-2).
4. The military logistics officer (S-4) coordinates with the local logistics section chief for food and facilities and internally provides logistics for mass decon equipment and supplies.

Most military officers are not aware that the IMS or ICS exists in the civilian response community. We advocate a basic IMS awareness course for military officers who respond to civilian missions. This model has already been combat tested in the wildfire incidents in the western United States. Marines and soldiers were given basic fire fighting and IMS training and divided into crews with a civilian liaison. This system worked well and continues to be used during fire seasons.

CHAPTER SUMMARY

In summary, there are 10 major points in this chapter that are critical for an effective incident management system:

1. The IMS is a functionally based system. The emphasis is on common terminology, a chain of command with effective span of control, and the assignment of resources on a priority basis.
2. The IMS is an all risk system that applies to any technological or natural disaster incident, and terrorism/tactical violence incidents.
3. Consequence management involves measures taken to alleviate the damage, loss, hardship, or suffering caused by emergencies, and is the responsibility of local/regional emergency response agencies.
4. The four major sections of the IMS are operations, logistics, planning, and administration. These sections are coordinated and directed by an incident manager and a management staff.
5. An incident action plan is dynamic and "on the fly" in the early stages of an incident. The plan is written and formalized on complex and long duration incidents and developed by the planning section.
6. The EMS branch is responsible for mass casualty operations and is divided into the sectors of triage, treatment, and transport.
7. A local community disaster plan must specify who is in charge. There can be a single incident manager, or a unified management team if several disciplines or jurisdictions are involved.
8. Terrorism/tactical violence incidents consume supplies/equipment quickly. An effective solution is pre-staged disaster caches that are rapidly deployed (push logistics).
9. The IMS provides a template for safe operations. A safety officer supervises safety operations and coordinates with safety officers

on special teams. A terrorism/tactical violence incident is the most unsafe workplace on earth.

10. Local emergency management agencies provide critical functions including planning, support, interagency coordination, exercise planning, and EOC/MACC operations.

Chapter Questions

1. What were the significant problems that prevailed in major wild-fires before the development of IMS?
2. Define consequence management and crisis management. What agencies are responsible for consequence management?
3. What are the positions on the management staff? Diagram and define the four sections of the incident management system.
4. What are the elements in the logistics section? Describe the critical logistics issues in terrorism/tactical violence incidents.
5. What is push logistics? Outline a system for placing disaster caches in your community including a supply list for the caches.
6. Describe the duties of the planning section. What is an IAP? What determines if an IAP is formal or informal?
7. Define and diagram the sectors of the EMS branch.
8. What other branches perform key operations in a terrorism/tactical violence incident? How do these branches coordinate and complement each other?
9. What determines who is in charge of a terrorism/tactical violence event? What is unified management and when should it be used?
10. How does the IMS provide a safer workplace? What are the major safety concerns at a terrorism/tactical violence incident?
11. What are the functions of emergency management? How can emergency management ensure coordination between diverse agencies?
12. What is an EOC? Define a MACC. What determines when an EOC/MACC is needed?
13. What are the staff functions in the military command and control system? How do these compare with the IMS? How can the IMS be used to coordinate with military or National Guard teams?

Notes

[1]For detailed information about the EMS incident management system, study *The EMS Incident Management System—EMS Operations for Mass Casualty and High-Impact Incidents,* by Hank T. Christen and Paul M. Maniscalco, Brady, 1998.

3
Terrorism/Tactical Violence Incident Response Procedures

Paul M. Maniscalco
James P. Denny
Hank T. Christen

Source: Courtesy Reuters/KNBC-TV/Archive Photos

Chapter Objectives

After reading this chapter, you will be able to accomplish the following objectives:

1. Understand the definition of convergent responders and how convergent responder agencies relate to first responders.
2. Recognize the critical importance of scene awareness in a dynamic terrorism/tactical violence event.
3. Have an awareness of the on-scene complications present in a terrorism/tactical violence incident.
4. List the responsibilities of the first arriving unit in a terrorism/tactical violence event.
5. Understand the principles of "2 in 2 out" and LACES (lookout, awareness, communications, escape, safety).
6. Outline the key elements in a terrorism/tactical violence response protocol.
7. Recognize critical hospital response issues.

Introduction to Response

Response to an emergency is a routine function of public safety agencies. Thousands of times a day across the world, EMS, fire, rescue, and law enforcement agencies go "out of the chute" and effectively handle a myriad of incidents. However, no terrorism/tactical violence event is a garden-variety incident. Initial responders are confronted with an unfamiliar, unpredictable, and unsafe scene. It is often a combination mass casualty incident, rescue, haz mat incident, and crime scene scenario. No matter how global an event becomes, it starts with convergent responders trying to assist (more on this later) and first responders being overwhelmed upon arrival at the scene.

While many emergency scenarios share some similar characteristics and response demands, as stated previously, none are "garden variety" and all pose complex and confusing environments for the arriving emergency responders. Let's take a minute to review the expected sequence of activity at a terrorism/tactical violence event.

Event: Explosives detonated at a football stadium to punish the "Great Satan" nation of America.

Jurisdiction—Local EMS, fire, hospital, and law enforcement with eventual state and federal support
Criminals—Foreign nationals
Patients—150 fans including eight children; 25,000 terrorized

Resolution—Convergent responders and emergency responders; medical facilities and prolonged emergency service presence due to criminal investigation and structural instability

Event: A street gang attacks another street gang with automatic weapons.

Jurisdiction—Local EMS, fire, hospital, and law enforcement
Criminals—The winning gang and the losing gang
Patients—Eight gang members and two citizens
Resolution—Convergent responders and first responders; medical facilities and short-term emergency service presence

Event: A fired employee tosses a grenade into a warehouse and shoots four employees.

Jurisdiction—Local EMS, fire, hospital, and law enforcement
Criminal—Ruckus Ralph who was fired for making threats to his boss
Patients—Eleven injured workers; 40 terrorized workers
Resolution—Convergent responders and first responders; medical facilities

In each scenario the common denominator in the event is a *local* incident that draws down upon *local* assets and requires an effective and robust emergency response plan to manage successfully. It does not matter about the jurisdictions, or whether the event is official terrorism; the locals have to get there first, and hold the fort for hours or a day before state and federal assistance arrives and supports the local effort. Reliance upon state or federal assets to assure a successful outcome of your response is unwise. The amount of time that it will take for these resources to arrive at most emergencies creates a vast disadvantage that may result in great detriment to the patients and your community. Clearly, it is in the best interests of all concerned to ensure that our personnel and organizations are capable of mounting an effective sustainable response to high impact/high yield events.

Convergent Responders

Convergent responders are citizens or individuals from nonemergency agencies that witness a terrorism/tactical violence event and converge on the scene. We call ourselves first responders, but we almost never arrive first (we are the first professionally trained responders); convergent responders get there first, we arrive second.

Many response professionals perceive convergent responders in a negative light. They are viewed as undisciplined and in the way. Reality is somewhat different than this myth. In many disaster and terrorism incidents, we have seen video footage of convergent responders digging victims out of rubble, manning hose lines or rendering first aid to victims. Convergent responders are the people who call 911 and report that a terrorism/tactical violence incident has occurred and provide vital incident information to the 911 operator or dispatcher. This information is often conflicting and sometimes hysterical, but multiple calls paint an initial picture that is extremely important in determining the nature of an incident and the level of response.

Realistically, convergent responders become victims, create a crowd, and may hinder initial response efforts. On the surface, it appears that the good and the bad aspects of convergent responders are beyond control. This is not the case. Response agencies are unaware that many convergent responders are from organized and disciplined agencies. At any moment, a local street may have convergent agencies, companies, or individuals performing work assignments. These organizations include:

1. Utility crews such as power, gas, telephone and cable
2. Postal workers and express delivery services (like FedEx or UPS)
3. Meter readers and inspectors
4. Transit authority, school buses and taxis
5. Public works crews
6. Social workers or probation officers
7. Private security agencies
8. Real estate agents
9. Crime watch and neighborhood watch volunteers

Many of these people are in radio-equipped vehicles or have cellular telephones and can provide early and accurate reports of a suspicious scene or a terrorism/tactical violence event in progress. Festivals, events, and public assembly buildings have security guards, ushers, ticket takers, and concession workers who are employees of formal organizations.

With training, convergent agencies are a positive initial response component. The level of training is similar to the hazardous materials awareness model. Members are exposed to basic awareness material in the following subject areas:

- A brief overview of terrorism/tactical violence history and local threats
- Recognition of potential threats such as suspicious people, weapons, or devices
- Procedures for reporting an incident and the critical information needed by 911 communications
- Safe scene control and personal safety
- Basic first aid techniques

While it may not be practical to conduct awareness training for most of the public, adoption of the Community Emergency Response Team (CERT) initiative, which is a familiar program in communities vulnerable to earthquakes, hurricanes, and tornados, may be a mechanism to afford these members of the community an awareness of emergency actions and the role that they may (or should) play at an incident.

It is also feasible to identify agencies that are possible convergent responders, solicit their participation, and assist them with basic awareness training. This is no different in concept than the CERT program or the law enforcement agency training programs for developing volunteer crime/neighborhood watch organizations. In summary, convergent responders are a viable force that the emergency service community needs to tap, for they will always get there first.

Scene Awareness

A terrorism/tactical violence event is a scene that resembles a boiling cauldron. The scene is a hot zone that can include chemical/biological/radiological hazards; individuals firing weapons (on both sides), partially exploded devices, secondary devices or booby traps, fires, collapsed structures, and multiple injured victims—many screaming for your assistance. On a time scale, first responders arrive when the event is getting started (we stumble into a can of worms), when it is already over (we're seldom that lucky), or somewhere in between (usually the case).

Scene awareness principles begin before the response in any incident (routine or terrorism). Being familiar with the neighborhood, the surroundings, and the violence history of the area is important. Does the area have a gang history? Are special events being held? Is the stadium full or empty? Has there been recent unrest such as political protests or union/labor issues? Are special religious ceremonies being held? These questions only scratch the surface of information that response agencies must consider before the 911 call. In fact, this type of information (intel) should be obtained pre-event if possible and incorporated into your organization's pre-incident response plans.

During an emergency response, scene awareness jumps into high gear. A terrorism/tactical violence 911 call seldom starts with an accurate description of the event. What sounds like a single shooting turns into a mass shooting with automatic weapons. A suspicious package report becomes a pipe bomb explosion, and a report of respiratory distress at a stadium evolves into a chemical release with contamination and mass casualties.

While responding, mentally explore the possibility that the scene may be far worse than the initial information. Replay your pre-response knowledge. For example, if you are en route to an abortion clinic for an "unknown medical," expect more than a simple gyn patient. Monitor the radio traffic; turn up the volume and really *listen*. You cannot afford to miss any additional information about scene conditions. Local protocol must emphasize that new information be immediately forwarded to all responding units. Radio traffic from convergent responder agencies and other emergency response agencies is also critical. Know the wind direction.

When you get close enough for the scene to appear in the distance, start really looking. Visually scan the entire scene periphery (this may be limited at night or in bad weather). On arrival, there is a tendency to get tunnel vision. EMS focuses on patients, firefighters focus on fires, and cops focus on a crime scene. These are habits based on years of practice that are detrimental in a complex terrorism/tactical violence incident. Force yourself to look around the incident. At this point you are still in the vehicle but slowing down. If you see threats to your safety, or if you have a sixth sense that something is wrong, stop and even retreat. Always trust your intuition on the street.

When exiting your vehicle, you are especially vulnerable. Look for indications of an unsafe scene. Start looking above, behind you, and for bad guys on roofs. Your head should be on a swivel. Look for any indication of people with weapons, explosive devices, or evidence of a chemical agent. The forward bodyline (FBL) may unfortunately define a hot zone. The FBL is a military term that describes the boundary, or forward line of bodies in a mass casualty zone. The FBL may be an indicator of a chemical hot zone. Remember that unsafe scene entry may result in emergency responders becoming the FBL.

Critical Factor: Do not become blinded by tunnel vision. Survey the entire scene, including the area above you, for threats to your safety.

In the structural fire service, there is a new safety guideline referred to as "2 in 2 out." This Occupational Health and Safety Administration (OHSA) guideline specifies that two members should enter a fire hot zone, remain in personal contact, and exit together. Two others are outside. This is the buddy principle that kids are taught in swimming lessons. The 2 in 2 out principle is a rule that applies to all first responders (EMS, fire, and law enforcement) in a terrorism/tactical violence incident when the scene is unstable. *Don't leave your partner!*

Another effective scene principle is one adopted from the wildland fire community, and suggested for terrorism by Assistant Chief Phil Chovan, Marietta (GA) fire/rescue. The principle is called LACES, and stands for lookout, awareness, communications, escape, and safety. These principles were developed after hard-learned lessons where wildland fires made sudden and unexpected changes in direction and/or intensity and trapped fire suppression crews. The same scene dynamics occur in a terrorism/tactical violence hot zone; especially when there is a chemical agent or automatic weapons fire.

Let's analyze the LACES principle:

L—Lookout: Someone is responsible for watching the overall scene from a safe distance and warning crews of danger.

A—Awareness: All members on the scene have situational awareness and are ready for unpleasant surprises.

C—Communications: Exposed crews must have effective communications which include direct voice or hand signals as well as portable radios.

E—Escape: Plan an escape route and an alternate route from any unstable scene.

S—Safety Zones: Escape to a safe area that provides distance, shielding, or upwind protection.

Consider a mass-shooting example where a 911 call describes shots fired with one possible victim in a warehouse. A first due EMS unit finds a single victim by the doorway. A law enforcement unit declares the scene secured. A second EMS unit and fire company arrives and enters a large open floor space with six victims. There is dead quiet (no pun intended). Things do not look or feel right. Fire crews work in pairs using the 2 in 2 out principle. An EMS commander arrives and places himself as a **lookout** watching the street and the crime scene. Crews in the area are looking around the periphery and above (**awareness**). The lookout suddenly spots three men with weapons moving on the far side of the building. He broadcasts an evacuation message (**communication**) to the fire and medical crews who run down an escape route and retreat behind an industrial dumpster (**escape** and **safety**). Heavy gunfire breaks out, but our people are safe because they used the LACES principle of lookout, awareness, communications, and escape and safety.

New Scenes—New Surprises

The twenty-first-century terrorism/tactical violence scene offers new problems previously unseen by civilian responders. It is important to understand that we are not heroes to everyone. In fact, the purpose of the event may be to harm the emergency response troops.

In an Atlanta area abortion clinic bombing, there was a secondary device (binary weapon) designed to detonate after EMS, fire, and law enforcement personnel arrived. In the video *Surviving the Secondary Device— The Rules Have Changed* (Georgia Emergency Management Agency), Assistant Chief Phil Chovan makes several important points:

1. On a bombing, suspect a partially exploded device or a second device.
2. If a second device is found or suspected, evacuate 1,000 feet in every direction (including above).
3. Patients should be removed as if they were in a burning vehicle; use minimal spinal precautions and omit invasive procedures until patients are in a safe area. A terrorism/tactical violence incident may be a diversion for a major crime or terrorist attack.

In Gainesville, Florida, a bank bombing resulted in a high-impact incident. Another bank was robbed while responders were at the original incident. In Texas, criminals placed explosive devices on a hazardous materials pipeline to create a diversion for an armored car robbery. Fortunately, the explosives did not detonate.

Remember that any terrorism/tactical violence incident is a high-impact event; there is a detrimental effect on a community's ability to deliver other 911 services. If possible, utilize the military principle of "uncommitted reserves" for 911 services and/or another terrorism/tactical violence incident. In small communities this principle requires early initiation of mutual aid and support. In summary, be aware of diversions; there's no rule against having two simultaneous terrorism/tactical violence events on a very bad day.

Another trend is tactical ultra-violence. Terrorists, criminals, political militias, and street gangs carry the latest automatic weapons and wear body armor. Often law enforcement is out-gunned. Responders are threatened with projectiles and splintering from concrete, glass, wood, and metals. There is also a danger of being caught in a crossfire between law enforcement and the criminals.

The best defense is avoiding entrance into a ballistic hot zone by observing the scene awareness principles. If you are exposed to shooting, distance and shielding are your only choices (run for cover). If possible, hide behind solid objects instead of vehicles. If you are in an area that requires body armor, you are in the wrong place. Obviously, law enforcement is the exception.

Along with the bombings and shootings, consider the brutal reality of a chemical/biological/radiological (CBR) hot zone. Biological mass casualties on a single scene are unlikely because biological effects take days or

FIGURE 3-1 Always remain aware of the environment to remain safe. *Source:* Courtesy Jamie Francis/AP/Wide World Photos

weeks to manifest themselves. Patients will be spread in ones and twos throughout a region, state, or the nation. Chemical attacks and radiological weapons are another story. First, the dispatch information is unlikely to paint a clear picture. The event may begin with a report of a single patient having respiratory distress in a stadium, auditorium, or airport. Second, the usual indicators of a haz mat incident will not be present. The location will be benign of haz mat storage or transportation facilities, and not have identifiable containers, placards, material safety data sheets (MSDS), or shipping papers. First responders may not immediately recognize a chemical incident; it will take longer (maybe days) to accurately identify the substance.

First responders must look for indicators and remember several important points:

1. Suspect a chemical agent if you are presented with several non-trauma patients with like symptoms.
2. Check for patients that may be scattered throughout a crowd or facility.

3. Look for convergent responders that are showing symptoms; beware of direct exposure or transfer of mechanisms of injury from patients to responders.
4. Does the patient area smell funny or unusual?
5. In extreme cases, an FBL indicates the hot zone (no man's land).
6. Listen for radio traffic from other units indicating multiple patients.
7. Establish a hot zone fast; get the walking patients out.
8. Call for special teams quickly; control hot zone entry.

Set up a decon area for mass casualty patients (see Chapter 6).

In summary, your scene awareness in a chemical attack can save your life and the lives of your patients. Act fast, establish a hot zone, and observe safe hot zone entry principles. In all terrorism/tactical violence events prepare before arrival. Use all of your senses; be suspicious of anything that does not sound, look, feel, or smell right. Use the safety principles of 2 in 2 out and LACES. Lastly, remember that the purpose of the event may be to kill you. Don't join the FBL!

The First Arriving Unit

No matter where you fit in the management hierarchy, someone has to get there first. The first arriving unit has a drastic effect (positive or negative) on the progress of the incident. Remember the key principle of IMS: Scene management builds from the bottom up. This means the first arriving unit is the incident manager, and is responsible for operations, logistics, and planning. Obviously, this is an impossible task without prioritizing. Getting help is the first priority. Make a quick scene survey and transmit a radio report. The first report is almost always inaccurate; that is okay, give the details later. In the initial report give your command post location (remember you are the incident manager at this point) and a basic description of the event such as "mass shooting victims" or "multiple non-trauma patients." Make sure the report is received by your communications center. Don't leave your vehicle until you get feedback confirming reception.

If the event is a nonviolent mass casualty incident, your partner or crew members can begin triage efforts. If the event is terrorism/tactical violence, stay with other crew members (2 in 2 out). Try to determine the scope of the hot zone, an approximate number of patients, and a mechanism of injury. Talk to convergent responders and make every effort to gain relevant information from the usual scene hysteria.

It is critical that you transmit scene threats over the dispatch radio system. Make sure dispatchers relay this information to other units and agencies. This includes information such as:

1. Shooters on the scene or perpetrators with weapons
2. Suspicious device(s)
3. A possible CBR hot zone

As help arrives, the first arriving unit assigns operational functions. These functions must be conducted with scene awareness and safety in mind.

Finally, command is relinquished by the first due unit when a senior officer, supervisor, or manager arrives. This process is done on a face-to-face basis and announced over the dispatch radio channel.

The following example demonstrates the responsibilities of the first arriving unit. A call is dispatched for respiratory difficulty at a religious institution conducting worship services. Rescue 7 arrives at the front entrance; already things don't look right. There are two patients on the building steps; respiratory difficulty with no apparent trauma. Several convergent responders are removing other patients from the building and everyone is coughing.

The unit transmits the following report: "Rescue 7 on scene; we have multiple respiratory patients; send two additional rescues and a chief officer; command post is in front of 5530 58th Street."

The paramedic sends her EMT partner into the building to begin triage and obtain a patient count. The EMT stops at the doorway after discovering at least ten patients inside gasping for breath. The building interior is too "hot" to enter.

The paramedic orders the EMT out of the area, and transmits the following report: "Rescue 7, priority traffic; we have multiple respiratory patients, at least ten in the building; declaring a hot zone in the interior and front entrance for unknown chemical agent; request a full first alarm fire response and the haz mat team; request additional law enforcement units; notify emergency management."

Critical Factor: Proper actions by the first responding units are critical for an effective outcome.

Scene Control

In any emergency incident, scene control is a difficult issue. Terrorism/tactical violence incidents present new and challenging scene control problems. The objective of scene control is to establish a secure perimeter around the scene/hot zone for the purpose of controlling entry and exit from the incident area. Entry control prevents civilians or media from converging on the area. Effective scene control also establishes entry points where personnel and units are logged in for accountability purposes. Unfortunately, terrorism/tactical violence hot zones are very dynamic (the scene can grow in many directions). Shooters on the move or rooftop snipers expand an incident by several blocks. The discovery of an unexploded device or a secondary device requires an evacuation area of 1,000 feet in every direction including up and maybe down.

Keeping people in the hot zone from leaving the scene is a new scene control issue unfamiliar to most of us. In a chemical, biological, or radiological incident, it is important to keep victims in an evacuation area. We do not want contaminated victims spreading the mechanism of injury. When patients leave in a hundred different directions, they contaminate vehicles, people, and buildings. In urban areas, commuters will get on trains or return home in their cars, only to later present at suburban emergency rooms. (Back to the scenario of contaminated people arriving at ERs everywhere.)

The solution to this problem is difficult. First, there's no corporate memory of a large civilian CBR event. However, if large-scale industrial

FIGURE 3-2   Students from Columbine High School are extricated from the hot zone during the tragic 1999 tactical violence incident. *Source:* Courtesy Hal Stoelzle/Denver Rocky Mountain News/Corbis/Sygma

accidents are indicators, there will be great difficulty in controlling patient exits. Many patients will leave before we get there, especially if untrained convergent responders are eager to transport them. Other victims will heed warnings to stay in place, but later grow impatient with a long line waiting for decontamination. Lastly, some patients will refuse the indignity of stripping down to their underwear to have themselves and their loved ones scrubbed by men or women in funny suits.

The answer is to do the best you can. Realize that many patients will initially escape. (That is why it is crucial, really crucial, for ERs to have an aggressive decontamination plan). Secondary patients have to be decontaminated as dictated by practicality. In most cases (not all), basic steps of clothing removal and wash down, done quickly, will suffice. If you lose control, at least settle for the clothing removal. Some alarmists raise the issue of using force to contain grossly contaminated patients to prevent further injury to rescuers or civilians. In practicality, such force will not be accepted, because the person exerting the force must be fully suited for protection from the patients (this is an opinion based on educated guesses and a few case histories). In the Tokyo sarin gas attack, patients were not effectively confined. They scattered from the hot zone to get breathable air and affected rescuers.

The following example demonstrates some practical scene control issues:

Event: A crime syndicate plans a multimillion dollar armored car robbery. To create a diversion, a street gang is subcontracted to explode a chlorine tank car on a downtown railroad siding. At 12:07 P.M., the tank car has a violent pressure rupture caused by a few pounds of strategically placed plastic explosives.

Casualties: In a second, 40 people are killed. Within minutes 160 people are injured from acute chlorine exposure. Thirty convergent responders and three police officers approach the scene and are immediately overcome by chlorine gas.

Response: The incident generates an immediate second alarm fire response and the arrival of two EMS units. Units approaching from the north see a large green fog accumulating in the low-lying area around ground zero. A chlorine cloud is seen drifting south. Units approaching from the south begin driving into the chlorine cloud and have to divert their response.

Victims: Mass casualties are reported with an FBL. Many patients are staggering in all directions from the scene. Some patients are leaving in taxis and private vehicles. Victims receiving minimal exposure are moving farther away or back to their offices.

Scene Control Procedures:
- There is a static hot zone at ground zero.
- There is a moving hot zone traveling to the south.
- Patients are diverted to three staging areas (west, north, east) for decontamination and medical treatment.
- An evacuation is conducted south of the incident.

Scene Control Issues:
- Many patients have left before scene control is established. Within 10 minutes the two nearest hospitals are inundated with contaminated patients arriving in private vehicles.
- In spite of a heavy chlorine odor, media, bystanders, and friends or relatives of the victims begin trying to enter the patient treatment areas.
- Because of a slow decontamination process, many "walking wounded" patients are becoming adamant about leaving to go home or get personal medical care from their private physicians.
- Within one hour, multiple 911 calls are being received for patients in offices, transit stations, and residences who were originally on the incident scene.
- For the next 48 hours, reports are continually received about patients presenting at suburban emergency rooms as far as 50 miles from the event.
- The scene requires entry by hundreds of EMS, fire, and law enforcement agencies.
- CNN breaks the story, opening the floodgates for every conceivable type of media response. Media pressure to get closer and closer to ground zero escalates.

Scene Control Solutions:
- Hospitals throughout the region are alerted. The importance of decontamination before admission is stressed.
- On-site monitoring is used to determine the extent of the hot zone. The perimeter is reduced accordingly.
- A strong law enforcement perimeter is established in the crime area. All evidence is properly preserved, photographed, cataloged, and removed.
- Scene entry points are established for public safety personnel to control warm zone and hot zone access. A local personnel accountability system is effectively utilized.
- All receiving hospitals initiate entry control procedures. Contaminated vehicles are diverted to a remote and secured parking lot (not the ER driveway). Arriving patients are diverted to a decon area outside the building for clothing removal and initial wash down. No patient is permitted entry into any hospital area without being decontaminated.

- 911 calls outside the incident area are handled by a beefed-up response force of mutual aid units and recall personnel. Records from all chlorine exposure patients are separately maintained for inclusion into a final after-action report. All cases are also reported to law enforcement for future investigation.
- The media is instructed to establish a media pool. The media pool is given a closely supervised escorted tour of areas cleared by the safety officer and law enforcement.

Effective control of an incident perimeter places a high drain on law enforcement resources. Consider controlling a four square block area. A chemical hot zone can easily get this big. This hypothetical area requires a minimum of 16 units for control. To place a unit halfway down each block on the perimeter requires 32 law enforcement units. This is a commitment of resources that severely taxes even the largest urban police or sheriff's department.

Another issue is maintaining law enforcement response times for 911 services unrelated to the major event. A third consideration is that many units will be engaged within the perimeter in a mass shooting or bombing scenario.

In summary, major terrorism/tactical violence incidents that require perimeter security are very high-impact law enforcement events. Effective sealing of a large urban area is very difficult and resource intensive under the best of circumstances. If possible, the scene area should be reduced as soon as practical. In the previous example, if the four square block area was reduced to two square blocks, the number of perimeter control units would be reduced from 32 to 16 units.

An uncontrollable factor in a chem-bio event is wind change. A 90 degree wind change, or a change in wind speed that optimizes a chemical plume footprint greatly changes the size and/or location of the hot zone. Sudden changes make effective perimeter control impossible in the short term because of a shifting and dynamic perimeter. Such changes require altering the evacuation zone; a step that cannot be done well on the run.

The last significant factor is public reaction—the "CNN factor." Informal observation by many peers suggests that a media evacuation announcement draws people to an area. These are not the helpful convergent responders that we discussed earlier. Amazingly, some people actually say, "Gee whiz, Martha, I've never seen a chemical attack before. Let's load up the kids and go watch." Other entry issues include friends or relatives rushing to a scene or parents entering an area to retrieve their kids. This situation will never change; onlookers and parents will always present scene control problems.

Response Training

In most emergency response agencies, the survival skills for living through a terrorism/tactical violence incident require development and training. The most important component is the implementation and daily use of the IMS. IMS must be the "gold standard" for the operation of response and support agencies (see Chapter 2, "The Basics of the Incident Management System").

Every agency must be trained in basic IMS as a starter. The IMS must pervade all areas of agency operations, not just emergencies. Daily business should be conducted using IMS forms and jargon. This means that IMS is a way of life. For example, Tad Stone, the previous public safety director for Citrus County, Florida, used the IMS boilerplate for meeting agendas. Items were listed under four columns entitled operations, logistics, planning, and administration. He also produced a biweekly plan using the official ICS incident action plan form. The point: Use IMS every day in all facets of your agency. When a major terrorism/tactical violence event unfolds, the teams will know how to play.

Convergent responder awareness is another important training objective. Trained convergent responders provide valuable crisis management information (intel) and assist early in the consequence response.

The first step in convergent responder training is to identify the government agencies and utilities. Identify the private business agencies on a separate list. Mandate training for government agencies and solicit cooperation from utilities and private businesses.

Using a traditional "brick and mortar" classroom to train a myriad of agencies in a convergent responders program is time consuming and expensive for all parties. Virtual training is one answer. Using the Internet, e-mail, and teleconference calling, information and basic awareness programs can be disseminated to any organization. Virtual technology is also being used to monitor certification and new employee orientation. By using the Internet, response agencies become a training source with minimal expenditure of personnel. Private businesses can determine when to utilize the material and schedule employee awareness sessions. At the very least, have a training video and supplement it with handouts.

On major high-threat events, specialized convergent responder awareness training should be conducted for security guards, staffers, ushers, maintenance personnel, concession workers, tour guides, and others. This includes events such as a papal visit, political conventions, presidential visits, political issue rallies, (pro-life, pro-choice, animal rights, etc.) and major sporting events. Before the 1996 Olympics, thousands of workers received terrorism/tactical violence awareness training. Such a program is time consuming and expensive, but a single truck driver reporting a "suspicious incident" can keep an attack in the crisis mode and prevent a consequence tragedy.

Special teams have established standards and training certification levels that must be maintained. This sounds like a given, but in some locales, special team activity is infrequent, and the specialists lose their edge. These teams also need terrorism/tactical violence awareness programs, including SWAT units, SWAT medics, search and rescue teams, and haz mat teams.

All emergency responders must be trained in scene awareness. The principles of 2 in 2 out and LACES (lookout, awareness, communication, escape, and rescue) should be in a written protocol and part of a scene awareness program. All terrorism/tactical violence incidents, especially the small ones, should be reviewed for scene awareness issues. An effective post incident analysis is also a good training aid.

Medical Facility Response

Medical facilities do not respond in the same sense as emergency responders. However, a terrorism/tactical violence incident requires facilities to alter their general mode of operation and respond to the demands of the event. Granted, hospitals do not respond by driving to a scene, but they do respond by preparing for unusual patients in mass numbers.

The initial element in hospital preparation that drives the rest of the hospital response system is communications. Medical receiving facilities must be alerted early in the event chain. This is the same process used in standard mass casualty procedures. Early warning gives facilities time to prepare for a patient onslaught. Information about the type of incident and numbers of patients is critical. For example, 10 mass shooting patients, 13 bombing victims, or 20 chemical attack victims all trigger different preparedness responses.

Communications are assured (or have a high potential for success) through the use of correct protocol and technology. Your local protocol must specify that terrorism/tactical violence events initiate immediate notification of appropriate receiving facilities. As EMS communications transmits scene information, medical facilities must be in the receiving loop. Medical control is a dispatch center or control medical facility that monitors local/regional bed status and specialties available and is a critical element.

A protocol for hospital communications must specify feedback from critical medical facilities. In many systems, EMS and/or fire communications are monitored in the ER. There are a million reasons why initial information about a terrorism/tactical violence event may not be heard on a busy night (okay, a million is an exaggeration, but you get the point). Don't depend on one-way monitoring. Require by protocol that medical receiving facilities acknowledge receiving notification of an unusual event.

Medical facilities should have several layers of technology to ensure receipt of communications. There must be auxiliary power and back-up systems for failure of private systems and electrical power. (A detailed discussion of communications technology is not within the scope of this text.) At the least, a secondary system must back up the telephone system.

Hospital security is a key nonmedical element in hospital response. Workplace violence and gang-related mass shootings might migrate from the scene to the ER. The number one cause of workplace death for physicians and nurses is gun violence. The assailants in several case histories have gone to the ER attempting to finish off their victims. In a 1998 incident in Toledo, Ohio, an assailant was killed near the ER. He was attempting to kill two children in the hospital after killing two women and wounding two fire department paramedics several miles away.

Hospital security should be immediately alerted when mass shooting victims are being transported to the facility. Armed officers should secure entry to the ER and related treatment areas.

Contaminated patients en route to an ER require a different type of security plan. Security should initiate a complete facility lock down. Every effort must be made to protect the facility from contaminated patients bypassing decon procedures. Erik Auf der Heide, in his excellent book *Disaster Response* (Mosby, 1989), points out that in mass casualty incidents, over 50 percent of the patients arrive at the hospital in private vehicles or by other means. Additionally, the Hazardous Substances Emergency Event Surveillance Annual Report indicates that only 18.5 percent of contaminated victims are treated at the scene of an exposure. The remainder seek out contamination treatment at medical facilities/hospitals. You cannot expect chemically exposed patients to arrive via EMS in a "clean" condition.

Critical Factor: Patients may also present at physician offices or emergicare centers hours or days later.

If the decon area is separate from the ER entrance, security must be positioned to direct arriving vehicles (EMS and private cars) to the decon corridor. In any terrorism/tactical violence incident, the CNN factor goes into hyper-drive. Victims' friends and relatives follow the media swarm. Both situations require security control. All private vehicles are assumed to be contaminated and must be diverted from driveways to a vehicle staging area. The vehicles can be decontaminated later after patient removal.

Unfortunately, some hospitals use contract security that is not permanently assigned to the facility. A guard assigned to the hospital one day may have been at a park on the previous day. This is especially true on weekends. For this reason, security checklists and protocols for each guard should be written in a pocket guide format and issued to each security officer, especially guards on rotation. The pocket guide procedures should be brief and consist of critical factors only. Forget the usual two-inch thick notebook. Remember that if your facility has contracted security that frequently rotates, the traditional methods of orientation and training will not work.

Critical Factor: Hospital/medical facilities *must* adopt terrorism incident protocols within their disaster plans as well as secure the necessary equipment to support actions related to these types of events.

Reliance upon local emergency response agencies to augment hospital capacity to manage patient load or decontamination is unwise. We discourage this dependency based upon the understanding that most, if not all, emergency assets will be either committed to the management of the incident (at the site) or sustaining 911 operations for calls unrelated to the terrorism incident.

CHAPTER SUMMARY

The key response issues relating to a terrorism/tactical violence incident are:

1. Local agencies will always be the cornerstone of an effective terrorism/tactical violence response. Plan to be self-sustaining for 12 to 24 hours before federal help arrives.
2. Convergent responders arrive before first responders. Identify convergent responder agencies and develop an awareness training program for them.
3. A terrorism/tactical violence scene is definitely a hostile workplace environment. Focusing on victims instead of overall scene awareness can get you killed. Use your senses; look around before charging in. Beware of a chemical hot zone, shooters in the area, and primary or secondary explosive devices.
4. Use the buddy system when entering an unsecured scene by applying the 2 in 2 out principle. Also apply the wildland fire fighting principle of LACES: lookout, awareness, communications, escape, and safety zone.
5. A trend of mass shootings and tactical ultra-violence means more exposure to ballistic hot zones. Examine the peripheral areas of a scene, including roofs or other high places. Use the principle of distance and cover for self-protection. If you're debating about ducking and running you should have already been doing it.

6. The IMS is the boilerplate for management of terrorism/tactical violence incidents. Learn it, implement it, train on it, exercise it, and use it.

7. Scene control is a critical factor in a terrorism/tactical violence event and has high impact on law enforcement. Victims, witnesses, and possible assailants must be kept on the scene. Other groups will attempt to enter the scene such as media, onlookers, and friends and families of the victims.

8. All emergency responders must be specially trained for terrorism/tactical violence incidents. This includes IMS proficiency, scene awareness, and special team training.

9. Medical facilities must initiate response protocols for processing and treating mass casualty terrorism/tactical violence patients. Facility response begins with effective communications to provide early scene information.

10. Hospital security is a critical factor in medical facility preparedness. In a mass shooting, the ER must be physically protected from possible perpetrators. In a chemical attack, contaminated patients must be diverted to the decon area and the facility should be locked down.

CHAPTER QUESTIONS

1. What are convergent responders? What are their strengths and weaknesses?

2. List the public and private convergent responder agencies in your community.

3. What are the unsafe conditions that may be present at a terrorism/tactical violence incident?

4. What is the 2 in 2 out principle? Discuss the LACES principle.

5. What is the importance of IMS in terrorism/tactical violence incidents?

6. List and discuss the major scene control issues in a terrorism/tactical violence event.

7. What are some of the security responsibilities of a medical facility when a terrorism/tactical violence incident is in progress?

8. What procedures should be initiated by a medical facility when contaminated patients are en route?

Simulation

Research the response procedures of your local fire, EMS, and law enforcement agencies. Do these procedures address tactical violence scenes? Develop a comprehensive terrorism/tactical violence operational procedure based on the concepts and key issues discussed in this chapter.

4
Planning for Terrorism/Tactical Violence

Paul M. Maniscalco
Hank T. Christen

Source: Courtesy H. Christen

Chapter Objectives

After reading this chapter, you will be able to accomplish the following objectives:

1. Understand the importance of planning as a front-end concept.
2. Recognize the importance of incorporating terrorism/tactical violence in an emergency operations plan (EOP).
3. Outline the key (IMS) elements in a consequence plan.
4. Distinguish between an EOP and a real-time (IAP).
5. Understand the importance of logistics in an emergency operations plan.
6. Understand the importance of liaison with other agencies in effective emergency planning.

Planning—A Front-End Concept

Effective consequence response to a terrorism/tactical violence event is perceived as action oriented. We picture quick and aggressive operations and tactics. This picture is hopefully accurate in a well-organized event. However, the use of tactical units never occurs without effective planning.

Advanced planning is a front-end concept. This means that for a positive outcome (efficient operations) to occur at the back end, we must heavily load the front end. No one is lucky enough to dynamically deploy in a terrorism/tactical violence incident and be successful without planning.

Critical Factor: Plan on the front end to ensure success on the back end.

A front-end plan is different than a reference guide. Many disaster plans are a two inch thick binder that includes radio frequencies, names and addresses, lists of vehicles, units, and descriptions of resources. These guides are important for reference information, but are not documents that yield "quick and dirty" guidelines in the heat of battle. There is nothing wrong with reference information; it's important, but it's not a plan that guides you through the critical steps of a disaster or terrorism/tactical violence incident.

An effective plan is an easy-to-read document that guides you through the critical factors of a dynamic event; the plan identifies operations and support functions that complement operations. In other words, the plan is an incident management system (IMS) guide.

IMS—The Boilerplate for Planning

IMS is not only a response system but also a template for planning. An effective plan guides you through the IMS functions. As discussed in Chapter 2, ("The Basics of the Incident Management System"), all emergency functions consist of a management staff, operations, logistics, planning, and administration. It makes sense to use the IMS model when developing effective operational plans.

An emergency operations plan (EOP) for terrorism/tactical violence incidents should identify key elements such as:

- Management staff
- Operations
- Logistics
- Administration
- Planning

Who Is in Charge?

Command turf wars have no place in a terrorism/tactical violence incident. Emergency response agencies have to sit down ahead of time and work out who will manage what type of event. This may not be easy, but it must be done. Federal and state agencies have elaborate plans and statutes that identify who (or what) will manage the event, but they are at least hours away and maybe days away from your community. If you are local, you will be there first, and you are on your own.

If an event meets the federal definition of terrorism, federal agencies will have jurisdiction. In accordance with PDD 39 (Presidential Decision Directive) the FBI (Department of Justice) has jurisdiction in crisis management and criminal investigation and the FEMA coordinates consequence management. The key word here is "coordinate," for FEMA does not have a response capability. FEMA can only coordinate federal teams with local teams. Even if everything goes perfectly, it will be many hours or longer before federal support is available.

The local community must be able to establish scene management immediately and maintain command throughout the incident. The critical step is to determine who is in charge. In most local governments the responsibility for scene management in terrorism/tactical violence events rests with the ranking law enforcement official. However, terrorism/tactical violence incidents are complex and require a number of agencies. As previously explained, the incident will involve a large EMS and fire/rescue commitment with the appropriate command responsibilities.

There are two solutions. The first solution is a single agency incident manager, such as a sheriff or police chief, with EMS and fire/rescue operating at

FIGURE 4-1 Identification of lead agencies prior to an incident, during the planning process, is good planning policy and avoids confusion. *Source:* Courtesy M. Cross

branch levels. The second solution is unified management (unified command). A unified management team is utilized when multiple agencies have jurisdiction in a complex incident. Consider a bombing with a building collapse and mass casualties; clearly, there are major EMS, fire/rescue, and law enforcement operations that must effectively coordinate. In this case, a command post with a joint EMS/fire/law enforcement management team is the solution.

Unified management requires that all managers be located in the same area (a command vehicle or an emergency operations center) and share information. The planning section makes this happen by effective status display and comprehensive interagency action plans. Separate command posts for each major agency never works. Each agency tends to freelance and coordination does not happen.

Unified management does not begin in the heat of battle. It starts with effective planning well before a terrorism incident. The responsibility of each agency must be specifically defined and written. Emergency management facilitates the formal development of unified management through the local comprehensive emergency management plan.

> **Critical Factor:** An essential step in consequence management planning is to determine who will be in charge.

In many ways, the informal development of unified management is more significant than the formal process. Managers must get to know each other. The corporate world uses the term "networking." It means that various agency managers initiate mutual support by breaking bread and sharing coffee. A community disaster committee is an excellent vehicle to schedule quarterly meetings where mutual incident management issues are discussed and agency heads get to know each other. In summary, managers cannot meet each other for the first time in a major incident, and expect to coordinate effectively.

Operations

The EOP must identify operations agencies in the local/regional area that are trained and equipped to handle specific operational problems. On the surface this may seem like an easy task. Obviously, EMS, fire, public health, and law enforcement have clearly defined and visible tasks. However, terrorism/tactical violence incidents present unique operational problems. Many of these issues require special teams not available in even large urban areas. Special terrorism/tactical violence operational problems include the following:

1. Heavily armed tactical teams to combat terrorists with automatic weapons.
2. Haz mat teams equipped to detect, penetrate, and decontaminate radiological incidents.
3. EMS teams that triage, treat, and transport large numbers of mass casualty patients.
4. A decontamination unit that can decon hundreds of patients in a chemical attack.
5. A public health unit that can detect and track mass disease patients in a biological attack (medical surveillance).
6. Search and rescue teams for structural collapse events.
7. Computer antiterrorist units.

The listed scenarios are not common incidents. At the time of this writing, there is not a single city in the United States that has the capability of managing all of these events. If special teams are not locally available, the plan must identify other sources. These sources include federal response teams, military units, state and regional agencies, and private response resources.

FIGURE 4-2   Pre-packaged caches of equipment transport ready are the most effective means for logistic support during a high-impact—high-yield incident. *Source:* Courtesy H. Christen

In reality, no single local government can afford all the anticipated resources. However, an effective threat assessment and planning process reveals areas of vulnerability and identifies possible operational units capable of threat response.

Logistics

Terrorism/tactical violence events are often destructive because equipment and supplies are consumed faster than they are replaced. We can manage a small bombing, but in an Oklahoma City type event, we run out of radio channels, people, vehicles, supplies, medications, and hospital beds. Examples of critical equipment needs in terrorism/tactical violence incidents are:

- People
- Weapons/crime scene supplies
- EMS units
- Protective equipment
- Medical supplies/ventilators
- ER/surgical facilities
- Detection and decontamination equipment
- Vehicles/aircraft

- Medical laboratories
- Medications/antidotes (pharmaceutical cache)
- Communications

In long duration incidents there is an added demand for crew rehabilitation, food/water, sleeping facilities, and sanitation measures.

An effective plan identifies logistics sources. The plan is based on the correct assumption that first response resources are immediately depleted. The availability of resources that address the previously listed problem areas are outlined in the plan. There are several solutions for critical logistics needs such as:

1. Logistics caches for regional support, such as a decontamination cache of washing supplies, protective equipment, and 100 Tyvek™ suits.
2. Mutual aid agreements, such as an agreement for a neighboring fire department to provide haz mat detection equipment.
3. Military support, such as a memorandum of understanding (MOU) with a local military installation for critical personnel or equipment.
4. Private contracting, such as an agreement with a chemical spill response company to provide chemical spill control or radiation equipment.
5. State/Federal support, such as procedures for requesting state and federal logistical support; nationwide pharmaceutical cache system.

Logistics caches must be packaged and stored for rapid deployment. Plastic carrying boxes, also called nesting boxes, are recommended. They are quickly loaded on a vehicle and rapidly transported. Avoid storing caches in a back room where they gather dust. Supplies should be accessible, packaged, and in good condition when needed for a "once in a career" incident.

Cost and quantities are other real world issues. How much should we buy and how much can we afford? These are tough questions. The history of the local area and the political climate greatly influence the financial commitment. A selling point is that equipment caches are needed for all types of disasters, not just terrorism. The question of quantities is just as complex. There is no formula based on population or threat assessment to determine how many Tyvek™ suits, body bags, or atropine injections a community needs. On the surface it seems obvious that high-threat urban areas should have the biggest caches, but what about a small college town that has a football stadium filled with 50,000 fans on a given Saturday? Again, there is no answer.

At a minimum, there should be enough medications and protective equipment for first responders and mutual aid personnel. This sounds self-serving, but the logic is irrefutable. We must protect ourselves and ensure

FIGURE 4-3 Remember in your planning to incorporate provisions to be self-sustaining for at least 48–72 hours. That is how long it will take for the federal special teams to arrive if you require their assistance. *Source:* Courtesy J. Dickens

our own survivability so we can take care of our customers. Key logistics points are:

1. Logistics takes planning.
2. Equipment and supplies must be pushed quickly to a scene.
3. Logistics caches must be accessible and maintained.
4. Budgets and political realities will always be logistics issues.
5. Estimates of logistics quantities are at best a semi-educated guess.
6. We need enough equipment and supplies to protect ourselves.

Administration

Administration functions are omitted from most emergency plans. In normal operations, individual agencies take care of the usual administrative duties such as finance/purchasing, workers compensation, and payroll records.

During major disasters, administrative requirements escalate. Normal administration is no longer suitable. Purchasing and contracting in the middle of the night, or tracking personnel from state and national agencies is a function that local agency administrative personnel have not experienced.

An EOP addresses administrative needs by establishing an administrative section chief who supervises the following:

1. Finance unit—performs purchasing/contracting duties, maintains records of all fiscal activities, develops post-incident financial reports for state/federal reimbursements.

2. Time unit—tracks all personnel and maintains hours and pay records; develops payroll report for state/federal reimbursement.
3. Compensation/claims unit—tracks and administrates all claims relating to the incident; tracks and handles submission of workers compensation claims.

The typical reader of this book is tactically oriented and may give little thought to administration until they have to account for expenditures approaching $1 million per day. If you are a mid-level or upper level manager, go back and read the administration paragraphs again. If an administrative section is not included in your EOP, your plan is inadequate.

Critical Factor: Don't allow your operations/logistics mind-set to blind you to the administrative needs of a major terrorism/tactical violence incident.

Planning Section

If there is no provision for planning, an EOP would not exist. The EOP is usually developed and maintained by emergency management, by a local interagency disaster committee, or both. An effective emergency manager plays a coordinating role in bringing competing agencies together and implementing the EOP. As many agency managers as possible should participate in the EOP development. The document should also be formally signed. When conflicts arise, agency heads are reminded of their responsibilities according to the EOP gospel.

The EOP should establish the position of planning section chief for disasters and terrorism/tactical violence incidents. The planning section chief is responsible for developing the IAP, conducting planning briefings, and supervising the following units:

- Resource unit—establishes an incident check-in procedure; maintains a master list of all incident resources; tracks location and status of all resources; assigns resources based on operational requests.
- Situation unit—collects and analyzes situation data; prepares incident map displays; displays critical incident information; prepares incident predictions at request of planning section chief; obtains and displays incident weather data.
- Demobilization unit—coordinates with resource unit to track incident resources; obtains incident manager's demobilization plans; establishes resource check-in; determines transportation and logistics needs related to demobilization.

- Documentation unit—responsible for maintaining accurate and complete incident files including duplication services, packing, and storing.
- Technical advisor(s)—specialists in any field relevant to the incident (e.g., a meteorologist, or an epidemiologist in a biological incident).

EOP Summary

The EOP is a comprehensive plan (sometimes called a comprehensive emergency management plan) that uses the IMS as a benchmark to establish an interagency plan of attack for terrorism/tactical violence incidents. The key steps in the implementation phase of an EOP are:

1. Coordinate with all convergent and local/regional response agencies.
2. Assign EOP responsibility to emergency management.
3. Conduct a terrorism/tactical violence threat assessment in your community.
4. Identify operational and logistics needs based on your threat assessment.
5. Produce a formal document signed by cooperating agency managers.
6. Perceive the EOP as an evolving document that is never done.

The EOP has the following key elements:

1. Specify who is in charge.
2. Make provisions for unified management in complex incidents. Base scene management on the overhead team concept. (An overhead team is the incident management team.)
3. Establish a management staff for public information, safety, and liaison.
4. Establish an operations section and identify operational agencies.
5. Establish a logistics section and identify logistics requirements.
6. Establish a planning section.
7. Establish an administration section.
8. Train section chiefs and unit leaders.
9. Conduct tabletop and operational exercises to test your plan.

Smaller communities are overwhelmed with the personnel demands of a full scale EOP implementation. Remember that in any disaster, overhead team positions are only filled as needed. The critical concept is that any function not assigned by the incident manager is his or her responsibility. It is very important to identify critical personnel from other support agencies or mutual aid agencies and train them to function as the overhead team. This is especially significant in locales that have inadequate staffing.

The IAP

An IAP is a plan of objectives for implementing an overall incident strategy. The IAP is a tactical plan for an operational period. Unlike the EOP, the incident action plan is related to a specific incident and a set of dynamic circumstances. The EOP is reference oriented whereas the IAP is action oriented.

On routine incidents or a small mass casualty event, a scene manager follows a protocol without a written plan. Planning is "on the fly" with the aid of a quick checklist. Major incidents need a formal IAP because an escalating event requires increased resources, increased variables, and an extended time period. The event also increases in geographical area requiring several divisions. Incidents of this nature present three major planning problems:

1. No individual can keep all the strategies in his or her head.
2. No single individual can plan all the strategies without consultation and help.
3. There is no way to convey the strategies, objectives, and assignments to others without a written document.

The solution is a formalized IAP. "When do you go formal?" is a valid question. In a short-duration incident, an informal plan communicated verbally will suffice. When an incident progresses beyond a 12-hour operational period, a written plan is prepared, briefed, and distributed to operational shifts. This is especially important if night operations are continued. If night operations are scaled down, a daily morning briefing is adequate.

The development of a 12-hour or daily IAP keeps a planning section chief busy. Fortunately, there is a nationally accepted format developed by the National Wildfire Coordinating Group. This format is fire oriented, but has been adapted for all risk type incidents, including terrorism/tactical violence events. There are several forms associated with the IAP that serve as checklists completed by the appropriate supervisor, and require information that greatly eases the IAP process.

The forms address critical planning areas:

1. ICS 202, Incident Objectives—includes basic strategy/objectives for the overall incident and includes critical areas such as safety concerns and forecasted weather.
2. ICS 203, Organizational Assignment List—includes operations sections with all branch directors and division/group supervisors; includes logistics section, planning section, and finance (administration) section with the respective units for each section.
3. ICS 204, Division Assignment List—a list for each branch (operations), divisions assigned to each branch, division managers, and units assigned to each division.

4. ICS 205, Incident Radio Communications Plan—lists administrative frequencies, operations frequencies, and tactical channels; lists telephone numbers for managers and key agencies; specifies an overall communications plan including secondary and tertiary communications networks.
5. ICS 206, Medical Plan—formalizes medical support for overhead team and on-scene responders; includes nearest hospitals, medical frequencies, and a roster of EMS units. *Note:* In mass casualty incidents, medical operations are delineated in ICS 204 relating to organizational assignments and division assignments.
6. ICS 220, Air Operations Summary Worksheet—lists all air units, air objectives, frequencies, and assignments.
7. Incident Map—a map, computer graphic, or aerial photo depicting the incident area.
8. Safety Plan—safety objectives and hazard warnings (prepared by the safety officer.) *Note:* In biological, chemical, and radiological events, safety procedures are technical and complex.

The formal IAP is not as overwhelming as it may appear. First, the forms serve as a checklist; you fill in the blanks. (Many agencies have their forms on notebook computers.) Second, the IAP is a joint effort. The incident manager, operations units, and specialized units such as medical, safety, weather, and communications contribute to the effort.

Critical Factor: The IAP forms serve as an effective planning checklist.

The IAP Briefing Cycle

In long duration incidents, the IAP is presented during a formal briefing every twelve hours. This is called a planning briefing cycle. The nature of the incident may dictate an eight-hour briefing cycle (at shift changes), or a 24-hour briefing cycle when there are diminished night operations.

The briefing is a very important formal process. All section level and division level commanders, along with appropriate unit leaders should attend the briefing. A 50-person audience or more is not unusual in a complex event.

The IAP is presented by the planning section chief and includes briefings by other specialists such as weather, safety, and technical experts who may include such specialties as medical, radiological, bio-weapons, etc.

Copies of the IAP are distributed to each attendee. An IAP can be 10 pages in length in a major disaster or terrorism/tactical violence incident.

FIGURE 4-4   Remember, if you have integrated military assets into the incident management they need to be included in your briefings. *Source:* Courtesy P. Maniscalco

The IAP copies become a reference for all managers, especially the sections on communications frequencies, unit assignments, and safety procedures.

The National Wildfire Coordinating Group publishes the following formal guidelines in the *Fireline Handbook*. In a 12-hour briefing cycle, IAP preparation progresses as follows:

1. Shift change—receive field observations; one hour.
2. Prepare for planning meeting; one hour.
3. Planning meeting with management staff, section chiefs, agency representatives; one hour.
4. Prepare incident action plan (IAP); four hours.
5. Finalize IAP; two hours.
6. Prepare for operations briefing; one hour.
7. Briefing of management staff, section chiefs, branch/division/unit supervisors; one hour.
8. Finalize reports; one hour.

The briefing cycle is a guideline, and is flexible. The cycle can be shortened or lengthened as appropriate.

> **Critical Factor:**   The IAP must be developed via a briefing cycle suitable for the incident.

Planning Scenario—Example

To demonstrate the use of an EOP and informal and formal IAPs, consider the following scenario:

It is 09:30 hours in Simulation City, California. There is an explosion originating from a parked van on Center Street. One person is killed, 14 people are injured, and windows are shattered throughout the block.

First due law enforcement units arrive at 09:32; fire/rescue and EMS units arrive at 09:35. At 09:41 there is a massive explosion in a complex of government buildings, immediately adjacent to the van explosion site. Many of the first responders are injured or killed. A five-story building collapses (estimated occupancy of 500 people). The major trauma center next to the building is heavily damaged; there are multiple injuries in the hospital from flying glass.

The EOP

The EOP has several sections directly related to an explosive attack on building complexes based on a previous emergency management threat assessment. Key response agencies immediately begin to run checklists based on elements of the EOP. Critical agency managers are immediately notified, as well as the state operations center. The EOP is based on the incident management system and identifies several critical areas:

1. Management—A unified management team is specified, with joint command between law enforcement and fire/rescue.
2. Operations—The three critical operations branches are law enforcement, fire rescue, and EMS. The EOP lists state/federal law enforcement mutual aid, procedures for fire mutual aid, and for requesting an urban search and rescue team (USAR), and procedures for medical mutual aid, including use of a disaster medical assistance team (DMAT).
3. Logistics—The logistics plan lists sources for scene control, vehicles, lighting, generators, back-up communications, fuel, emergency food, construction equipment, and lumber for shoring.
4. Administration—Specifies that expenditures, claims, worker's compensation issues be tracked and establishes the city purchasing director as the supervisor of expenditures.
5. Planning—Establishes the activation of the emergency operations center by emergency management and the establishment of a fully

staffed planning section if the incident becomes protracted, including a resource unit and situation unit.

The Informal IAP

Initial response managers begin arriving and consult checklists developed from the EOP. It is apparent that a major incident is in progress. The chief of police and fire chief establish a command post four blocks from the incident.

An informal IAP is developed in minutes by identifying critical factors. This plan is communicated verbally and by radio to response managers and units. The key elements are:

1. All units search their operational and staging areas for possible secondary devices.
2. Three branches are established: collapse branch, Center Street branch (including the van explosion), and trauma center branch (the EOP never addressed the loss of the trauma center).
3. A recon group is established to assess damage on all sides of the original explosion.
4. Immediate control of the scene perimeter is established.
5. Appropriate EMS, law enforcement, and fire units are assigned to groups/divisions.
6. Triage, treatment, and transport of MCI patients throughout the incident area are addressed.

As hours pass, new problems such as an area power failure and loss of the downtown communications repeater arise. There is also disturbing news that many patients appear to have chemical injuries and a combination explosive/chemical attack is suspected. As these problems evolve, the IAP is affected accordingly.

The unified management team becomes aware in the first hour that this will become a complex, long-duration incident. As a result, they request a pre-established incident team for full staffing of incident management positions. This overhead team is comprised of certified people from a multitude of local and state response agencies.

The scenario progresses to day two:

Day Two—The Formal IAP

The planning section, in coordination with the unified command team and the logistics and operations section chiefs, develops the IAP. Emergency management also establishes a multiagency coordination center (MACC).

The formal action plan is developed using a laptop computer and ICS forms 202–206 (see pages 79–92). Copies are made for each member of the overhead team and all branch directors and division supervisors.

Day Two also dawns with the arrival of federal assistance. The FBI has a full response team assigned to law enforcement operations. The U.S. Marine Corps CBIRF is assigned to the haz mat branch for detection and decontamination. CBIRF strike teams are also available for divisions requiring haz mat support. Lastly, a state National Guard unit is assigned to law enforcement operations for perimeter security.

The following pages demonstrate a completed IAP for an incident of this level. These pages include an incident radio communications plan (ICS 205), medical plan (ICS 206), and an air operations summary (ICS 220). See pages 79 to 92.

CHAPTER SUMMARY

Planning for terrorism/tactical violence is a front-end concept. For a successful tactical outcome on the back end, effective planning must occur at the front end.

The model of an effective emergency operations plan (EOP) is the incident management system (IMS). The plan addresses the key IMS functions of management staff, operations, logistics, planning, and administration. The management component identifies who is in charge and recognizes the concept of unified management. The operations section identifies operations agencies/teams based on an emergency management threat assessment.

Terrorism/tactical violence incidents and disasters consume logistics rapidly. The logistics section of an emergency operations plan must identify logistics needs and agencies or organizations that provide the appropriate people, supplies, and equipment. In a major event logistical support may be regional, state, or federal. Critical logistics requires logistics caches (push logistics) that are quickly deployed to a scene.

An EOP also identifies an administration section and a planning section. The administration section includes a time unit, procurement unit, and a compensation unit. The planning section consists of a resource unit, situation unit, and mobilization/demobilization unit.

An EOP is a reference tool, and not a tactical guide. Incidents are extremely dynamic; critical events change in seconds or minutes. In the "fog" of combat the incident manager develops an informal and verbal incident action plan (IAP).

A long-duration incident (longer than a day) requires a written IAP developed by the planning section chief in coordination with the incident manager and other section chiefs. The National Wildfire Coordinating Group has developed forms for the IAP. The forms serve as a checklist for organizing the event. All section groups and divisions are given a daily briefing along with copies of the IAP.

INCIDENT OBJECTIVES	1. INCIDENT NAME Simulation City explosion	2. DATE PREPARED 3/1/00	3. TIME PREPARED 05:37

4. OPERATIONAL PERIOD (DATE/TIME) 08:00 to 20:00

5. GENERAL CONTROL OBJECTIVES FOR THE INCIDENT (INCLUDE ALTERNATIVES)
Scene control entry/exit
Detailed secondary search
Evidence recovery and preservation
Chemical detection and decontamination
Heavy rescue
Equip and re-open trauma center

6. WEATHER FORECAST FOR OPERATIONAL PERIOD
Heavy fog restricting visibility to 10:30
Wind light from 270 deg.
50% chance rain from 17:00 to 19:00

7. GENERAL/SAFETY MESSAGE
Type of chemical(s) not confirmed in collapse area; treat entire area as "hot zone."
Full ppe required in hot zones
Bio precautions for all divisions
Possible non-detonated explosives; possible secondary devices
Lightning in afternoon thunderstorms

8. ATTACHMENTS (X IF ATTACHED)

- ORGANIZATION LIST (ICS 203) **XXX**   INCIDENT MAPS (2)   Safety Message **XXX**

- DIVISION ASSIGNMENT LIST (ICS 204) **XXX**   TRAFFIC PLAN   Homestead Map

- COMMUNICATIONS PLAN (ICS 205) **XXX**   - Air Operations   Structural Fire Plan
       Summary (ICS 220) **XXX**

- MEDICAL PLAN (ICS 206) **XXX**

202 ICS 3/80	9. PREPARED BY (PLAN- NING SECTION CHIEF)	10. APPROVED BY (INCIDENT COMMANDER)

ORGANIZATION ASSIGNMENT LIST		1. INCIDENT NAME Simulation City explosion		2. DATE PREPARED 3/1/00	3. TIME PREPARED 06:01
5. INCIDENT COMMANDER AND STAFF POSITION	NAME	4. OPERATIONAL PERIOD (DATE/TIME) 08:00 to 20:00 3/1/00			
INCIDENT COMMANDER	Christen/Maniscalco	9. OPERATIONS SECTION			
SAFETY	P Chovan	CHIEF		C Lynne	
		DEPUTY			
INFORMATION OFFICER	T Blackmon			L Foley	
TECHNICAL SPECIALISTS:	J Denney	BRANCH DIRECTOR	I	R Carmine	
		GROUP	A	J Knowles	
7. PLANNING SECTION		GROUP	B	R Sampson	
CHIEF	D Chamberlin	GROUP			
SITUATION UNIT	R Gallagher	BRANCH DIRECTOR	II	M McGuire	
RESOURCES UNIT	D Chavis	GROUP	C	J Sanford	
DOCUMENTATION UNIT		GROUP	D	C Poliseno	
DEMOBILIZATION UNIT		GROUP			
		BRANCH DIRECTOR	III	T Weatherford	
STATUS/CHECK-IN RECORDER		GROUP	E	S Barney	
		GROUP	F	G Solomon	
TECHNICAL SPECIALISTS:	E Robbins				
		BRANCH DIRECTOR	IV	R McAllister	
		GROUP	G	H Tiffany	
		GROUP	H	R Colbert	
8. LOGISTICS SECTION		GROUP			
CHIEF	M Hopmeier	AIR OPERATIONS BRANCH			
SUPPORT BRANCH DIR	L Adams	AIR OPER.BR.DIRECTOR		J Hughes	
SUPPLY UNIT	J Hawkins	HELIBASE MANAGER			
FACILITIES UNIT	R Holden	AIR ATTACK SUPERVISOR			
GROUND SUPPORT	R Pitts	AIR SUPPORT SUPERVISOR			
SERVICE BRANCH DIR	S Katz	HELISPOT MANAGER			
COMMUNICATIONS UNIT	R Stancliff	10. FINANCE SECTION			
MEDICAL UNIT	K Burkholder	S Fallon			
FOOD UNIT	B Dennis	CLAIMS UNIT		R Cohen	
		CHIEF		TIME UNIT	
FOR FORMER BRANCH III		PROCUREMENT UNIT		G Collins	
COORDINATION CONTACT		COST UNIT		R Antonio	
		ADMIN PAYMENT TEAM			
		COST UNIT		R Antonio	
203 ICS 1/82					

1. BRANCH I Collapse	2. DIVISION/GROUP A	DIVISION ASSIGNMENT LIST ICS204
3. INCIDENT NAME Simulation City explosion		4. OPERATIONAL PERIOD DATE 3/1/00 TIME 08 to 20

5. OPERATIONS PERSONNEL

OPERATIONS CHIEF C Lynne
BRANCH DIRECTOR _ R Carmine

DIV/GROUP SUPERVISOR J Kowles
AIR ATTACK SUPERVISOR NO.

6. RESOURCES ASSIGNED THIS PERIOD

STRIKE TEAM/TASK FORCE/ RESOURCE DESIGNATOR	LEADER	NUMBER PERSONS		DESCRIPTION	
FBI	J Wilson	5		Evidence task force	
USAR	F Domino	35		Fl TF-1 urban search & rescue	
Fire/Rescue	J Redner	16		Eng16 eng4 eng6 trk4	
DMAT	G Moore	5		Type II Fl-2 medical task force	
TOTAL		61			

7. OPERATIONS

.Victim search/ collapse rescue; medical support

8. SPECIAL OPERATIONS   Evidence location/removal

9. MEDICAL UNIT   DMAT task force

10. FREQUENCIES   USAR tac 1   Sim City freq 2

PREPARED BY (RESOURCE UNIT LEADER)	APPROVED BY (PLANNING SECTION CHIEF)	DATE 3/1/00	TIME 07:24

1. BRANCH I Collapse	2. DIVISION/GROUP B	DIVISION ASSIGNMENT LIST ICS204

3. INCIDENT NAME Simulation City explosion	4. OPERATIONAL PERIOD DATE 3/1/00 TIME 08 to 20

5. OPERATIONS PERSONNEL

OPERATIONS CHIEF C Lynne   DIV/GROUP SUPERVISOR R Sampson
BRANCH DIRECTOR _ R Carmine   AIR ATTACK SUPERVISOR NO.

6. RESOURCES ASSIGNED THIS PERIOD

STRIKE TEAM/TASK FORCE/ RESOURCE DESIGNATOR	LEADER	NUMBER PERSONS		DESCRIPTION	
FBI	L Freeh	6		Crime scene task force	
USAR	D Salinger	32		Va TF-1 urban search & rescue	
Fire/Rescue	P Williams	17		Eng1 eng58 sq4 trk11	
DMAT	G Moore	5		Medical task force	
TOTAL		60			

7. OPERATIONS

.Victim search/ collapse rescue; medical support

8. SPECIAL OPERATIONS   Evidence removal

9. MEDICAL UNIT   DMAT task force

10. FREQUENCIES   USAR tac 2   Simulation City freq 3

PREPARED BY (RESOURCE UNIT LEADER)	APPROVED BY (PLANNING SECTION CHIEF)	DATE 3/1/00	TIME 07:24

1. BRANCH II Trauma center	2. DIVISION/GROUP C	DIVISION ASSIGNMENT LIST ICS204
3. INCIDENT NAME Simulation City explosion		4. OPERATIONAL PERIOD DATE 3/1/00 TIME 08 to 20

5. OPERATIONS PERSONNEL	
OPERATIONS CHIEF C Lynne BRANCH DIRECTOR _ M McGuire	DIV/GROUP SUPERVISOR J Sanford AIR ATTACK SUPERVISOR NO.

6. RESOURCES ASSIGNED THIS PERIOD

STRIKE TEAM/TASK FORCE/ RESOURCE DESIGNATOR	LEADER	NUMBER PERSONS	DESCRIPTION	
DMAT	E Robbins	35	MA-1 primary care	
DMAT	K Allen	32	OH-1 emer room	
DMAT	C D'Angelo	34	CA-2 clinic	
TOTAL		101		

7. OPERATIONS

Maintain ER operations, support EMS, operate treatment clinic, support primary care

8. SPECIAL OPERATIONS
.

9. MEDICAL UNIT   N/A

10. FREQUENCIES   DMAT tac 4, Simulation City EMS Med 2

PREPARED BY (RESOURCE UNIT LEADER)	APPROVED BY (PLANNING SECTION CHIEF)	DATE 3/1/00	TIME 07:26

1. BRANCH II Trauma center	2. DIVISION/GROUP D	DIVISION ASSIGNMENT LIST ICS204

3. INCIDENT NAME Simulation City explosion	4. OPERATIONAL PERIOD DATE 3/1/00 TIME 08 to 20

5. OPERATIONS PERSONNEL

OPERATIONS CHIEF C Lynne
BRANCH DIRECTOR _ M McGuire

DIV/GROUP SUPERVISOR C Poliseno
AIR ATTACK SUPERVISOR NO.

6. RESOURCES ASSIGNED THIS PERIOD

STRIKE TEAM/TASK FORCE/ RESOURCE DESIGNATOR	LEADER	NUMBER PERSONS		DESCRIPTION	
EMS strike team	Chief Neal Dolan	10		Sim City EMS 6, 14, 8, 7, 2	
LAFD res 27	Chief Neil Cross	3		Heavy rescue	
Orange Co 62	Lt. Reza Golesorkhi	2		ALS unit	
Orange Co 24	EMT M. Griswold	2		BLS unit	
TOTAL		17			

7. OPERATIONS

City wide EMS response to support local 911 system

8. SPECIAL OPERATIONS
.

9. MEDICAL UNIT   N/A

10. FREQUENCIES   EMS med 4

PREPARED BY (RESOURCE UNIT LEADER)	APPROVED BY (PLANNING SECTION CHIEF)	DATE 3/1/00	TIME 07:26

1. BRANCH III Center St.	2. DIVISION/GROUP E		DIVISION ASSIGNMENT LIST ICS204	
3. INCIDENT NAME Simulation City explosion			4. OPERATIONAL PERIOD DATE 3/1/00 TIME 08 to 20	

5. OPERATIONS PERSONNEL

OPERATIONS CHIEF C Lynne
BRANCH DIRECTOR _ T Weatherford

DIV/GROUP SUPERVISOR S Barney
AIR ATTACK SUPERVISOR NO.

6. RESOURCES ASSIGNED THIS PERIOD

STRIKE TEAM/TASK FORCE/ RESOURCE DESIGNATOR	LEADER	NUMBER PERSONS		DESCRIPTION	
FBI	SSA W. Drivet	10		Crime scene unit	
Simulation City PD	Chief Patricia O'Brien	6		Crime scene unit	
Medical Examiner	Dr. K.A. Holtermann	3		Body/remains recovery	
Fire/rescue	Chief Don Hiett	8		Strike team	
TOTAL		27			

7. OPERATIONS

Evidence and body recovery; scene control

8. SPECIAL OPERATIONS   Bio protection and bio waste disposal

9. MEDICAL UNIT   N/A

10. FREQUENCIES   Simulation City PD channel 1 Fire freq 3

PREPARED BY (RESOURCE UNIT LEADER)	APPROVED BY (PLANNING SECTION CHIEF)	DATE 3/1/00	TIME 07:27

1. BRANCH III Center St.	2. DIVISION/GROUP F	DIVISION ASSIGNMENT LIST ICS204

3. INCIDENT NAME Simulation City explosion	4. OPERATIONAL PERIOD DATE 3/1/00 TIME 08 to 20

5. OPERATIONS PERSONNEL

OPERATIONS CHIEF C Lynne   DIV/GROUP SUPERVISOR G Solomon
BRANCH DIRECTOR _ T Weatherford   AIR ATTACK SUPERVISOR NO.

6. RESOURCES ASSIGNED THIS PERIOD

STRIKE TEAM/TASK FORCE/ RESOURCE DESIGNATOR	LEADER	NUMBER PERSONS		DESCRIPTION	
ATF	SA M. Maniscalco	4		Bomb evidence recovery	
FBI	SSA Connie Patton	4		Crime scene unit	
EMS rescue 23	PM Minga	2		ALS medical unit	
Simulation City PD	Capt. M. Newburger	12		PD strike team	
TOTAL		22			

7. OPERATIONS

Center Street damage assessment
Perimeter control

8. SPECIAL OPERATIONS   Evidence detection, photo evidence, and recovery

9. MEDICAL UNIT   EMS rescue 23

10. FREQUENCIES   Simulation City PD channel 2 Fire freq 4

PREPARED BY (RESOURCE UNIT LEADER)	APPROVED BY (PLANNING SECTION CHIEF)	DATE 3/1/00	TIME 07:27

1. BRANCH IV Haz mat	2. DIVISION/GROUP G	DIVISION ASSIGNMENT LIST ICS204

3. INCIDENT NAME Simulation City explosion	4. OPERATIONAL PERIOD DATE 3/1/00 TIME 08 to 20

5. OPERATIONS PERSONNEL

OPERATIONS CHIEF C Lynne   DIV/GROUP SUPERVISOR H Tiffany
BRANCH DIRECTOR _ R McAllister   AIR ATTACK SUPERVISOR NO.

6. RESOURCES ASSIGNED THIS PERIOD

STRIKE TEAM/TASK FORCE/ RESOURCE DESIGNATOR	LEADER	NUMBER PERSONS		DESCRIPTION	
Simulation City haz mat	Gene Chantler	12		Bomb evidence recovery	
Orange Co. haz mat	Bill Lewis	14		Crime scene unit	
USMC CBIRF	Bob Morrone	20		ALS medical unit	
Johnson Co. EMS medic 4	Matt Streger	4		Haz mat medical support	
TOTAL		50			

7. OPERATIONS

Chemical detection and identification
Decontamination for on-scene personnel

8. SPECIAL OPERATIONS

.

9. MEDICAL UNIT   Johnson Co medic 4

10. FREQUENCIES   Simulation City haz mat channel

                         Orange Co tac 1

                         USMC bravo channel

PREPARED BY (RESOURCE UNIT LEADER)	APPROVED BY (PLANNING SECTION CHIEF)	DATE 3/1/00	TIME 07:27

1. BRANCH IV Haz mat	2. DIVISION/GROUP H	DIVISION ASSIGNMENT LIST ICS204
3. INCIDENT NAME Simulation City explosion		4. OPERATIONAL PERIOD DATE 3/1/00 TIME 08 to 20

5. OPERATIONS PERSONNEL

OPERATIONS CHIEF C Lynne   DIV/GROUP SUPERVISOR R Colbert
BRANCH DIRECTOR R McAllister   AIR ATTACK SUPERVISOR NO.

6. RESOURCES ASSIGNED THIS PERIOD

STRIKE TEAM/TASK FORCE/ RESOURCE DESIGNATOR	LEADER	NUMBER PERSONS		DESCRIPTION	
USMC CBIRF	Sgt. Maj. A.S. Maniscalco	22		Chemical detection	
USMC CBIRF	Sgt. R. Christen	18		Patient decontamination	
Johnson Co Sheriff Ofc	Deputy P. Chovan	17		Perimeter/scene control	
TOTAL		57			

7. OPERATIONS

Chemical detection and decontamination in trauma center

8. SPECIAL OPERATIONS

9. MEDICAL UNIT   N/A

10. FREQUENCIES   Johnson Co S/O freq 4

                           USMC alpha channel

PREPARED BY (RESOURCE UNIT LEADER)	APPROVED BY (PLANNING SECTION CHIEF)	DATE 3/1/00	TIME 07:27

INCIDENT RADIO COMMUNICATIONS PLAN

1. INCIDENT NAME	2. DATE/TIME PREPARED	3. OPERATIONAL PERIOD (DATE/TIME)
Simulation City explosion	3/1/00 05:50	08:00 to 20:00

4. BASIC RADIO CHANNEL UTILIZATION

BRANCH/SYSTEM/CACHE	CHANNEL	FUNCTION	FREQUENCY/TONE	ASSIGNMENT	REMARKS
Simulation City haz mat	Tac 1	Haz mat teams	152.250	Haz mat branch	Haz mat ops only
Orange Co	Tac 1	Haz mat team	800.500	Haz mat branch	Haz mat ops only
Johnson Co Sheriff	Freq 4	Dispatch channel	457.400 tx 445.120 rx	Haz mat branch	

5. PREPARED BY (COMMUNICATIONS UNIT)

205 ICS 9/86

INCIDENT RADIO COMMUNICATIONS PLAN

1. INCIDENT NAME	2. DATE/TIME PREPARED	3. OPERATIONAL PERIOD (DATE/TIME)
Simulation City explosion	3/1/00 05:50	08:00 to 20:00

4. BASIC RADIO CHANNEL UTILIZATION

BRANCH/SYSTEM/CACHE	CHANNEL	FUNCTION	FREQUENCY/TONE	ASSIGNMENT	REMARKS
USAR	Tac 1	Rescue teams	172.250	Branch I A	
USAR	Tac 2	Rescue teams	177.500	Branch I B	
DMAT	Tac 4	Medical at trauma center	174.200	Branch II C	For internal team com
Simulation City fire	Freq 2	Collapse area tac & command	458.100 tx 453.600 rx	Branch I A	
Simulation City fire	Freq 3	Collapse area tac and command	457.265 tx 453.700 rx	Branch I B	
Simulation City EMS	Med 2	Med dispatch		Branch II C	
Simulation City EMS	Med 4	Med dispatch		Branch II D	
Simulation City PD	Ch 1	Tac and command	457.100 tx 453.100 rx	Branch III E	
Simulation City PD	Ch 2	Tac and command	456.950 tx 454.015 rx	Branch III F	

5. PREPARED BY (COMMUNICATIONS UNIT)

205 ICS 9/86

MEDICAL PLAN	1. INCIDENT NAME Simulation City explosion	2. DATE PREPARED 3/1/00	3. TIME PREPARED 06:30	4. OPERATIONAL PERIOD 08:00 to 20:00

5. INCIDENT MEDICAL AID STATIONS

MEDICAL AID STATIONS	LOCATION CONTACT THRU DISPATCH	PARAMEDICS	
		YES	NO
Trauma Center 3 DMATs with physicians	123 Pratt St	XXX	
Center St branch II	704 Center St	XXX	

6. TRANSPORTATION A. AMBULANCE SERVICES

NAME	ADDRESS	PHONE	PARAMEDICS	
			YES	NO
Simulation City EMS & mutual aid	City-wide 754 Main Ave	555-2376	XXX	
Johnson Co EMS	County-wide 117 Wilson St	555-2311	XXX	

B. INCIDENT AMBULANCES

NAME	LOCATION	PARAMEDICS	
		YES	NO
Orange Co 62, 64	Trauma center	XXX	
Simulation City EMS 23	Center St	XXX	
Johnson Co medic 4	Haz mat operations – Center St	XXX	

7. HOSPITAL NAME	ADDRESS	TRAVEL TIME (Hr)		PHONE	HELIPAD		BURN CENTER	
		AIR	GRD		YES	NO	YES	NO
Simulation City Trauma Center	123 Pratt St	N/A	1 min	555-2624	XXX			
Baptist Hospital	2766 Mullen Dr	10	30	555-4555	XXX			
Mount Sinai	1749 125th Ave	5	15	555-4002	XXX		X	

8. MEDICAL EMERGENCY PROCEDURES

All pediatric patients to Baptist – burn patients to Mount Sinai

Trauma Center patients admit directly to DMAT tents

All divisions have EMS coverage – requests for additional EMS go to operations section chief

206 ICS 8/78	9. PREPARED BY (MEDICAL UNIT LEADER)	10. REVIEWED BY (SAFETY OFFICER)

AIR OPERATIONS SUMMARY

1. INCIDENT NAME	2. OPERATIONAL PERIOD	3. DISTRIBUTION
Simulation City explosion	08:00 to 20:00	PD air unit, Lifeflight, medical unit leader

4. PERSONNEL AND COMMUNICATIONS

	NAME	AIR/AIR FREQUENCY	AIR/GROUND FREQUENCY
AIR OPER. DIRECTOR	Chief E. O'Neill	122.50	123.75
AIR ATTACK SUPER.			
HELICOPTER COOR.			
AIR TANKER COOR.			
HELIBASE MANAGER			

5. REMARKS (Spec. Instructions, Safety Notes, Hazards, Priorities)

PD helicopter dedicated to incident site and perimeter

Lifeflight available on-call basis

6. LOCATION/ FUNCTION	7. ASSIGNMENT	8. FIXED WING		9. HELICOPTERS		10. TIME		11. AIRCRAFT ASSIGNED	12. OPERATING BASE
		NO.	TYPE	NO.	TYPE	AVAIL.	COM-MENCE		
Simulation City PD	Perimeter and traffic surveillance			1	4			PD 1	PD hdqtrs
Baptist Hosp	EMS response			1	3			Lifeflight	Baptist Hosp
13. TOTALS				2					

14. AIR OPERATIONS SUPPORT EQUIPMENT	15. PREPARED BY J Hughes (Include Date & Time) 3/1/00 07:01

220 ICS 3/82

NFFS 1351

CHAPTER QUESTIONS

1. Define the front-end concept of planning.
2. What are the key elements of the incident management system and how do they relate to planning?
3. Discuss at least four operational problems related to terrorism/tactical violence incidents.
4. Why is administration important in a long-duration terrorism incident?
5. List at least eight critical equipment needs in a terrorism incident.
6. What are the key steps in the implementation of an EOP?
7. What are the key elements of an EOP?
8. What determines if an IAP is formal or informal?
9. Define an IAP briefing cycle. What are the related steps in the cycle?

Simulation I

Obtain an after-action report for a major event in your community or state. Based on the incident report, develop an IAP based on the event by using copies of blank ICS forms on pages 79–92. Establish IMS sections, and use the branch/division concept.

Simulation II

You have been appointed as emergency manager in your community. Your elation is short-lived when you find out your first assignment is to develop an EOP. Develop a community EOP by observing the following principles:

- Obtain a realistic threat assessment or design a hypothetical threat assessment.
- Identify key operations agencies.
- Determine who will be the incident manager in various types of incidents.
- Identify logistics sources on a local and regional level.
- Identify sources of support personnel and support agencies.

5
Weapons of Mass Effect: Explosives

Hank T. Christen
Robert Walker

Source: Courtesy Liaison Agency, Inc.

Chapter Objectives

After reading this chapter, you will be able to accomplish the following objectives:

1. Recognize the significance of explosive devices in terrorism and tactical violence events.
2. Understand the categories of explosives and their characteristics.
3. Outline the basic elements in the explosive train.
4. Understand the basic initiating elements in explosive devices.
5. Outline the critical safety steps that must be utilized when operating in an environment where explosive devices are suspected or present.

Introduction

One of the first explosives was black powder. The Chinese invented black powder in A.D. 600. History has not recorded the first use of explosives for terrorism, but there is little doubt that soon after the invention of black powder, someone used it to blow up someone else.

Today there are many types of explosives designed for industrial use, military operations, and entertainment. All of these explosives are available to people through various means (legal and otherwise) for clandestine use. Some explosives can be made at home with common chemicals using "recipes" easily accessible to anyone seeking the information.

Explosive devices are effective for three basic reasons:

1. They create mass casualties and property destruction (a WMD).
2. Explosives are a major psychological weapon. An explosion instills terror and fear in survivors and the unaffected population (a WME).
3. Secondary explosive devices render a site unsecured, greatly complicating medical, rescue, and suppression efforts (WME).

Critical Factor: Explosives are very effective weapons for creating mass casualties and fear.

There are many historical examples of the terrorist use of explosives. Factions throughout Europe, the Middle East, Asia, and Africa have used long-term bombing campaigns. In the United States we have witnessed the horror of the World Trade Center and Oklahoma City explosions, but fail to realize that there are several detonations per week and numerous devices disarmed that do not get coverage beyond the local media.

There is every indication that emergency responders in the United States will see an increase in explosive terrorism and tactical violence. The Internet abounds with information about simple explosives and simple timing devices that can be made at home. Commercial explosives are readily available, and military explosives can be accessed in world black markets.

Explosive Physics

How do explosives work? How do explosives differ? What causes some explosive devices to fail? The answers to these questions fall under the general category of explosives physics (the science of explosives). Explosive physics is important to emergency responders. These are the scientific laws that kill you and your patients, and the laws that determine whether you will live through an event.

An explosive material is a substance that is capable of rapidly converting to a gas with an extreme increase in volume. This rapid increase in volume causes heat and noise, and a shock wave that travels outward from the detonation. Chemists and physicists like to point out that an explosion is not "instantaneous." Academically, they are correct because explosives require several nanoseconds to develop. To human observers, however, explosions are instantaneous. More importantly, significant injury and property damage also occurs "instantly."

The most damaging by-product of an explosion is the shock wave. The shock wave is an energy wave that originates at the source and travels outward in all directions. It behaves much like ripples on the surface of water when a pebble is dropped into a pond. The wave travels the course of least resistance, reflects off hard objects such as strong walls or buildings, and becomes concentrated in spaces such as hallways or areas between buildings. Shock waves can also be reflected back to the source.

The strength and characteristics of explosives are measured by the speed of the shock waves they produce. This is measured in feet per second (fps) or meters per second (mps). Their velocity of detonation determines the dividing line between low explosives and high explosives. A more precise and scientific definition is that a low explosive is one that deflagrates into the remaining unreacted explosive material, at less than the speed of sound. A high explosive is an explosive that detonates into the remaining explosive material faster than the speed of sound. A low explosive may become a high explosive by the way it is contained or initiated. Black powder, when burned in an open area, will not detonate. If you confine the powder in a container such as a pipe bomb, the outcome is very different. The same applies with the initiation of high explosives. When C4 is ignited it will burn without detonating. If you introduce a shock to C4 via a blasting cap, you get an explosive detonation.

Critical Factor: Explosives produce a very high speed, damaging shock wave.

Some explosives have a shock wave that produces a pushing effect. Detonation or deflagration that is slower than the speed of sound causes this push effect. Deflagration is a very rapid combustion that is less than the speed of sound. These explosives push obstacles and are commonly used for applications such as quarrying, strip-mining, or land clearing. Black powder, smokeless powder, and photoflash powders are examples of deflagrating or low explosives. A deflagrating effect or low explosive effect is similar to what you feel when a car is next to you with deep bass speakers at full volume.

High explosives have a sharp, shattering effect. This shattering effect is referred to as the explosive's brisance and is comparable to the high-pitched voice of an opera soprano that causes crystal glass to shatter. High explosives are very brisant, and produce shock waves greater than the speed of sound. For example, military explosives such as C4 produce a shock wave of 24,000 fps. High explosives (high brisance) have a very sharp and shattering effect. These explosives do extensive damage, causing severe injuries with a high percentage of fatalities.

The devastating effect of land mines is a product of brisance. The shock wave literally pulverizes bone and soft tissue in the lower extremities. In improvised explosive devices (IED) the shock wave causes severe barotrauma injuries, major internal organ damage, head injuries, and traumatic amputations. A lethal secondary effect is fragmentation. Concrete, glass, wood, and metal fragments are expelled at ballistic speeds. The effect causes multiple fatalities and critical injuries.

An explosive shock wave creates another effect called blast overpressure. Air in the vicinity of the explosion is compressed and expands creating a pressure higher than atmospheric pressure. Blast overpressure causes barotrauma damage in the form of air embolisms and damage to tethered organs. This pressure also causes severe structural damage to buildings. A blast pressure of 5 pounds per square inch (psi) does not sound high. However, on a standard door (80 by 30 inches), the total impact pressure is 12,000 pounds. On a wall that is 8 feet high and 10 feet long, the total pressure is 50,000 pounds.

In summary, the physics of explosives explain the effects that kill people and severely damage property. The most damaging by-product is a shock wave that travels very fast and is unseen. The shock wave causes fragmentation, blast overpressure, and barotrauma injuries.

Types of Explosives

Explosives are designed to detonate with maximum power when initiated, yet be extremely stable when stored or transported. One of the most widely known civilian explosives is dynamite. The invention of dynamite was a major breakthrough in explosive technology. The prime ingredient in dynamite is nitroglycerin (nitro), an extremely unstable liquid that detonates violently, with even minor shocks. In dynamite, the nitro is mixed with sawdust and other ingredients to stabilize the nitro.

Dynamite is a high explosive that generates a shock wave of 14,000 to 16,000 fps. It is readily available and legally procured in states that issue a blaster's permit. Quantities are stored on construction sites and are frequently stolen. Dynamite is also used on farms for digging, land clearing, and stump removal. Due to its availability, ease of use, stability, and explosive power, dynamite is a popular choice for IEDs.

Black powder and smokeless powder are also popular IED explosives. They can be easily purchased in small quantities in gun shops that cater to ammunition reloading hobbyists. These explosives are frequently used in pipe bombs. Black powder is a deflagrating explosive that detonates with extreme force when stored in a confined container. Pipe bombs were used in the Atlanta Olympics bombing and in many abortion clinic bombings.

Ammonium nitrate is another common civilian explosive. Ammonium nitrate fertilizer, when mixed with a catalyst, will detonate with violent force. This explosive is frequently used in agricultural operations, and was used in the Oklahoma City bombing.

Military explosives are extremely powerful, even in small quantities. The most well-known type is a plastic explosive called C4. It is soft and pliable, resembling a block of clay, and may be cut, shaped, packed, and burned without detonating. When detonated, C4 explodes violently and produces a very high-speed shock wave. Just two pounds of C4 can totally destroy a vehicle and kill its occupants.

C4 is not easily obtained, but is illegally available on the black market. Similar plastic explosives are available on foreign markets. A military plastic explosive called Semtex was used to make the IED that caused the Pan American crash in Lockerbie, Scotland. Other military explosives include TNT, Tritonal, RDX, and PETN.

All explosives (civilian and military) require an initial high-impact and concentrated shock to cause detonation. A small explosive device called an initiator produces this initiating shock. Initiators are a key step in a chain of events called the explosive train. The most common type of initiator is a blasting cap.

The first step in the explosive train is a source of energy to explode the initiator. This source is usually electrical, but can be from thermal, mechanical, or a combination of the three sources. The initiator contains a small amount of sensitive explosive, such as mercury fulminate. The detonation of the initiator produces a concentrated and intense shock that causes a high-order detonation of the primary explosive. The explosive train is diagramed as follows:

Initiating energy = initiator explosion = main explosive detonation

It is critical that all elements of the explosive train function properly. Any malfunction or separation of the elements breaks the explosive train resulting in a failed detonation.

Improvised Explosive Devices (IED)

An IED is any explosive device that is not a military weapon or commercially produced explosive device. In essence, IEDs are homemade. It is important to realize that homemade devices can vary from simple to highly sophisticated. Do not perceive IEDs as a high school product constructed from an Internet bomb recipe.

Approximately 80 to 90 percent of IEDs are made from smokeless powder or dynamite according to the Eglin Air Force Base, Florida, EOD School. Devices made from C4 or Semtex are rare, and usually lead investigators to suspect foreign sources.

A crucial element in an IED is a timing device. For many reasons, bomb makers do not want to be present when the device is initiated. Because of security and scope, this text does not cover timing devices in detail. Timers can be chemical, electrical, electronic, or mechanical. Simple timers include watches or alarm clocks that close an electrical circuit at a preset time. Electronic timers operate in a similar fashion, but are more reliable and precise. Some electronic timers or initiating devices can be activated from radio

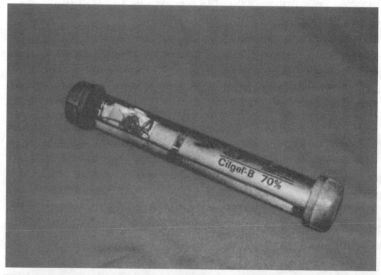

FIGURE 5-1 Pipe bombs account for 26 percent of all improvised explosive devices according to the FBI Bomb Data Center. The above photo is a confiscated pipe bomb constructed with a stick of Cilgel-B dynamite. *Source:* Courtesy R. Walker

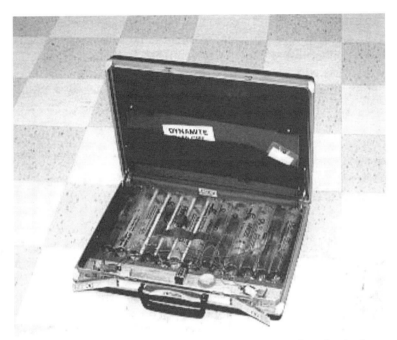

FIGURE 5-2 Briefcase rigged with dynamite and multiple detonation devices. *Source:* Courtesy R. Walker

signals from a remote site. In most cases, timers cause electrical energy to be routed from batteries to an initiator (usually an electric blasting cap).

Other devices have no timer, and are designed to detonate when people or emergency responders trigger the detonation. These devices are called booby traps. In simple devices, a trip wire or mechanical switch initiates the detonation. When the wire is touched or the device is tampered with, an explosion occurs. In more sophisticated devices, an invisible beam that is broken by people walking through it causes the detonation. Other high-tech booby traps include light, sound, or infrared triggering systems.

Critical Factor: Improvised explosive devices vary in the type of explosive, form of initiation, and degree of sophistication.

Chemical, Nuclear, and Biological IEDs

An IED may be used to initiate a chemical, biological, or nuclear event. In these cases, the improvised explosive is used to scatter a chemical or biological pathogen or toxin. The history of such devices is scarce, but increased use of these devices is anticipated.

An especially "dirty" weapon is an improvised nuclear device (IND). An IND does not involve a nuclear explosion like a military nuclear weapon. In an IND, conventional explosives are used to scatter radioactive materials. The device is considered dirty because the radioactive contamination can render an area radioactively "hot" for thousands of years. Presently, there is no history of an IND incident, but the potential is there.

Critical Factor: Conventional explosives can be used to disperse chemical or radiological agents.

Secondary Devices

High threats to emergency responders are secondary devices (review Chapter 3, "Terrorism/Tactical Violence Incident Response Procedures"). Secondary devices are timed devices or booby traps that are designed and placed to kill emergency responders. The objective is to create an emergency event, such as a bombing or fire, that generates an emergency response. The secondary device explodes and may cause more injuries than the original event. In one of the Atlanta abortion clinic bombings, a secondary device in a dumpster exploded after EMS, fire, and law enforcement responders arrived. In the Columbine High School shooting, multiple devices scattered throughout the school greatly restricted the tactical operations of EMS units and SWAT teams.

Secondary devices can be used to create an entrapment situation. Beware of a situation that lures responders into narrow areas with only one escape route. A narrow, dead-end alley is a classic example. An incident such as a fire or explosion at the end of the alley is the initial event that causes emergency responders to enter the area. The secondary device (a booby trap or timed IED) is placed in the alley. When the IED detonates, there is only one narrow escape route that lies in the path of a concentrated shock wave.

A key to surviving an entrapment situation is to recognize the scenario by surveying the overall scene. A narrow focus (called tunnel vision) obscures the big picture. Look around! Do not concentrate on a small portion of the incident scene. Look for trip wires, suspicious packages, and objects that appear to be out of place. Be especially aware of dumpsters or abandoned vehicles. Question bystanders familiar with the area if possible. Try entering by an alternate route. In summary, look for a setup that could kill you.

Critical Factor: Beware of secondary devices!

FIGURE 5-3 Environmental awareness is critical to remaining safe at explosives or threat scenes. In the United Kingdom the general public is enlisted through a public awareness campaign and poster placement in areas of public assembly. *Source:* Courtesy P. Maniscalco

Safety Precautions

Many of the safety precautions for explosive devices were discussed in Chapter 4. Several safety steps bear repetition.

1. Avoid radio transmissions within at least fifty feet of a suspected device. Electromagnetic radiation (EMR) from radio transmissions can trigger an electric blasting cap or cause a sophisticated device to detonate.
2. Avoid smoking within fifty feet (or further) from a suspicious device.
3. Do not move, strike, or jar a suspicious item. Do not look in a suspicious container or attempt to open packages.

4. Memorize a clear description of suspicious items.
5. Establish a hot zone for 500 feet around small devices, and 1,000 feet around large devices or vehicles. (Large zones may not be practical in congested downtown areas). Maintain the required hot zone until bomb technicians advise otherwise.
6. Try to stay upwind from a device; explosions create toxic gases.
7. Take advantage of available cover such as terrain, buildings, or vehicles. Remember that shock waves bounce off surrounding obstacles.

Basic Search Techniques

Emergency responders often conduct primary searches or assist bomb experts in conducting a thorough search for explosive devices. Remember that emergency responders are not trained to clear an area of explosive devices; only bomb technicians perform this function.

Critical Factor: Bomb technicians are the only personnel qualified to clear an area or remove/disarm an explosive device.

In building searches, always search from the outside in. Building occupants are an excellent source of information, because they know what objects are supposed to be in a given location. Occupants can tell you that a trash basket has always been there, or that a paper bag is Joe's lunch. Likewise, they can point out that the innocent looking newspaper machine was never there before. In building interiors, custodians can assist in unlocking areas and pointing out obscure storage areas.

Search from the floor to the ceiling. Often objects that are not at eye level are unseen. Adopt the habit of making a floor level sweep, followed by an eye level sweep, and finally a high wall and ceiling sweep.

Begin vehicle searches from the outside to the inside (just like buildings). If the driver is present, assign one person to distract the driver from observing advanced search techniques. Leave the trunk and doors closed, and concentrate on the outside. Avoid touching the vehicle; touching can activate motion switches. Never open the vehicle until trained technicians

FIGURE 5-4 Suited in explosive protective ensemble EOD personnel will require special attention from on-scene EMS resources. EOD techs are prone to hyperthermia, dehydration, and in the event of device detonation during inspection, a whole blast of trauma-related injuries. *Source:* Courtesy P. Maniscalco

arrive. If the driver is present, have the driver open doors, the trunk, and dash compartments.

Always emphasize the safety precautions previously discussed in this chapter. When in doubt, wait for bomb technicians. You can save lives by establishing a hot zone and exercising effective scene control.

Chapter Summary

The use of explosives for terrorism goes back many centuries. Explosive devices are very effective weapons of mass effect. Bombings create mass fatalities and mass casualties. Bombs are also effective psychological weapons; they create fear in survivors and the community at large. Lastly, bombs can be used as secondary devices to kill or injure emergency responders.

An explosive is a material that converts to a gas almost instantly when detonated. This detonation creates a shock wave, which is a measure of the explosive power of a given material. In a low-order detonation, a shock wave travels through the remainder of the unexploded material at a speed less than the speed of sound. High-order explosives create shock waves greater than the speed of sound. High explosives have a sharp, shattering effect called brisance.

There are many types of explosives, with black powder being the earliest type. When confined in a device such as a pipe bomb, it has considerable explosive force. The first commercial type of explosive was dynamite, which can produce a shock wave of 14,000 to 16,000 feet per second. Ammonium nitrate (fertilizer), when mixed with a catalyst, is a low-order explosive. Military explosives are extremely powerful. They have high brisance and create shock waves that are as high as 24,000 feet per second.

Improvised explosive devises (IEDs) are homemade weapons that contain an explosive material, a power source, and a timer. The explosives are usually dynamite or black powder. The timing devices can be chemical, electrical, or electronic. Special devices called booby traps contain a triggering mechanism such as a trip wire. These are secondary devices designed to injure emergency responders.

Secondary devices can be used to create an entrapment situation. Entrapment is a situation with a device in a narrow area, such as an alley, with no escape route. A key prevention step is to survey the entire scene before entry, and look for trip wires or other initiation devices.

Key safety steps in an unsecured area are:

- Avoid radio transmissions or smoking within 50 feet of a suspected device.
- Do not move, strike, or jar a suspicious item.
- Establish a hot zone 500 feet around a small device and 1,000 feet around a large device or vehicle. (These distances may not be practical in urban areas).

Emergency responders often assist in searching an area for suspicious devices. Bomb disposal experts are the only personnel that can clear an area or safely remove an explosive device.

Chapter Questions

1. Name three reasons why explosives are effective WMD/WME weapons.
2. Define and discuss the most damaging product of an explosion.
3. What is blast overpressure? What are the injury and damage effects of blast overpressure?
4. Name and briefly describe at least three types of explosives.
5. List four types of explosive timers.

6. List and discuss seven safety precautions relating to secondary explosive devices.
7. What is the role of emergency responders in a basic search for explosive devices?

Simulation

Research the previous year's history of explosive attacks in the United States. Ascertain trends in the types of explosives used, their effectiveness (casualties), and the primary motives for the attacks. What was the number of explosive detonations in the United States last year? (Note—sources can include publications, news articles, or Web sites for the ATF, FBI, Department of Justice, or other law enforcement sources.)

6
Mass Casualty Decontamination

Michael V. Malone

Source: Courtesy H. Christen

Chapter Objectives

After reading this chapter, you will be able to accomplish the following objectives:

1. List the three stages of decontamination.
2. Describe several methods used by fire departments for gross decontamination.
3. Recognize several considerations for setting up a decontamination area.
4. Define the decontamination requirements for hospital joint accreditation.
5. Understand the principles of mass casualty decontamination.
6. Recognize the decontamination requirements for various agents.
7. List features of biological agents that affect decontamination for biological agents.
8. Understand weather factors that affect decontamination.
9. Discuss considerations in local protocols for the establishment of triage procedures for contaminated patients.

Introduction

Decontamination is defined as the process of removing or neutralizing a hazard from the environment, property, or life form. According to the Institute of Medicine National Research Council, the purpose of decontamination is to prevent further harm and enhance the potential for full clinical recovery of persons or restoration of infrastructure exposed to a hazardous substance. This chapter will focus on mass casualty decontamination, and will discuss these areas:

- the traditional decontamination process used by fire departments and hazardous material response teams
- the decontamination capabilities of hospitals or health care facilities
- military types of decontamination
- methodology and principles applied to a mass casualty incident resulting from weapons of mass effect or an accidental release of a harmful substance
- containment procedures
- mass casualty decontamination, including decontamination requirements for victims with conventional injuries
- site selection, environmental, weather, and responder requirements during the decontamination process

Basic Principles of Decontamination

The management and treatment of contaminated casualties will vary with the situation and nature of the contaminant. Quick, versatile, effective, and large capacity decontamination is essential. Casualties must not be forced to wait at a central point for decontamination. Decontamination of casualties serves two purposes; it prevents their systems from absorbing additional contaminants, and protects health care providers and uncontaminated casualties from contamination. Review of after-action reports and video-tapes of the Tokyo subway incident in 1995 emphasizes this requirement.

Fire departments and hazardous materials response teams define the two types of decontamination as *technical decon* and *medical* or *patient decon*. Medical or patient decon is the process of cleaning injured or exposed indi-viduals. This process, performed by haz mat teams, is far less common than technical decon. Personnel decon methods are traditionally established for haz mat team members and have not been applied in a mass casualty setting. The method of self-decontamination, or team decontamination, is considered a part of technical decontamination. Shower systems with pro-visions for capturing contaminated water runoff are commercially available and may provide a degree of victim privacy. This type of system does not have the capacity to treat a large number of casualties. The main limitations are availability of equipment and haz mat personnel.

Fire departments are equipped and structured for rapid and effective decontamination. Many fire departments have developed procedures that use existing low-tech equipment. A common practice is the use of two en-gines parked 20 feet apart with three ground ladders placed on top of the engines and spanning the gap between them. A fourth ladder is placed per-pendicular on top of the other ladders at the midpoint of the span. This serves as a girder to support a hanging tarp creating two corridors (male and female). Tarps are stretched over the top of the ladders and down the middle of the corridor to create a male/female decontamination route. Hand lines and/or engine discharges with low pressure (60 psi) fog noz-zles are utilized for water spray. The pumps are shut down and supplied by a distant engine to reduce noise in the decon area.

Fire departments with aerial devices utilize effective elevated deluge systems (low pressure fog) in conjunction with engine companies. Aerial ladders, extended horizontally, can also be used with tarps to create a de-contamination corridor for privacy.

Stages of Decontamination

The process for decontamination of casualties involves three stages called *gross, secondary,* and *definitive* decontamination.

Gross decontamination:

1. Evacuate the casualties from the high-risk area. With limited personnel available to conduct work in the contaminated environment or hot zone, a method of triage needs to be established. First, decon those who can self-evacuate or evacuate with minimal assistance to decon sites, then start decontamination of those who require more assistance.
2. Remove the exposed person's clothing. The removal and disposal of clothing is estimated to remove 70 to 80 percent of the contaminant[1]; others estimate 90 to 95 percent.[2]
3. Perform a one-minute, head-to-toe rinse with water.

Secondary decontamination:

1. Perform a quick, full-body rinse with water.
2. Wash rapidly with a cleaning solution from head to toe. A fresh solution (0.5 percent) of sodium hypochlorite (HTH chlorine) is an effective decontamination solution for persons exposed to chemical or biological contaminants. Undiluted household bleach is 5.0 percent sodium hypochlorite. Plain water has been found to be equally effective because of ease and rapidity of application. With certain biological agents, the sodium hypochlorite solution may require more than 10 minutes of contact. This is not possible in a mass casualty incident requiring rapid decontamination.
3. Rinse with water from head to toe.

Definitive decontamination:

1. Perform thorough head-to-toe wash until clean. Rinse thoroughly with water.
2. Dry victim and have them don clean clothes.

Critical Factor: The stages of decontamination are gross, secondary, and definitive.

Methods of Initial Decontamination

A first response fire company can perform gross decontamination by operating hose lines or master streams with fog nozzles at reduced pressure. The advantage of this is that it begins the process of removing a high percentage

FIGURE 6-1   Simulated patient undergoes gross decontamination process at chemical terrorism exercise in Newark, NJ. *Source:* Courtesy P. Maniscalco

of the contaminant in the early stage of an incident. Methods to provide privacy and decontamination for non-ambulatory casualties must be addressed. Decontamination considerations include:

1. Prevailing weather conditions (temperature, precipitation, etc.), which affect site selection, willingness of the individual to undress, and the degree of decontamination required.
2. Wind direction.
3. Ground slope, surface material, and porosity (grass, gravel, asphalt, etc.).
4. Availability of water.
5. Availability of power and lighting.
6. Proximity to the incident.
7. Containment of runoff water if necessary or feasible. The Department of Mechanical and Fluid Engineering at Leeds (U.K.) University has determined that if a chemical is diluted with water at the rate of approximately 2000:1, pollution of water courses will be significantly reduced[3] (Institute of Medicine National Research Council). Examples of containment devices or methods: children's wading pools, portable tanks used in rural fire fighting, hasty containment

pits formed by tarps laid over hard suction hoses or small ground ladders, diking with loose earth or sandbags covered with tarps.

8. Supplies including personnel protective equipment and industrial-strength garbage bags.

9. Clearly marked entry and exit points with the exit upwind, away from the incident area.

10. A staging area at the entry point for contaminated casualties. This is a point where casualties can be further triaged and given self-decontamination aids, such as spray bottles with a 0.5 percent solution of sodium hypochlorite solution of Fullers Earth.

11. Access to triage and other medical aid upon exit, if required.

12. Protection of personnel from adverse weather.

13. Privacy of personnel. (This will be a media intensive event; an example is B'nai B'rith, Washington, D.C., 1997).

14. Security and control from site setup to final cleanup of the site.

Decontamination Triage

In a mass casualty event, decontamination of chemically exposed patients must be prioritized or triaged. The intent of this process is similar to the triaging of trauma patients in a conventional incident. The objective is to first decontaminate salvageable patients that are in immediate need of medical care. Patients that are dead or unsalvageable should not be immediately decontaminated. Patients that are ambulatory and non-symptomatic are the lowest decontamination priority. Again, the primary objective is to immediately decontaminate patients who are exposed, yet salvageable.

Critical Factor: First decontaminate victims who are severely exposed, yet salvageable.

The U.S. Army Soldier and Biological Chemical Command (SBCCOM) published a guide called *Guidelines for Mass Casualty Decontamination During a Terrorism Chemical Agent Incident* (January 2000). The SBCCOM guidelines suggest the following factors for assigning decontamination triage priorities:

1. casualties closest to the point of release
2. casualties reporting exposure to vapor or aerosol
3. casualties with liquid deposition on clothing or skin
4. casualties with serious medical signs/symptoms (shortness of breath, chest tightness, etc.)
5. casualties with conventional injuries

The major question in decontamination triage is the criteria for determining where or when not to treat/decontaminate a non-ambulatory patient that is symptomatic. Emergency response agencies must adopt a local protocol that should be based on the following issues:

- What is the nature of the incident? Severe exposure to nerve agents with major symptoms usually result in death.
- Are there high quantities of antidotes available? For example, nerve agents require very high doses of atropine and valium (for seizures).
- Are personnel available to move and treat mass numbers of non-ambulatory patients? A single non-ambulatory patient requires two to four responders.
- Ambulatory patients who are symptomatic or have been severely exposed should be immediately decontaminated.
- Ambulatory patients who are non-symptomatic should be moved to a treatment area for possible clothing removal and medical evaluation.
- Non-ambulatory patients should be evaluated in place while further prioritization for decontamination occurs (SBCCOM).
- Patients who are in respiratory arrest, grossly contaminated with a liquid nerve agent, having serious symptoms, or fail to respond to atropine injections should be considered deceased or expected to die ("expectant" in military terminology).
- In extreme cases, a patient in a hot zone may require immediate treatment prior to decontamination. Treatment usually consists of immediate antidote administration and airway maintenance. Clothing removal is the only expedient method of field decontamination, with decontamination by showering or flushing later, if appropriate.

HOSPITAL DECONTAMINATION STANDARDS

The Joint Commission on Accreditation of Healthcare Organizations (JCAHO) requires hospitals to be prepared to respond to disasters including hazardous materials accidents. The majority of hospitals that have decontamination capabilities utilize existing indoor infrastructure and do not have the ability to expand to accommodate mass casualties. Outside the standard universal protection procedures followed by the medical community, required protective equipment and trained personnel are limited in the hospital system.

A hospital standard practice for haz mat response is to call the fire department. Due to the stress placed on the response system mitigating the effects of a large incident, haz mat teams will not be available. The hospitals are at risk when the response system is stressed to the point that patients start self-referring or independent sources deliver patients to the hospital.

> **Critical Factor:** Hospitals are required by joint accreditation standards to have de-
> contamination procedures and equipment.

The military has identified two types of decontamination: personnel and equipment. Personnel decontamination has been divided into two sub-categories: hasty and deliberate. Specialized units within the military (U.S. Marine Corps Chemical Biological Incident Response Force and the National Guard's Civil Support Teams) have further subdivided deliberate decontamination to encompass ambulatory and non-ambulatory personnel.

Hasty decontamination is primarily focused on the self-decontaminating individual using the M258A1 skin decontamination kit. This kit is designed for chemical decontamination and consists of wipes containing a solution that neutralizes most nerve and blister agents. Another type of kit, the M291

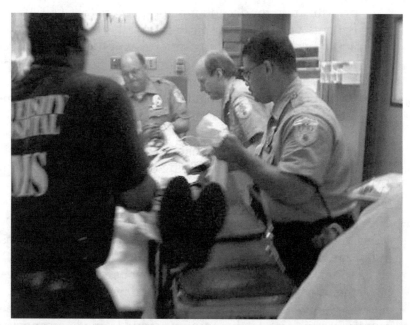

FIGURE 6-2 Hospitals must train personnel and equip facilities to conduct patient decontamination. There is no guarantee that all patients who arrive at your facility will be clean or have been through decontamination on-site at the emergency. Only 18.5%* of contaminated victims are treated at the scene of an exposure. The remainder seek out contamination treatment at medical facility/hospital. *Hazardous Substances Emergency Event Surveillance, Annual Report 1999. *Source:* Courtesy D. Gerard

decontamination kit, uses laminated fiber pads containing reactive resin, which neutralizes and removes the contaminant from a surface by mechanical and absorption methods. (These kits require user training, and are not usually available for civilian emergency response organizations.)

The procedure of removing and exchanging (donning and doffing) personnel protective clothing is also considered hasty decontamination. Deliberate decontamination is required when individuals are exposed to gross levels of contamination or for individuals who were not dressed in personnel protective clothing at time of contamination. The established process is to completely remove the individual's clothing, apply a decontamination solution (0.5 percent HTH or water) followed by a freshwater rinse, then use a chemical agent monitor (CAM) to detect the presence of nerve and blister agents or M-8 paper to validate the thoroughness of the decontamination process. At the end of this process the individual is provided new clothing and equipment. If the individual presents symptoms, he or she will be processed through the heath care system.

Decontamination Site Setup

The decontamination site should be established with the following considerations:

1. upwind from the source of contamination
2. on a downhill slope or flat ground with provisions made for water runoff
3. water availability
4. decontamination equipment availability
5. individual supplies
6. health care facilities
7. site security

Mass Casualty Decontamination

Specialized military units have developed personnel decontamination sites that can process large numbers of contaminated personnel, both ambulatory and non-ambulatory. These systems or sites are capable (agent dependent) of processing up to 200 ambulatory or 35 non-ambulatory personnel per hour depending upon the agent(s) involved. The sites are set up in a tent that incorporates a shower system that sprays a decontaminant followed by a rinse.

Step one of this process is removal of the patient's clothing. Ambulatory patients use a similar process that military personnel use

FIGURE 6-3 The USMC CBIRF establishing a decontamination line at an exercise in Tampa, Florida. *Source:* Courtesy P. Maniscalco

during their doffing procedures. Non-ambulatory casualties' clothing is cut off by decon specialists.

Step two is to place clothing into disposable bins, which are sealed.

Step three is to remove personal effects, tag them, and place them into plastic bags. Disposition of the personal effects will be determined later. These items may be crime scene evidence.

Step four is to apply a decontamination solution. For ambulatory casualties, this is done through a shower system. Non-ambulatory casualties are sponged down.

Step five is for individuals to use brushes to clean themselves, or be cleaned by a decon specialist. This step aids in the removal of the contaminant and allows for a three-minute contact time for the decontaminating solution.

Step six is a freshwater rinse.

Step seven is to monitor for the agent or contaminant. This is conducted using a CAM or M-8 paper for chemical agents, or using a radiation meter for radiation.

Step eight is to don dry clothing.

Step nine is medical monitoring. Individual documentation is developed.

Step ten provides for individuals' release or transport to a medical facility.

The non-ambulatory site uses the same steps; however, the casualty is moved along a series of rollers and cleaned by decon specialists. Care must also be taken at the non-ambulatory site to decontaminate the roller surface with a 5 percent solution of HTH between patients. These sites are self-contained, require a water source, and provide:

- heated water (if required; warm water opens the pores of the skin and could accelerate dermal exposure)
- water runoff capture
- decontamination solution
- protection from the elements
- privacy
- medical monitoring during the decontamination process
- post-decontamination checks
- clothing
- site control

The specialized decontamination assets just described are from pre-positioned military units and not usually available for rapid response to civilian incidents. These units are highly competent and professional, but limited by numbers and location. The military refers to them as low density, high demand assets. The U.S. Public Health Service has developed a similar capability resident in the Metropolitan Medical Response System (MMRS) and the National Disaster Medical Response Teams (NMRT).

Radiation Decontamination

Radiation injuries do not imply that the casualty will present a hazard to health care providers. Research has demonstrated that levels of intrinsic radiation present within the casualty from activation (after exposure to neutron and high-energy photon sources) are not life threatening. If monitoring for radiation is not available, decontamination for all casualties must be conducted. Removal of the casualty's clothing will reduce most of the contamination with a full body wash further reducing the contamination.

Wearing surgical attire or disposable garments such as those made of Tyvek will reduce the potential exposure of health care providers. Inhalation or ingestion of particles of radioactive material presents the greatest cross-contamination hazard. Care must be taken to capture runoff or retrieval of the material. Industrial vacuum cleaners are commonly used. The vacuum cleaner output air should be filtered with a HEPA filter to prevent rerelease of the material into the air.

FIGURE 6-4 North Carolina–Special Operations Response Teams (SORT) of the National Disaster Medical System (NDMS) participate in multiple training and response exercises yearly to maintain a heighten sense of readiness. NC–1 SORT is one of the best trained and equipped organizations in the world for response to these types of incidents and are deployable anywhere. *Source:* Courtesy P. Maniscalco

Decontamination Requirements for Various Agents

Decontamination requirements differ according to the type of chemical agent or material to which individuals have been exposed. Water is the accepted universal decontaminant. The importance of early decontamination cannot be overemphasized due to the mechanism of action with organophosphorus compounds (nerve agents). Nerve agents may be absorbed through any surface of the body. Decontamination of the skin must be accomplished *quickly* to be fully effective. Liquid agents may be removed using Fullers' Earth. Persistent nerve agents pose the greatest threat to health care providers. Once a patient has been decontaminated or the agent is fully absorbed, no further risk of contamination exists.

Critical Factor: Early decontamination is critical for severe exposure to nerve agents.

Exposure to a vesicant (blister agent) is not always noticed immediately because of the latent effects. This may result in delayed decontamination or failure to decontaminate at all. Mucous membranes and eyes are too sensitive to be decontaminated with normal skin decontaminant solutions. Affected sensitive surfaces should be flushed with copious amounts of water or, if available, isotonic bicarbonate (1.26 percent) or saline (0.9 percent). Physical absorption, chemical inactivation, and mechanical removal should decontaminate skin. Chemical inactivation using chlorination is effective against mustard and lewisite, and ineffective against phosgene oxime. If water is used, it must be used in copious amounts. If the vesicant is not fully removed, the use of water will spread it.

Critical Factor: Vesicant contamination may not be immediately noticed.

Choking agents will not remain in liquid form very long due to their extremely volatile physical properties. Decontamination is not required except when used in very cold climates. Choking agents are readily soluble in organic solvents and fatty oils. In water, choking agents rapidly hydrolyze into hydrochloric acid and carbon dioxide.

Blood agents will not remain in liquid form very long due to their extremely volatile physical properties. Decontamination is not required.

In the case of incapacitants, total skin decontamination should be completed with soap and water at the earliest opportunity. Symptoms may appear as late as 36 hours after a percutaneous exposure, even if the individual is decontaminated within one hour of exposure.

Personnel exposed to riot control agents should be moved to fresh air, separated from other casualties, faced into the wind with eyes open, and told to breathe deeply. Clothes should be removed and washed to preclude additional exposure from embedded residue.

Biological Agents

Biological agents are unique in their ability to inflict large numbers of casualties over a wide area by virtually untraceable means. The difficulty in detecting a biological agent's presence prior to an outbreak, its potential to selectively target humans, animals, or plants, and the difficulty in protecting the population conspire to make management of casualties (including decontamination) or affected areas particularly difficult. The intrinsic features of biological agents that influence their potential use and establishment of management criteria include virulence, toxicity, pathogenicity, incubation period, transmissibility, lethality, and stability.

If a dermal exposure is suspected, it should be managed by decontamination at the earliest opportunity. Exposed areas should be cleansed using the appropriately diluted sodium hypochlorite solution (0.5 percent) or copious quantities of plain soap and water. The patient's clothing should also be removed as soon as possible.

Secondary contamination of medical personnel is a concern and can be avoided by strict adherence to universal medical precautions. Biological agents, for the most part, are highly susceptible to environmental conditions, and all but a few present a persistent hazard.

Anthrax is a very stable agent; however, in a non-aerosolized state it presents only a dermal (requiring breaks or cuts in the skin) or ingestion hazard. The strategy recommendations for potential exposure to anthrax are:

1. Gather personal information from the potentially exposed individual(s).
2. Explain the signs and symptoms of the disease.
3. Give them a point of contact to call if they show symptoms.
4. Send them home with the following instructions: remove clothing and place it in a plastic bag, securing it with a tie or tape. Shower and wash with soap for 15 minutes.
5. The individuals should be informed of the lab analysis results of the suspected agent as soon as possible. If results are positive, the correct medical protocol will be administered.

Effects of Weather on Decontamination

Weather effects will impact the manner in which an agent will act in the environment and will have an impact on decontamination requirements. A release of chemical agents or toxic industrial materials always has the potential to cause injuries to unprotected people proximal to the point of release. Strong wind, heavy rain, or temperatures below freezing may reduce effects. Weather will be of great importance for the respiratory risks expected at different distances from the point of release. Weather conditions will also influence the effect of ground contamination.

High wind velocity implies a short exposure time in a given area, reducing the number of casualties in an unprotected population. Low wind velocity will increase the exposure time, increasing the number of casualties, and may cause effects at a greater distance.

Critical Factor: Weather is an important determination in the effectiveness of a chemical attack.

To a high degree, the gas/aerosol concentration in the primary cloud depends on the air exchange or turbulence of the atmosphere. In clear weather, at night, the ground surface is cooled and inversion is formed (stable temperature stratification). Inversion leads to weak turbulence, resulting in the presence of a high concentration of material. Unstable temperature stratification occurs when the ground surface warms, resulting in increased turbulence. The effect is decreased concentration, particularly at increased distances from the point of release.

The concentration in the primary cloud may also decrease in cold weather, particularly at temperatures below −20°C (−4°F), due to a smaller amount of agent(s) evaporating during dispersal. However, this will increase ground contamination at the point of release. Precipitation also reduces concentration, but can increase ground contamination.

Low temperatures will increase the persistency of some agents. Some agents may cease to have an effect at very low temperatures due to their freezing point, however, they present a problem when temperatures increase or if they are brought into a warm environment.

Biological agents are potential weapons of mass destruction and generally have the following characteristics: odorless and tasteless, difficult to detect, and can be dispersed in an aerosol cloud, over very large downwind areas. Ideal weather conditions for dispersal include an inversion layer in the atmosphere, high relative humidity, and low wind speeds. Incubation periods can be as long as several days, therefore, wind speed and direction are a primary weather concern to determine the exposed population and predict the effects upon that population. Ultraviolet (UV) light has a detrimental effect on many biological agents, making periods of reduced natural sunlight the optimal time for release.

Most biological agents will not survive in extremely cold weather and it is difficult to aerosolize live biological agents in freezing temperatures. Toxins are less affected by cold weather, however, cold weather tends to provide a temperature inversion that prolongs the integrity of an aerosolized cloud.

CHAPTER SUMMARY

A common sense, well-informed approach to decontamination should be adopted. The following are additional considerations for decontamination operations in a mass casualty setting:

1. Establish a local protocol for decontamination triage.
2. Decontaminate as soon as possible to stop the absorption process.
3. Establish multiple decontamination corridors.

4. Establish security and control measures to contain contaminated casualties and prevent non-contaminated/nonresponders from entering the affected area.
5. Decontaminate only what is required.
6. Decontaminate as close to the point of contamination as possible (100 m or 328 ft) outside, if the point of contamination was inside a building; 1 km (0.6 miles) for an outside release.
7. Involve the patient in the process, allowing as much self-decon as possible.
8. Use existing infrastructure.
9. Monitor the patients throughout the process.
10. Provide privacy if possible with use of tents, available facilities, and/or removal of the media.

Organizations that have potential requirements to provide decontamination support for a mass casualty incident should focus on existing inherent capabilities. With modifications and enhanced training, a good, thorough decontamination system can be effectively implemented.

CHAPTER QUESTIONS

1. List and discuss the three stages of decontamination.
2. Discuss at least five considerations for setting up a decontamination area.
3. Discuss lockdown procedures for controlling entry of contaminated patients at medical facilities.
4. Outline the 10 steps in mass casualty decontamination.
5. Outline triage procedures for mass casualty decontamination.
6. What factors determine the severity or effectiveness of a given biological agent?
7. How do the following weather elements influence the effects of a WME agent?
   • wind direction and speed
   • temperature
   • atmospheric stability

Simulations

1. Develop a mass decontamination procedure for your community. Consider training, equipment, protocols, and triage procedures.
2. Develop a mass decontamination plan for a medical facility. Consider security and lockdown, training, equipment, and control of contaminated vehicles.

Notes

[1]Cox, R. D., *Annals of Emergency Medicine,* 23, 761–770, 1994.

[2]NATO Handbook on the Medical Aspects of NBC Operations, 1991.

[3]Institute of Medicine Research Council, *Improving Civilian Medical Response to Chemical or Biological Terrorist Incidents: Interim Report on Current Capabilities.* Washington, D.C.: National Academy Press, 1998.

7
Crime Scene Operations

Neal J. Dolan
Paul M. Maniscalco

Source: Courtesy P. Maniscalco

"Wherever he steps, whatever he touches, whatever he leaves, even unconsciously, will serve as silent evidence against him. Not only his fingerprints or his footprints, but his hair, the fibers of his clothing, the glass he breaks, the toolmarks he leaves, the paint he scratches, the blood or semen that he deposits or collects—all these and more bear mute witness against him. This is evidence that does not forget. It is not confused by the excitement of the moment. It is not absent because human witnesses are. It is factual evidence. Physical evidence cannot be wrong; it cannot be wholly absent. Only its interpretation can err. Only human failure to find it, study and understand it, can diminish its value."

Presiding Judge
Harris v. United States 331 US 145 (1947)

Chapter Objectives

After reading this chapter, you will be able to accomplish the following objectives:

1. Define a crime scene.
2. Recognize the value and importance of physical evidence.
3. Understand the evidence "theory of exchange."
4. Recognize the evidence classification of objects, body material, and impressions.
5. List key crime scene observations that should be made by initial responders.
6. Understand the key steps for emergency responders in preservation of evidence.
7. Understand the concept of "chain of custody."

Introduction

The significance of physical evidence at a crime scene cannot be overestimated. It is the only thing that will help prove who committed the crime. Proper training and technique are necessary to maintain the integrity and value of evidence. Each day emergency responders travel to emergency scenes to render aid. These emergency personnel shoulder a formidable burden to accomplish their mission and cause no further harm to the people or the scene. Crime scenes are exciting, chaotic, and dangerous places. They are replete with hidden clues that hold the answer to the question, "Who committed this crime?"

Emergency responders often carry out their duties in conflict with important crime scene procedures. Emergency responders are focusing on the preservation of life and not the preservation of evidence. EMS responders may not be aware that the clothes they are cutting off and discarding from a shooting victim may contain valuable evidence to solve the crime. Firefighters may be employing legitimate fire fighting techniques at an explosion scene that are destroying evidence of who committed the offense.

It is possible to carry out the emergency responders' mission without creating more problems for the crime scene. This is best accomplished through training and awareness of potential crime scenes, and acting to minimize damage to the area and its contents.

The Crime Scene—Physical Evidence

A crime scene is any area in which a crime may have been committed. It is anywhere the criminal was during the commission of the crime and the egress from the scene. The exact dimensions of the scene will be determined by the nature and type of crime. For example, a shooting crime scene could be as large as the room or building where the victim was discovered. A terrorist incident could be several blocks or even miles in diameter. The Oklahoma City Federal Building incident had a 20-block perimeter established and a critical piece of evidence, the crankshaft from the rented Ryder truck, was found two blocks from the explosion site.

One key to uncovering the vast amount of information and physical evidence present at the crime scene is an awareness of what constitutes physical evidence. Evidence is something legally submitted to a competent tribunal as a means of ascertaining the truth in an alleged matter under investigation. Physical evidence is one form of evidence. It can be defined as anything that has been used, left, removed, altered, or contaminated during the commission of a crime by either the victim or the suspect.

Critical Factor: Emergency responders have a major role in assisting law enforcement agencies with identifying and preserving physical evidence.

The benefits of physical evidence are best summarized in the opening paragraph by the issuing judge in the case of *Harris v. U.S.* (1947). Physical evidence does not lie, forget, or make mistakes. It has no emotional connection to anyone or anything. It is demonstrable in nature and not dependant on a witness. It is the only way to establish the elements of a crime.

In order to heighten the awareness of responders, it is necessary to explain how physical evidence evolves at the scene. Forensic scientists propose the *theory of exchange* to describe this process. Whenever two objects

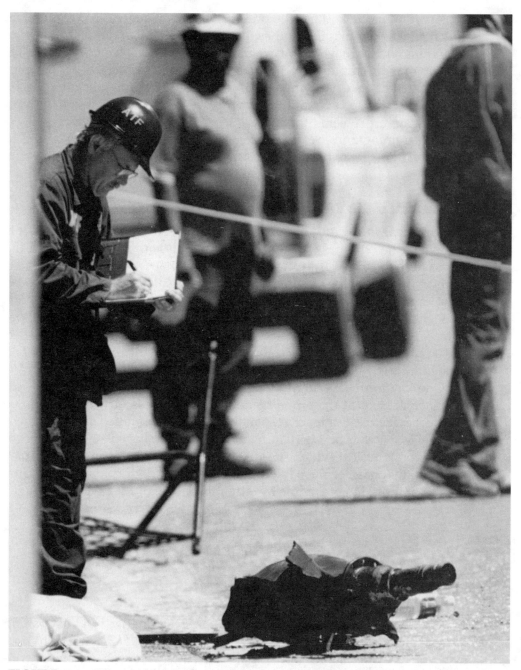

FIGURE 7-1 Proper identification, preservation, and collection of physical evidence often can mean the difference between conviction or acquittal of a suspect. *Source:* Courtesy J. Pat Carter/AP/Wide World Photos

come in contact with each other, each will be altered or changed in some way. When a rapist comes in contact with a victim, numerous substances will be exchanged. The suspect or the victim could deposit or remove skin traces, blood, body fluids, carpet fibers, soil, and many other items. Bombing victims may have chemical traces on their clothing or fragments of evidence embedded in their bodies that may prove to be important in the investigation and prosecution of the perpetrators. These evidence sources have been invaluable to law enforcement investigators in the past, including high profile cases such as the bombing of a Pan Am airliner arriving in Honolulu, Hawaii, from Narjita, Japan, in 1982, as often taught by forensics expert Rick Hahn (retired FBI). Changes in the objects may be microscopic and require detailed examination to establish the variations. However, responders should be cognizant that exchanges will take place and are not always noticeable to the naked eye.

Physical evidence can be almost anything. Table 7-1 gives some examples of items that could be encountered by responders working at a potential or actual terrorism/crime scene.

Being aware of potential hazards at a scene is not new to EMS, firefighters, or haz mat responders. Scene safety, sizing up the scene, or just taking a minute to examine the environment of a scene can minimize the impact of costly mistakes of overzealous responders.

Table 7-1   Possible Items of Evidence at a Crime Scene

Objects	Body Material	Impressions
Weapons	Blood	Fingerprints
Tools	Semen	Tire traces
Firearms	Hair	Footprints
Displaced furniture	Tissue	Palm prints
Notes, letters, papers	Sputum	Tool marks
Matchbook	Urine	Bullet holes
Bullets	Feces	Newly damaged areas
Shell casings	Vomit	Dents and breaks
Cigarette butts		
Cigar butts		
Clothes		
Shoes		
Jewelry		
Bomb fragments		
Chemical containers		
Mechanical delivery systems		

Actions of First Arriving Units

Literature in the EMS, emergency management, and fire/rescue fields stresses initial scene evaluation. However, few texts elaborate on the importance of viewing an event as a crime scene and analyzing the hot zone accordingly.

First arriving units are usually overwhelmed. The scene is chaotic and dynamic. Any observations at this early stage are very important to law enforcement investigators.

Critical Factor: An initial scene evaluation should include a basic crime scene evaluation.

Several key observations are important for initial responders. There is not time to write anything; just remember key crime or evidence observations and report them to the incident manager or the law enforcement branch as soon as possible. Important observations include:

1. chemicals on the scene that would not normally be present
2. damage, debris fields, and fragmentation that indicate an explosion
3. suspicious people; people hiding or running
4. statements issued by bystanders
5. unusual odors on the scene
6. evidence of gunfire (shell casings, bullet holes, or gunshot wounds)
7. weapons in the area
8. suspicious casualties (patients may be terrorists)
9. multiple fires that appear to be from separate sources
10. suspicious devices

Evidence Preservation by Emergency Responders

What do we do with physical evidence when we find it? There are several answers. Observations should be written down on a notepad or electronic device as soon as practical. Admittedly, this step may take place hours later. Observations of weapons, suspects, or devices must be communicated to the incident manager or law enforcement branch immediately. Other observations should be conveyed when emergency response tasks are completed (put out the fire and treat the patients first).

There are several important rules in preserving physical evidence:

FIGURE 7-2 The Murrah Building bombing (April 1995) in Oklahoma City posed many issues for emergency responders with respect to evidence collection and recovery. *Source:* Courtesy P. Maniscalco

1. Do not touch or move evidence. Law enforcement knows how to photograph, document, package, and remove evidence.
2. If evidence must be moved for tactical reasons, note the original location and report it to law enforcement investigators.
3. If possible, photograph evidence removal during tactical operations. Forensic photographers will photograph normal evidence removal during an investigation.
4. Avoid evidence contamination caused by walking through the scene. Stretch a rope or scene tape into the crime scene area and instruct personnel to walk along the established path.
5. Minimize the number of personnel working in the area.
6. Check the soles of boots or shoes when personnel exit the crime scene because fragments or fibers may be imbedded.
7. Clothing or personal effects removed from victims are considered evidence. Ensure that law enforcement personnel practice biohazard safety procedures when examining "red-bagged" evidence or clothing.

Emergency responders can also become victims. A classic case was the Sarin gas attack in the Tokyo subway system. This incident was initially reported to be a normal call until emergency physicians realized they were dealing with a nerve agent as the cause of the sickness. The importance of preparation procedures and the use of protective equipment is paramount. Every day police, fire, and emergency medical services encounter dangerous situations during the normal course of performing their services. However, the potential for lethal hazards and long-term effects that result from terrorist incidents are much greater.[1]

Another unique hazard of terrorist incidents is the probability of a secondary device targeting the responders to the incident. Remember that the goal of the terrorist is to create chaos and fear, and what better way to accomplish this than to turn the responders into victims. Bombing incidents in Atlanta, Georgia, and Birmingham, Alabama, offer real examples of this scenario. In both cases, secondary devices were detonated. Emergency responders must be alert, aware, and suspicious of their surroundings when responding to incidents that have the potential to be terroristic in nature.

Crime Scene Analysis

The thorough analysis of a crime scene consists of the identification, preservation, and collection of physical evidence as well as the recording of testimonial evidence. Without adherence to this basic assertion during the initial stages of a crime scene investigation, the potential to disrupt the integrity of the evidence is great. Hawthorne states that this could result in the evidence being challenged by the defense in a court of law, which in turn could lead to dismissal of the charges or the finding of a lesser offense against the criminal defendant.[2] More often than not, the proper collection of physical evidence from a crime scene is the definitive portion in the resolution of a criminal offense. Admissible physical evidence has the potential to (1) establish that a crime has occurred; (2) place a suspect in contact with the victim and/or the scene; (3) establish identity of those associated with the crime; (4) exonerate the innocent; (5) corroborate the victim's testimony; and (6) cause a suspect to make admissions or confess.[3]

The crime scene should be approached as if it will be the only opportunity to gather the physical evidence present.[4] Attention should be initially directed toward observing and recording the information present at the crime scene, rather than taking action to solve the crime immediately.[5] Careful consideration should also be given to other case information or statements from witnesses or suspects.

This chapter was prepared with the intention of providing the reader with rudimentary principles of crime scene investigation, from the initial

FIGURE 7-3   Evidence preservation and recovery at a terrorism scene can involve thousands of pieces of physical evidence. With the TWA Flight 800 investigation federal investigators reassembled the fuselage from numerous pieces. *Source:* Courtesy Mark Lennihan/AP/Wide World Photos

approach of the crime scene to final disposition of physical evidence found at the crime scene. Although the methods used to initially approach a crime scene are virtually universal in terms of application of use, it should be noted that at some point, the investigation may begin to take on unique characteristics that may be atypical or unorthodox in nature. Therefore, it is impossible to propose a single, step-by-step procedure that will ultimately resolve every type of crime scene[6] (Department of Justice, 2000).

However, regardless of the unique nature that a crime scene may take on, thorough crime scene analysis, effective interviews and interrogations and the use of common sense will make it less likely that evidence will be overlooked, improperly collected or preserved, or that mistakes will be made.[7]

A review of the literature reveals that a common set of generalized categories for crime scene procedures exists. These procedures are listed as follows:

1. protection of the crime scene
2. identification of evidence
3. documentation of evidence
4. collection of evidence
5. marking of evidence
6. packaging of evidence
7. transportation of evidence

Law Enforcement Responsibilities

Upon initial arrival at the scene of a crime, the first responders are tasked with a grand responsibility. It is their task to set the foundation for what Hawthorne termed the process of analyzing a crime scene. The basic elements of the process are: (1) approach; (2) render medical aid; (3) identify additional victims or witnesses; (4) secure the crime scene and physical evidence, and (5) make appropriate notifications. While adhering to these principles, the first law enforcement responders will be certain to provide subsequent investigators and technicians with a sound foundation from which they can conduct a comprehensive analysis of the crime scene.

When approaching a crime scene, the first law enforcement responder must maintain professional composure regardless of the often overwhelming factors associated with the task to be completed.[8] He must be vigilant and able to recognize anything, whether it be animate or inanimate, which seems to have a connection to the crime committed. Furthermore, the relationship of items at rest as they relate to the position of other items present at the crime scene should be noted in terms of the distances and the angles that separate them. The first law enforcement responder must be objective in his initial approach of a crime scene and resist the temptation to form conclusions as to what occurred.

Upon arrival at a crime scene, the paramount concern should be the preservation of human life and/or the prevention of additional injuries. The first law enforcement responders must be able to provide adequate first aid and/or request professional medical assistance. According to Hawthorne if law enforcement responders are providing medical assistance and the crime scene or physical evidence becomes contaminated, altered, or

> **Critical Factor:** The paramount concern at a crime scene is the preservation of life and injury prevention.

lost, that is a price that must be paid. The preservation of life outweighs the preservation of evidence at a crime scene.

After satisfying the immediate medical issues, the search for additional victims or witnesses should commence. This should be done for various reasons. These reasons include: (1) additional victims may require medical assistance and the need for additional medical personnel; (2) they may provide needed information that will aid the law enforcement responder in determining the extent of the crime, the crime scene, and any physical evidence; (3) they may also serve to corroborate what actually happened and provide needed information to establish the elements of the crime, suspect descriptions, vehicle descriptions, and avenue of escape. If there is more than one witness, the law enforcement responder should make arrangements to separate, and keep separated, those witnesses who have something to say about what they saw, in an attempt to prevent collaboration. There is always the possibility that the witnesses could have collaborated before the law enforcement responder's arrival, and the law enforcement responder should take all possible steps to ascertain if that was, in fact, what occurred. After obtaining all the facts from any additional victims and/or witnesses, the law enforcement responder now has knowledge that will enable him or her to implement the security of the scene and/or any physical evidence.[9]

It is the task of the first law enforcement responder to coordinate with emergency responders in properly identifying and securing the crime scene and its contents. The first law enforcement responder must continually question the scope of the crime scene and not limit the scope of his or her investigation. All possibilities must be considered regardless of their degree of improbability. Once the crime scene has been established, an account of personnel coming into and leaving the scene must be maintained through the use of a crime scene log. Such a log will lessen the possibility of unauthorized personnel entering into and contaminating the crime scene.[10] This log must be coordinated with the EMS/fire personnel accountability system.

The final step in what Hawthorne termed the process is making notification. This simply entails notifying supervisors as well as investigators or detectives who will be handling the case, and those people who will be ultimately responsible for documenting the scene and collecting the evidence.

The first law enforcement responders must be prepared to make split-second decisions on arrival at a crime scene. These decisions can have a lasting impact on victims, witnesses, the accusatory process, and even the community in which the crime occurred. For these reasons and others, the first law enforcement responders must be well trained in the significance of crime scene preservation, enabling the crime scene to be analyzed with as little disruption as possible. When this task is done properly, a successful investigation and conclusion of the case can be achieved.[11] Otherwise, all of the advanced technology and expertise at the disposal of law enforcement may potentially be rendered virtually useless.

Processing of Crime Scene/Physical Evidence

To achieve the maximum benefit from physical evidence, the investigator must not only be skilled in its identification, preservation, and collection, he or she must know how to handle and care for the evidence beyond the time of collection in order to preserve it for the development of leads, for laboratory examination, and/or for presentation in court. Such handling and care involves documenting and storing the evidence to retain the integrity of the item in its original condition (as nearly as possible), maintaining a chain of custody for the item to assure responsibility, and to ensuring its evidentiary value and its disposition when it is no longer of evidentiary value.[12]

The proper processing of a crime scene begins with properly documenting the evidence found within its boundaries. The investigator who first receives, recovers, or discovers physical evidence must be able to identify such evidence positively, at a later date, as being the specific article or item obtained in connection with a specific investigation.[13] This is best accomplished by utilizing various proven techniques of recording the nature of the scene and its contents as they are obtained or collected.[14] This process simply entails providing pertinent data about the evidence as it relates to a particular crime scene investigation.

Chain of Custody

In order for physical evidence collected from a crime scene to be considered admissible in a court of law, a valid chain of custody must be established.[15] The chain of custody, which ensures continuous accountability, is comprised of all those who have had custody of the evidence since its acquisition by a law enforcement agency. It begins when the item is collected and is maintained until its disposition. Each person in the chain of custody is responsible for the safekeeping and preservation of an item of evidence while it is under his or her control. Because of the sensitive nature of evidence, an evidence custodian often assumes responsibility for the item when it is not in use by the investigating officer or other competent authority involved in the investigation.[16]

Once the evidence from a crime scene has been properly identified, collected, and stored, it must be processed by a multitude of professionals who will analyze the evidence until its evidentiary value is no longer of use. It is at this point that the evidence may be considered for disposal. To determine when an item of evidence should be disposed of, the evidence custodian consults with the investigator who originally produced it, and any other investigator who has an official interest, to make sure the item is no longer needed as evidence.[17]

CHAPTER SUMMARY

Law enforcement history has shown that when mistakes are made, they predominantly occur during the initial stages of an investigation or at the crime scene.[18] More cases are lost or unresolved because the crime scene was not processed properly.

Furthermore, there are numerous incidents where police officers were careless and valuable evidence was not identified, not collected, or lost resulting in a poor follow-up by the investigating officers. Worse yet, this carelessness has, in some situations, lost the only evidence with which to prove or disprove that a crime was committed and to identify who the perpetrator might have been.

The critical nature of evidence simply cannot be ignored.[19] The responsibility of ensuring this does not happen belongs to all of those involved, from the first law enforcement responder to the investigators and technicians. Everyone within the system needs to know the importance of the crime scene and how it should be processed.[20]

CHAPTER QUESTIONS

1. Define a crime scene.
2. Discuss the theory of exchange in the evidence process.
3. What are the three major classifications of evidence? List several examples in each category.
4. List and discuss at least four crime scene observations that should be made by emergency responders.
5. List and discuss five key steps for first responder preservation of evidence.
6. Discuss the concept of chain of custody.

Simulation

Consult with at least two separate law enforcement agencies. Examine their training modules for evidence preservation and collection. Examine their standard operating procedures for evidence preservation and recovery. Based on your findings, write a comprehensive on-scene procedure for an emergency response agency relating to crime scene preservation.

NOTES

[1]Burke, Robert (2000). *Counter Terrorism for Emergency Responders.* Boca Raton, FL: Lewis Publishers.

[2]Hawthorne, Mark R. (1999). *First Unit Responders: A Guide to Physical Evidence Collection for Patrol Officers.* Boca Raton, FL: CRC Press.

[3]Fisher, Barry A. J. (2000). *Techniques of Crime Scene Investigation.* (6th ed.). Boca Raton, FL: CRC Press.

[4]Department of Justice (2000). *Crime Scene Investigation: A Guide for Law Enforcement.* Washington, DC: GPO.

[5]Hawthorne.

[6]Department of Justice.

[7]Adcock, James M. (1989). *Crime Scene Processing.* Dba JMA Forensics.

[8]Hawthorne.

[9]Ibid.

[10]Ibid.

[11]Ibid.

[12]Schultz, Donald O. (1977). *Crime Scene Investigation.* Upper Saddle River, NJ: Prentice Hall.

[13]Fox, Richard H., and Carl L. Cunningham (1973). *Crime Scene Search and Physical Evidence Handbook.* Washington, DC: U.S. Department of Justice.

[14]Schultz.

[15]Hawthorne.

[16]Schultz.

[17]Ibid.

[18]Adcock.

[19]Hawthorne.

[20]Adcock.

8
Technology and Emergency Response

Michael J. Hopmeier

Source: Courtesy R. Christen

Chapter Objectives

After reading this chapter, you will be able to accomplish the following objectives:

1. Recognize factors that have changed significantly in technology.
2. Understand the important linkage of technology with doctrine.
3. Recognize the limits of technology.
4. Have an awareness of technology use for personnel accountability.
5. Understand use of technology for situational awareness.
6. Understand technology applications that improve survivability.

Introduction

Any sufficiently advanced technology is indistinguishable from magic.

Arthur C. Clarke

Much discussion has taken place recently concerning technology as it relates to the new class of threats (specifically WMD), and applications for response to these threats. Many assessments are based on partially understood problems or partially understood technologies, and seldom reflect a true *system* approach. As a result, technology developers are often disappointed by the lack of acceptance of their ideas, and technology users rapidly become disillusioned about technology's ability to help them.

This chapter discusses issues associated with assessment of technology needs, and acquisition/purchase/design of technology solutions that help the first responder or public safety professional. The primary focus is on operators, not management, and as a result management issues are addressed only as they relate to field operations.

Background

New threats, especially WMD, have often been attributed to new technologies. With very few exceptions, this is not the case. Whether chemical or biological in nature, *new* threats are *not* the result of new technologies. In most cases the technology, and in fact its application to warfare, have been around for hundreds or thousands of years. From poisoning of wells with dead bodies to catapulting plague cadavers over the walls of castles, biological warfare has been used for over 1,000 years. Smoke, burning liquids, and even gases have been used for almost as long.

The exceptions to this are nuclear/radioactive threats. These threats are addressed directly, as there has been an enormous amount of writing, discussion, and preparation for these incidents over the past 50 years. In most cases it is not a need for new technologies or doctrine, but simply for re-learning what was implemented over the years of the Cold War. Our focus is on other classes of threats including chemical and biological, man-made as well as natural.

Several factors have changed significantly including:

- **Greater Recognition**—While many of these technologies have been used for many hundreds of years, we are only now becoming cognizant of them. It is only recently that they have entered the public and political consciousness, so it is easy to assume they never existed prior to current thought about them (the ostrich head-in-the-sand syndrome).
- **Greater Vulnerability**—For a variety of reasons, society is much more vulnerable to attacks of this nature than ever before, especially American society. From greater population densities to less robust infrastructure, society overall is less able to respond to *any* threat, let alone the catastrophic ones addressed in this book. Couple this with increasingly easier travel over longer distances and shorter times, as well as greater reliance on information technology with less understanding of it, and the vulnerability is obvious.
- **Greater Awareness**—With the increasing accessibility of information from the popular press and the Internet as well as other sources, the public has more and more information. Unfortunately, there is little ability to interpret this information and, as a result, even less understanding. This generally results in knee-jerk responses to the crisis *du jour*, and these responses are seldom correct.

Technology Considerations

This chapter will **not** address specific systems, manufacturers, or devices (they change rapidly and there are other sources of information on specific systems), but instead will discuss generic considerations in choosing technologies or systems. For specific data concerning devices and manufacturers, refer to various standards and evaluation organizations.

Technology must be used to improve job performance.—Much of today's focus is on development, deployment, and marketing of technologies only for terrorist and WMD incidents. Some developers have lost sight of the fact that terrorist/WMD incidents seldom occur, but fires, haz mat accidents, explosions, and earthquakes occur much more frequently. As the old adage goes, "you fight as you train and you train as you fight." This is true in the public safety community. If technologies do not help in everyday operations and support the first responder on a regular basis, they will not be used (the training and support infrastructure needed to sustain them will never be absorbed). The end result is that vast quantities of effort and resources are expended as long as external funding is available, and thereafter fall into disuse, amounting to wasted effort. Technologies must be beneficial in raising overall preparedness, or not be pursued at all.

Technology without a plan is useless.—All too often it is assumed that a new technology (black box) will be a panacea and solve all problems. It will not. It is vital to have a way to use it when it arrives. Technology alone will never solve anything. Consider the issue of medical anti-shock trousers (MAST) in emergency medical services. The technology is sound, namely, squeezing the lower extremities to increase blood pressure. However, the protocols for the use of MAST trousers are still highly debated at medical conferences.

Training and sustainment.—When evaluating a technology, consider what is needed to maintain proficiency. If it is a long, arduous task to learn how to use a technology, and it will seldom be used, it will probably never be used at all. When a crisis develops that requires the technology, it will be unused because there is no time to relearn how to apply it. Consider computer software: We are all aware that Microsoft Windows has an enormous number of resources and capabilities, but few have mastered or recall all of them. As a result it is often easier to fall back on old ways of doing things (especially if we have a deadline to meet and it is coming up fast) than to try and figure out how to make the document look just right. The same thing happens with technology.

Maintenance, repair, and calibration.—It is often necessary to repair, adjust, or perform preventive maintenance on a technology, but this is not always factored into the cost of the new system. Consider the recent introduction of automatic external defibrillators (AED). Many underfunded volunteer fire departments received AEDs through grants, only to discover that the cost of the required yearly calibration and inspection was prohibitive. Also, many of today's highly accurate sensor and sampling devices require periodic calibration and adjustment that must also be factored into the support costs.

Understand the problem.—Often technologies are obtained to solve a perceived problem, but do little to address the actual problem. Consider, for example, personnel accountability. Exact location of personnel on the fire ground or at a crime scene may not be needed. It may be sufficient to know simply who is in the area of interest and be able to recall them, en mass, as needed. As a result, a simple inventory management system is better than a global positioning system (GPS) location system.

Recognize the limitations of technology.—As noted earlier, technology is not a panacea; it must be examined in the context of the entire problem. Make sure the limitations of technology are clearly recognized before use. As an example, uses of night vision goggles by police are a real improvement over simply having a flashlight. But low light level imaging can be spoofed or rendered inoperable through either intentional or unintentional means (shine a flashlight at the goggles or simply have someone turn on a porch light). All technologies have limitations; understand the limitations of the ones you plan to use.

Technology never replaces training and judgment.—Technology, no matter how good, can never replace proper training, skills, and good old-fashioned common sense. Always remember that the person on the ground is the ultimate tool and technology. Their training, preparedness, and ability to respond to and adapt to changing circumstances are paramount. Any technology, no matter how good, is only a tool and support method to extend the ability of the person on the ground. Technology must support the user; never make the user support the technology.

The user knows best and is the final arbiter.—Remember that no matter how many degrees or years of experience a technologist or scientist may have, he or she is not the one whose life is on the line and will depend on the technology. No matter how good a technology may look in a laboratory or during a demonstration, the true test is always in the field. When considering new technologies, always ask the question, "How will this help me do my job better?" If you don't know, don't buy it.

Strive for the acceptable solution, not the perfect one.—It is often very expensive to achieve an absolute, custom, and perfect solution. It is also nearly impossible. Instead, consider what would be acceptable (albeit not necessarily perfect), and consider optimizing the overall system and application of the technology. Can you make due with something less than perfect now, as opposed to waiting for perfection in a year or more? These questions must be asked and answered before embarking on a technology quest.

Ensure that a technology will be used.—If a technology is too time consuming or uncomfortable to be used, it won't be. Often the human factors associated with a technology are overlooked in the rush to get something into the market. If a technology is not comfortable, easy to use, and does not provide some capability that the user wants, it will be ignored.

Legacy system (hardware and procedural).—A legacy system is the existing system of hardware or procedures in a response organization. It is seldom successful to completely change the way something is done to fit a new technology. Instead, strive for *revolutionary* capabilities through *evolutionary* means. New systems must be compatible with existing technologies and legacy systems so that an upheaval is not required to introduce a new capability.

Technologies

Rather than providing a catalog of different technologies, this chapter is structured around expressed needs. Numerous studies have been done to define the needs of the emergency responder. The following is a compendium of the results. First the need is discussed briefly, and then potential technology solutions are addressed.

A major requirement in consequence response is personnel accountability. The questions of "where are you," "how are you," and "do you need help" are the most critical questions asked and answered during any operation. The ability to maintain accountability and knowledge of personnel assets on the ground or during an operation is paramount. Information such as individual location with sufficient accuracy to locate, identify, and render service if needed is crucial. The need to call for help in a crisis or the ability to render a determination as to whether help is required are both key. Furthermore, solutions must be economical, easy to use, and compatible with existing doctrine, protocol, and technologies within the emergency services.

Consider this issue in the context of inventory management or control. Industry manages its assets through use of various tags and points of entry/exit. Most of the classic solutions involve trying to track an individual, usually through some form of GPS-based system. This presents many problems, however. Among them is the difficulty of using GPS in built-up areas as well as in buildings. What may make more sense is to use some form of inertial tracking and navigation system.

There are currently many technologies (generically referred as taggants) that can be used for tracking commodities and personnel. Consider using point of entry/exit control systems such as those used for inventory management in warehouses and supermarkets. These portals coupled with various forms of radio frequency (RF) identification tags, or even barcodes such as those used to identify automobiles going through tollbooths, could be very effective in this role.

Various attempts over the years have been made to create individual status/biotelemetry systems (the personnel status monitor (PSM) being a good example) that have all failed. Most have failed because of the designer's lack of knowledge as to what is actually needed. In general, physiologic status is *not* necessary to meet the needs of the incident commander in maintaining knowledge of his/her personnel and their status. Further, the need for physiologic monitoring creates the need for probes and sensors directly attached to the user. This is often uncomfortable, impractical, or both. As a result, the technology is seldom used accurately or effectively. Consider the minimum amount of technology and information needed to protect the user: systems that meet that need without getting overly complicated or complex.

Analysis and Evaluation of Emergency Response Data

While a large amount of data is currently being collected on emergency personnel and their operations, very little is being used to determine ways in which to improve effectiveness of the system. To determine which technologies and efforts should be pursued, and which of those have the highest potential payoff, it is vital that some methodology and analysis be created to assign benchmarks (also called metrics) to emergency personnel and system performance. As new technologies or techniques are brought online for evaluation and use, their various capabilities can be evaluated to determine what needs to be changed, dropped, pursued, or enhanced. This capability is vital to ensure that high value projects are pursued and marginal projects are discontinued.

The ability to assess the impact of new technologies on operations is paramount. The goals of a technology must first be defined, and then applied when a new technology or capability is assessed. To do this effectively, it is vital that the true problem be understood. Take the problem of firefighters being trapped in a zero visibility environment. The difficulty is not that they are unable to see, it is that they become disoriented, confused, and run out of air. Many die as a result of running out of air while trying to find their way out of a structure. In this case, knowing where they are is of little help without a detailed map of the structure. Therefore, the issue is trying to locate them in the building. One possible solution may be an inertial tracker that would let them simply walk back through the path they had taken, without knowing exactly where they are. This is an example of clearly understanding the problem, and the benchmarks (metrics) needed to assess the problem before attempting to obtain technology.

Improved Situation Awareness

Perhaps the most important aspect for any emergency responder is awareness of their surroundings (situational awareness). This is vital not only to allow the first responder to complete their mission, but to make sure that the team does the same in a safe manner. This awareness includes the ability to sense their surroundings, especially through improved sight in degraded conditions (thermal and acoustic imaging, image processing, radar vision, etc.). Individuals must know where they are situated, where their partners and other teams are located, and where major assets such as the fire truck, escape routes/safe zones, and supplies like oxygen and water are located. What type of atmosphere are they in (is it poisonous, too hot, contaminated)? What is the status of the building around them (will it collapse shortly, is a wall too hot, is an electrical short occurring nearby)? Are there signs of chemical, biological, or nuclear contamination in the atmosphere around them, on them, on their patients, or partners? Of equal importance is how the information should be provided (heads-up displays, wrist worn indicators, voices, image displays)? What is the status of their equipment (amount of air, water, chemical agent, and power)?

Critical Factor: Responders must have situational awareness: an awareness of their surroundings.

Many of these questions have different answers depending on the environment in which they are asked, the community or department asking them, and the other resources available as infrastructure. The specific integrated systems, while unique, will still be able to be made from the same basic sets and systems of components. There are four areas/issues that need to be considered:

1. *Sensor technologies.* These are individual sensors that the responder can use such as temperature detectors, chemical sensors, thermal imagers, etc.
2. *Onboard/man information processing.* How is the data presented to the user? Heads-up displays? Voice presentation? Vibration? All at once, in individually controllable pieces, etc.?
3. *Externally available information transmission/display.* How much information goes back to the command post and incident commander? Back to headquarters? Back to the rest of the world? How much is recorded?
4. *How information is integrated into existing systems.* Is there an existing accountability system or mapping/situational awareness system that needs to be used? Are there already maps of city buildings available electronically and can they be accessed? Can this information be overlaid on an existing framework or incorporated into existing situational awareness systems?

Sensor technologies are expanding at an increasing rate. In the area of imagery, night vision scopes that function in the near infrared (IR) are available for less than $150.00. Uncooled thermal imagers (for example, new micro-bolometer technologies) are just starting to reach the mass market and will shortly provide thermal imaging and far IR capabilities for well under $1,000.00.

In the area of chemical/biological sensors, there is an enormous amount of work and effort going on. Much of the focus is on individually operated monitors and detectors designed for use by the first responder, which provide them with specific identification of individual agents. The first responder needs the ability to determine simply whether the environment is safe or not. The actual cause of the hazard is secondary and can be determined by other specialized units.

During the Tokyo sarin incident the "chemical detectors" used were parakeets. The responders knew upon arrival that they were dealing with some form of unknown chemical. However, they were not prepared to deal with any particular agent. Knowing exactly what agent they were dealing with at this level of response was of questionable value at best and useless at worst. Instead, what was needed was a simple safety detection device (safe/unsafe) with identification of the agent being performed at some other level of response (laboratory, hospital, etc.). The only real need is to determine whether the environment is safe to remove gear or whether the casualties have been properly decontaminated.

Until recently, chemical detectors consisted almost exclusively of carbon monoxide (CO) and lower/upper explosive limit detectors. Poisonous chemical agents were considered to only come from combustion products, and these products were correlated with CO concentrations. Therefore, when the CO concentration fell below a certain level, the other agents were considered to be below that level as well. Specialized gear, however, existed for use in specific, highly dangerous environments (chemical processing plants, rocket fueling areas, etc.). Specialized training went along with these areas.

Today that is no longer the case. In spite of the focus on chemical warfare agents, the real problem is, and continues to be, hazardous materials. Many chemical warfare agents are industrial chemicals transported throughout the country in bulk transporters (i.e., phosgene). As a result, it is necessary for technologies to be used in a variety of applications and circumstances, not just for terrorist incidents.

Tools and Technology to Improve Survivability

Improved hospital care.—Dealing with shock (hypo-perfusion), airway maintenance, and vital signs monitoring are all issues of concern that improve the survivability of the injured patient. Better ways to provide this prehospital care are of importance. These techniques and technologies need to be rugged, relatively easy to use, require minimal training and maintenance, and be cost effective.

Monitoring responder health conditions and performance.—The status of the emergency personnel during operations is vitally important. At a minimum, are they healthy, injured, or under unacceptable stress (i.e., heat exhaustion, dehydration, etc.)? Can this data provide a prediction as to their likely abilities and capability to continue operations? This information not only improves the safety of the individual emergency responder, but also their ability to perform their jobs. With sufficient information, improvements in training, equipment, procedures, and doctrine can be made.

Field performance predictive methods.—It is difficult to predict under non-stress conditions how a person will perform physically. Whether it is a masked or unknown cardiac condition or perhaps an allergy to specific chemicals that might be encountered, the need to be cognizant of these conditions is paramount. Issues such as buildup of chemical dosages (i.e., CO poisoning) that might need time to clear from a system, or longer-range impact (i.e., radiation) need to be monitored, accounted for, and used to help place and utilize emergency personnel to minimize danger to themselves and their colleagues.

Improved voice and data communications for intermodal use.—The transmission of data from the scene of an incident back to some central point, and vice versa, is vital. This data includes, but is not limited to, analog (i.e., voice) and digital (i.e., video) data. It might also include system status, maps, blueprints, and real-time access to databases. The communication system must be compatible with urban points of interference (such as buildings and other broadcasters), as well as rural environments (longer range, no repeaters). It must also be compatible with individual communications systems (battalion chief or incident commander's communication system). The system must be compatible with other equipment (i.e., trucks), as well as supporting legacy systems to minimize cost.

Improved voice and data communications for individuals.—Each individual on the scene must have the ability to communicate with the person next to him, every responder on the scene, or headquarters, and do so selectively and with ease. The capability to transmit voice, video, and status data is also important. The system must be compatible with the intermodal communications systems as well as individual equipment (i.e., self-contained breathing apparatus [SCBA], available batteries, water, smoke, etc.). It must function in urban areas (inside buildings with lots of electrical interference, including compatibility with other transmission sources such as radio stations, TV, etc.), and in rural areas (work at extended ranges in the woods, open fields, etc.). Additionally the system must support reception of data maps, graphics, personnel status, etc.

Measurement, prediction, and improvement of interpersonal skills.—Interpersonal and communication skills between emergency personnel and their various chains of command, and the community as a whole, should be monitored, measured, and improved through training. The ability to evaluate individual traits and capabilities to predict these skills can lead to improved operations and better interaction. This also provides a basis for focusing training and other resources where they can be the most effective. Issues concerning environment (room setups, facility design, etc.) will also be taken into account to make the emergency personnel as effective as possible.

Improved environmental data.—When engaging a fire or hazard, the personnel need to have as much information as possible about the environment around them, information such as the layout of the building and material stored in each room (i.e., are hazardous materials in danger of igniting and/or exploding). Are poisonous compounds or accelerants nearby? What walls and floors are the strongest or weakest? Other information would include where the standpipes, power and gas lines, and structural components are located. What is the current structural status (is the building about to collapse, is a particular joist or main support weakened from heat or fire?)? What is the micrometeorology (local weather); will it rain, will the wind shift, is there lightning in the area? Real-time maps and geographic information are required to better locate the scene of an incident, or the best way to approach it (avoid mud, traffic congestion, small roads, etc).

Critical Factor: The data that relates to the surrounding environment is vital to emergency responders.

Improved threat assessment and intelligence.—Accurate information concerning likely threats and threat scenarios is vital to ensure proper training, equipment, and engagement of incidents. This information might range from terrorist threats to new forms of arson. Responses might include applying new methods or techniques of combating these incidents, to looking for specific early indications of a future incident that could be mitigated. Better methods of communicating information, analyzing its import, and determining actions based on this information is vital. This might include, but not be limited to, a central clearinghouse for information, better dissemination and communication of information, improved analysis and distribution, etc.

After-action analysis.—After an incident, it is vital to analyze and understand not only the cause, but also the effectiveness of the response. Better forensic analysis, record keeping, and logging of events correlated with the results of the response and the effects are important. The end goal is to reduce the effects of the response through mitigation and improved engagement techniques.

Remote analysis.—Many situations are so hazardous (biological, chemical, nuclear) that remote observation and initial analysis are the only safe means of determining the situation. Methods of remotely detecting contamination, heat sources, casualties, etc., are vital. Whether detection is by robotic or autonomous means, or through the use of remote sensing, this is crucial.

Robotics and autonomous devices.—Often, situations arise where a remote piloted or autonomous device may be needed. Requirements include the ability to maneuver through doors and up/down stairs; be self-powered and possibly self-directing; provide heavy lift (i.e., more than a person is capable of); and provide evacuation, breaching of barriers, auxiliary power, enhanced sensing, and other tasks that either augment or replace personnel.

Forced entry and breaching of barriers.—Depending on the incident, it may be necessary to breach security barriers, such as locked doors or chained gates, or if structural damage has occurred, to penetrate through debris. Power rams, hydraulic spreaders, pneumatic tools, etc., are all used; still better means are required. Barriers might include doors, bars and chains, walls, floors and ceilings, reinforced concrete walls, and pavement. Debris might include buckled beams, fallen concrete, crushed or damaged vehicles, timber, rock slides, etc. Technologies need to be safe and nonlethal (i.e., explosives generally create a greater hazard than not using them), man-portable, and require minimum support and training for their use.

Energy storage, control, transport and discharge.—Many missions require the application of external force or energy. Hydraulic tools, chain saws, and explosives are all examples. The capability to transport these energy sources to the scene and be able to apply the forces required is important. Current techniques include gas powered hydraulic pumps and air compressors, but these are often bulky, heavy, or unwieldy. Furthermore, because of the use of gas and the exhaust fumes, these techniques may not be suitable for all situations. New sources of easily applied power, compatible with the incident environment, are needed. These power sources must be compatible with existing tools so that an entire new system of equipment and ancillary devices need not be purchased.

CHAPTER SUMMARY

The so-called new threats of weapons technology are actually new or revised applications of old technology. Radioactive threats are an obvious exception.

There are several technology considerations:

- Technology must be used to improve job performance.
- Technology without doctrine is useless.
- Technology requires training and ongoing use.
- Technology requires maintenance, repair, and calibration.

- Technology has limitations.
- Technology never replaces training and judgment.

The user should be the final arbiter in technology considerations. The true test is in the field, not the laboratory. The technology solutions available will never be perfect due to human imperfection and cost. Instead, acceptable solutions should be the end state rather than perfect solutions.

New technology must be compatible with existing systems (legacy systems). It is not practical to change all existing technologies to be compatible with a new technology.

New technology requirements in the emergency response field include:

- tracking of resources and assets
- bio-monitoring with telemetry
- tracking of responders in a hot zone or building
- improved situational awareness
- sensor capability including biological, chemical, thermal, etc.
- survivability improvement
- improved voice and data communications
- improved environmental data
- improved threat assessment and intelligence

CHAPTER QUESTIONS

1. Discuss three factors relating to technology and threat vulnerability that have changed significantly.
2. What is the relationship between technology and doctrine?
3. Discuss at least three limits of technology.
4. How can technology be utilized for personnel accountability?
5. Discuss how technology can be used to enhance situational awareness.

Simulation

Select a major technology that has evolved in the emergency response or military arena in the past 20 years. Examples include noninvasive monitoring in EMS, water additives in fire operations, public health surveillance for disease agents, or DNA matching in law enforcement. Trace its evolution including early development to the present time, a success/failure analysis of products and manufacturers, costs, support, and training issues. Discuss how doctrine or operational procedures did or did not evolve with the technology. Conclude with a discussion of the outcome (end-state) of the technology and a prediction for the future of the technology you selected.

Part II

Mass Casualty and High-Impact Incidents: An Operations Guide

9

The Basics of Incident Management Systems

Paul M. Maniscalco
Hank T. Christen

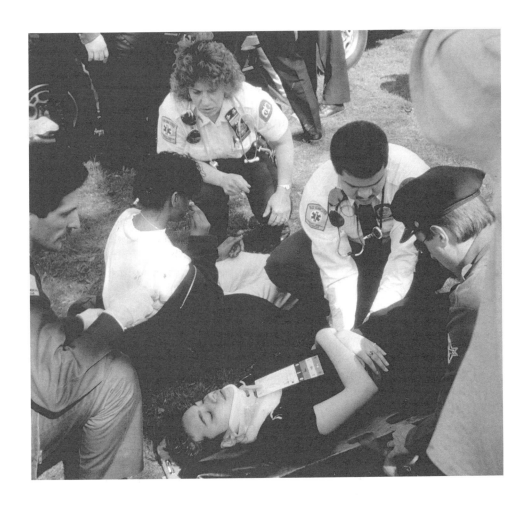

Chapter Objectives

After reading this chapter, you will be able to accomplish the following objectives:

1. Understand the history of incident management.
2. Recognize the parallels between incident management and military command structures.
3. Understand the development of fire command systems.
4. Recognize the modern management principles that are inherent in incident command systems.
5. Have a basic knowledge of the EMS Incident Management System.

The Early Times

How far back in history do basic organizational principles go? You might guess that incident command principles were first discussed by Phoenix Fire Chief Alan Brunacini in the 1970s. Others would suggest that the writings of Peter Drucker in the 1950s and 1960s were early works on the subject. Management scholars select the writings of Henri Fayol, Chester Barnard, or Fredrick Taylor, dating back to the turn of the century. Actually, management principles were discussed several thousand years ago.

Military Influences

In pre-Roman times armies were disorganized hordes. Looting and plundering were the plan of the day. The leader was the person that killed his upstarts. In a battle, the leader was always in the middle of the melee with his troops. (This still happens in many emergency medical organizations.)

The Romans changed military history. A centurion class of military professionals evolved. The famous Roman Legions were structurally organized into succinct units. The various divisions were headed by highly trained and professional leaders. Significantly, these leaders coordinated with the central commander in accordance with a plan. This form of organization continued to develop through centuries.

During the Civil War, weapons development received historical attention. The fact that improved management and control made an equal contribution to military prowess was not recognized.

In World War II several failed invasions revealed the need for developing a modern battle plan. Military leaders learned that dedicated soldiers and modern weapons were not enough. Management techniques were recognized as having equal importance with fighting skills.

These management concepts were fine tuned in Korea and Vietnam. The concepts of command, control, and communications were refined to a science in the Persian Gulf.

The management lessons learned in combat operations were also applied to the management of casualties. The first ambulances in America were wagons assigned to carry wounded soldiers in the Civil War. Patients were transported to large casualty assembly areas behind the lines.

In World Wars I and II, large field hospitals were established. For the first time, triage was developed. Patients were sorted, with the least critical receiving emergency treatment and being sent back immediately to the fighting lines. Critical patients were forwarded to surgical wards and hospital ships.

In the Korean War, the first use of helicopter patient transfer occurred. Field hospitals (MASH units) were established close to the battle front. The time from a severe wound to a surgical suite was greatly reduced. In Vietnam this time was a matter of hours. There was extensive use of helicopter transport from the immediate battle scene to sophisticated surgical units. Effective triage and advanced medical techniques led to reduced loss of life.

The lessons learned from the military operations lead us into the modern area of incident management. The lessons of war became the foundations of the first civilian incident management system.

Modern Fire Command Systems

In the 1970s, a series of catastrophic brush fires destroyed thousands of structures. Fire units were not coordinated. There were horror stories about incompatible radio frequencies, lack of priority resource allocation, and poor coordination and control among a myriad of federal, state, and local agencies.

The lessons learned by the Roman Legions had to be relearned. The result was the California Firescope (Firefighting Resources of Southern California Organized Against Potential Emergency) Program. Key agencies began to meet and talk about mutual problems.

During the development of Firescope, emergency agencies and planners agreed on several objectives:

1. A system of command, where a single individual (or unified command team) is responsible for the ultimate outcome of the incident.
2. A system of common terminology. All agencies should understand each other.
3. A system of coordination among diversified agencies.
4. A communications system with shared frequencies and common radio language.
5. A system for resource allocation, including prioritizing and staging.

A national Incident Command System (ICS) evolved. It was determined that situations had the components of administration, planning, logistics, and operations. These sections were coordinated by an Incident Commander, supported by the Command Staff.

ICS was recognized as a system for fire agencies. Other agencies, on the outside looking in, pushed for a system that incorporated non-fire organizations into the command plan. This system was the evolutionary step that lead to the National Interagency Incident Management System (NIIMS).

ICS and NIIMS were criticized in some fire service circles as being wildfire/California oriented. The urban fire service in the 1970s began to move in its own directions. New York City developed a command system based on operational sectors. In Phoenix, Chief Alan Brunacini developed the command system that made him famous through his excellent NFPA Fire Command Seminars. Simultaneously, David Chamberlin, former Atlanta Fire Chief, developed the incident command system taught at the Emergency Management Institute at Emmittsburg, Maryland.

Equally important components of the emergency response community other than fire service (law enforcement, Emergency Medical Services, etc.) began to rally for an incident command system that met the needs of their specific functional areas.

The functional area of Emergency Medical Service (EMS) found itself confronted with being buried in the existing ICS organizational chart as a small block labeled "medical unit." The "medical unit" is located in the service branch of the logistics section with no real delineation of the primary tasks required for successful EMS MCI operations.

The importance of a standard command system for EMS operations cannot be disputed, but what would the standard be? What should it be? Many different individuals and organizations have toiled over these questions. Most recently we have witnessed organizations such as the National Fire Academy, Emergency Management Institute, and the National Fire Service Incident Management Consortium assist with this standardization process by producing documents and educational programs to aid the local EMS provider with quickly ascending the command system learning curve.

The purpose of this text is to take the basic command principles set forth in those models and bring them to the student in a non-confusing, "real world" EMS fashion. The grasp of a theory is at times relatively easy. The application of that theory, successfully, is another story. It is our intent to share with you the specifics of the EMS Incident Management System and the successful application of the tasks from a "real world EMS" viewpoint.

Modern Management Principles

All the command systems discussed use basic management principles. These principles are the cornerstone of business management, military command systems, and emergency incident management.

Critical Factor: Medical disasters can and must be managed. Management principles used in routine functions must be applied to the non-routine disaster.

Unity of Command

Unity of command means someone is in control. This concept can mean that a "team" is in charge. (See Chapter 10.)

Every component, section, or unit has an individual responsible for performance. Unit members understand and recognize this authority. Managers understand their relationship to their superiors, their subordinates, and their peers.

Span of Control

The number of subordinates responsible to a leader is called the "span of control." An ideal span of control is three to five people but varies with the operations.

If a span of control is too narrow, the organization becomes management top heavy (lots of chiefs, too few Indians.) If the span of control is too wide, individual leaders cannot effectively manage the units or people under them. They cannot process the information overload from too many units.

Chain of Command

"Chain of command" is linked to unity of command and span of control and is defined as the flow of information from one command level to another.

There is an old military expression that says certain things (expletive deleted) flow downhill. We know information must flow vertically through the chain of command (uphill), as well as downward.

Line and Staff (Operations and Support)

Traditional business management models divide organizational functions into line functions and staff functions. The line function is the company's mission. Examples include making "widgets" in a manufacturing business or printing manuscripts for a publisher.

Staff functions provide support to the line functions. Staff responsibilities include areas such as finance, personnel, marketing (sales), etc. In incident management systems, the terms operations and support replace the business management terms of line and staff.

Operations, in the EMS Incident Management System, includes the triage, treatment, and transport of patients. Support functions include supplies, communications, planning, media coordination, and liaison with outside agencies.

A key concept of operations/support (or line and staff) is balance within the management system. Often operations are emphasized and support is minimized. The result is decreased operations. In summary, the right hand must complement what the left hand is doing.

Critical Factor: In the EMS Incident Management System, balance between operations functions and support functions is vital.

C Cubed I (C³I)

Modern military command systems have a balanced command structure instead of a focus on operational tactics. The military jargon is command, control, communications, and intelligence. It is written C³I, pronounced "see-cubed-eye."

This command and control system is similar to civilian public safety command systems. There is emphasis on coordination of operational functions (military tactics) with support functions.

Desert Storm was the classic example of effective military management. Throughout the conflict, commanders discussed their management successes instead of battle tactics. The media devoted as much coverage to logistics, planning, and communications as they did to the fighting. During interviews, top commanders often talked about destroying the enemy "command and control" structure rather than its weapons.

For years experts will analyze Desert Storm as a management model. The conclusion is: We won because of an effective management system. (As one Army officer said, "We had good C-cubed.")

The Checklist Mentality

Many incident management systems consist of checklists for every conceivable problem. Incident management control then involves following the rigid checklists.

Checklist systems tend to fail. First, if you encounter an incident that is not on the checklist, the management system falls apart. As an example, you may have a checklist for a fire, a tornado, or an airplane crash. None of these checklists is useful during a mass shooting or an earthquake.

Second, a checklist for an incident cannot be all inclusive. Disasters are full of surprises. It is impossible to think of everything. The checklist will never include surprises. (Remember: No plan survives contact with the enemy.)

Last, checklists do not address the coordination between elements in a management system. There must be assignments (based on checklist items) and interrelations between the people receiving the assignments. Management systems address these relationships; checklist systems do not.

Checklists have their place. Detailed and repetitive procedures are well-suited to checklists. Inspecting a hand-held radio or setting up an oxygen cascade system requires a checklist. Equipment needs are a resource checklist. Just remember, checklists are not management systems.

Management Focus versus Task Focus

Tasks require the manual skills necessary to carry out an operational plan. Most tasks are hands-on operations. This includes skills such as CPR, IV therapy, bandaging, or splinting. Obviously, tasks are the essence of incident operations. When tasks are applied without management (command/control), there is no effective system. More importantly, there is no coordination and individuals (or units) operate in a freelance style. Their task skills may be excellent, but are applied at the wrong place or the wrong time.

Consider a mass casualty incident with task focus only. All the medics are treating patients and no single person is in charge. The order of treatment is "first come, first served." (The management concept of triage is missing). There are no support functions since everyone is concentrating on individual tasks. As the incident progresses, there is a depletion of EMS supplies, a breakdown in communications, and a loss of transportation resources, with no one responsible.

Whereas on a daily basis we applaud independent actions, at the scene of the MCI there is no room for independent actions. Independent actions, in these instances, lead to "freelancing," and often the actions of "freelancers" yield results that are contrary to the commanders' strategies or cause safety problems. It is evident that many EMS providers do not recognize the need for senior supervision, yet the orientation of all members of an EMS system to the behavioral requirements of the Incident Management System is a must.

The required transition is one from relationship behavior to task behavior. Usually an EMS provider has the luxury at most emergency and non-emergency calls to discuss and reason with his or her partners regarding actions to take, treatment protocols to follow, and hospitals to which to transport. This participatory decision-making process can be termed an example of relationship behavior. When an EMS crew is operating at an MCI, its actions are being dictated by a Sector Officer and crew members might find themselves being transferred from one sector to another based upon the requirements of the incident. The directions given by the Sector Officer must be followed to ensure that the overall tactics and strategies are applied as intended by the Incident Manager or Branch Director. These actions are examples of task behavior.

When a crew is operating in the MCI arena, there is no time for relationship behavior. The directions of the Sector Officer must be followed in order to ensure the efficacy of the operation and safety of all involved.

The IMS Model

The national Incident Management System (IMS) is a management model that incorporates all the sound management principles discussed earlier in this chapter.

The individual in charge is called the Incident Manager. The Incident Manager is assisted by a Management Staff, a group of specialists coordinating as a Manager's support team.

There are four major sections under the Management Staff. These sections are Administration, Planning, Logistics, and Operations. (See Figure 9-1.) In many cases, Administration does not justify full section status. In these situations, Administration can become a unit in another section.

This model is the basis for all public safety management systems. The system, as diagrammed, incorporates all of the elements previously discussed.

- Unified Command—There is a single person (or management team) in charge.
- Span of Control—No individual manages more than three to five sections or units.
- Chain of Command—There is a clear flow of information up or down. (Remember: Sometimes the "expletive deleted" has to flow uphill.)

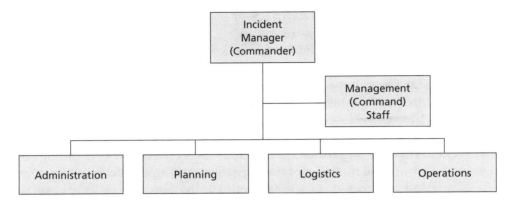

FIGURE 9-1 Basic Structure of the Incident Management System.

- Line and Staff—There is a line function (operations), supported and co-ordinated with staff functions (logistics, planning, and administration).
- C³I—There is a system of command, control, communications, and intelligence. (We call intelligence reconnaissance, recon, or threat assessment, in the public safety world.)
- Flexibility—The system applies to any incident (or management problem). It is not a system of checklists.

This model is generic and not specific to medical disasters. In the next section, we will develop the incident management model into the EMS Incident Management System.

Incident Classifications

A medical incident (non-routine) is classified as either a routine event or a mass casualty incident, also known as a multiple-casualty incident (MCI). An MCI is an event that

- Produces several patients.
- Produces a minimal number of casualties but has unusual events surrounding the incident (e.g., Haz Mat, multiple vehicle accident, rail, aircraft, or marine incident, etc.).
- Affects local hospital(s) receiving the patients to the point that normal EMS operations become hindered, thereby having a negative impact on system efficacy.
- Generally may "draw down" the system resources, or the number of patients outnumbers the resources of initial rescuers.

A disaster is a type of MCI that involves hundreds or thousands of patients. It strikes anytime, anywhere. It takes many forms—a hurricane, an earthquake, a tornado, a flood, a fire or a hazardous spill, an act of nature or an act of terrorism. It builds over days or weeks, or hits suddenly, without warning. Every year millions of Americans face disasters and their terrifying consequences. The medical and public safety infrastructure may suffer considerable damage. Resources will be needed from the state and federal government. Operations will be conducted in what the military calls a "resource scarce environment." In a disaster, a complete EMS Incident Management System will be needed to provide planning, administration, and logistical support to operation teams.

The term MCI should be transmitted via the designated communications system. If the meaning of this term is clearly understood, other units can respond accordingly. They can activate the appropriate checklists in communications centers and medical control. All responding agencies must know the meaning of an MCI and should identify an incident as such.

A medical disaster is not declared by a responding unit. A disaster declaration unfolds after a period of damage assessment or after several days of emergency operations. In many states a governor's official declaration of emergency is required to obtain state and federal resources.

EMS Incident Management builds from the bottom level upwards. As operation units survey their situation, they build the incident management system. It begins from a single patient incident to an MCI and finally to a medical disaster, which is really an expanded MCI (Figures 9-2, 9-3, and 9-4).

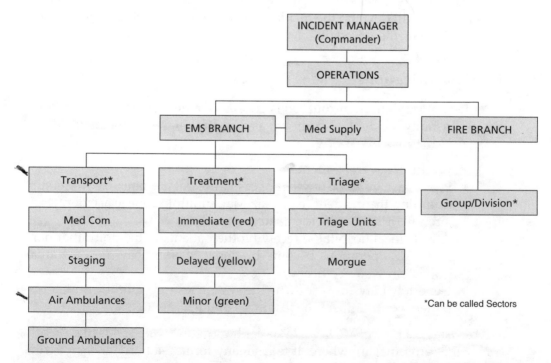

FIGURE 9-2 Mass Casualty Incident.

EMS Incident Management System

The principles and organizational structure in the Fire Incident Command System are easily adopted into an EMS Incident Management System (EMS/IMS). The key components are triage, treatment, and transportation. Staging is an additional sector in a medical disaster. These tactical activities are coordinated by an EMS Branch.

The Incident Manager is supported by a Command Staff consisting of a liaison, as well as safety, public information, and trauma intervention program (TIPs) personnel. All of these sectors, and the sectors described below, may require expansion depending on the situation.

The Planning Section provides documentation (medical records), planning, and administration. Rarely is an incident large enough to justify separate Administration and Planning Sections.

The Logistics Section provides support in the form of communications, medical supplies, facilities, and mobilization.

The Operations system in Figure 9-3 applies to major incidents. All diagrammed functions are not necessary in small-scale situations.

In a routine automobile accident with two patients, a single paramedic team can perform the required functions. The senior member is in charge. The team triages the patients, selects the proper supplies, applies treatment, communicates, and transports the patients.

In a larger incident, management systems must begin to function. Consider a bus accident with 15 patients.

A supervisor must assume command. The supervisor should not be touching patients. One team must concentrate on triage, since patient treatment must be prioritized. Normal transport resources will become overwhelmed. Transportation coordination becomes a function assigned to a transportation unit. Additional supplies are sent by transporting a disaster cache to the scene. One medic is assigned responsibility for EMS Supply.

A Public Information Officer (PIO) reports to the scene to coordinate media relations. A trauma intervention team is activated to conduct a post incident stress debriefing session.

In this incident the local EMS delivery system is stressed. Management functions (according to IMS) are assigned as needed. There is a system of control and coordination.

Finally, suppose a medical disaster natural event has devastated an area. There are several hundred casualties. A disaster team from the region or from out-of-state must respond.

It is necessary to fully implement IMS. The Incident Manager must deal with a large-scale and long-term operation. A full Command Staff will be necessary in addition to the PIO and TIPs. A Liaison Officer will be needed to integrate outside agencies, and a Safety Officer will be needed to coordinate safety operations.

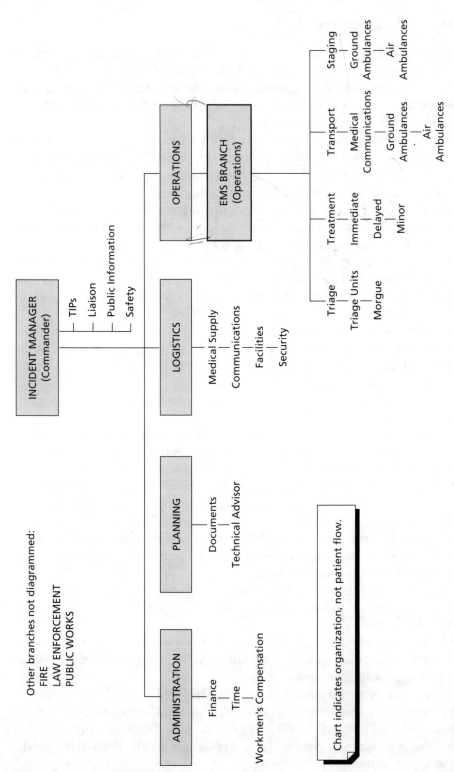

Other branches not diagrammed:
FIRE
LAW ENFORCEMENT
PUBLIC WORKS

INCIDENT MANAGER (Commander)
TIPs
Liaison
Public Information
Safety

ADMINISTRATION
Finance
Time
Workmen's Compensation

PLANNING
Documents
Technical Advisor

LOGISTICS
Medical Supply
Communications
Facilities
Security

OPERATIONS

EMS BRANCH (Operations)

Triage
Triage Units
Morgue

Treatment
Immediate
Delayed
Minor

Transport
Medical Communications
Ground Ambulances
Air Ambulances

Staging
Ground Ambulances
Air Ambulances

Chart indicates organization, not patient flow.

FIGURE 9-3 Expanded Mass Casualty Incident—An Incident Major in Scope and/or Duration.

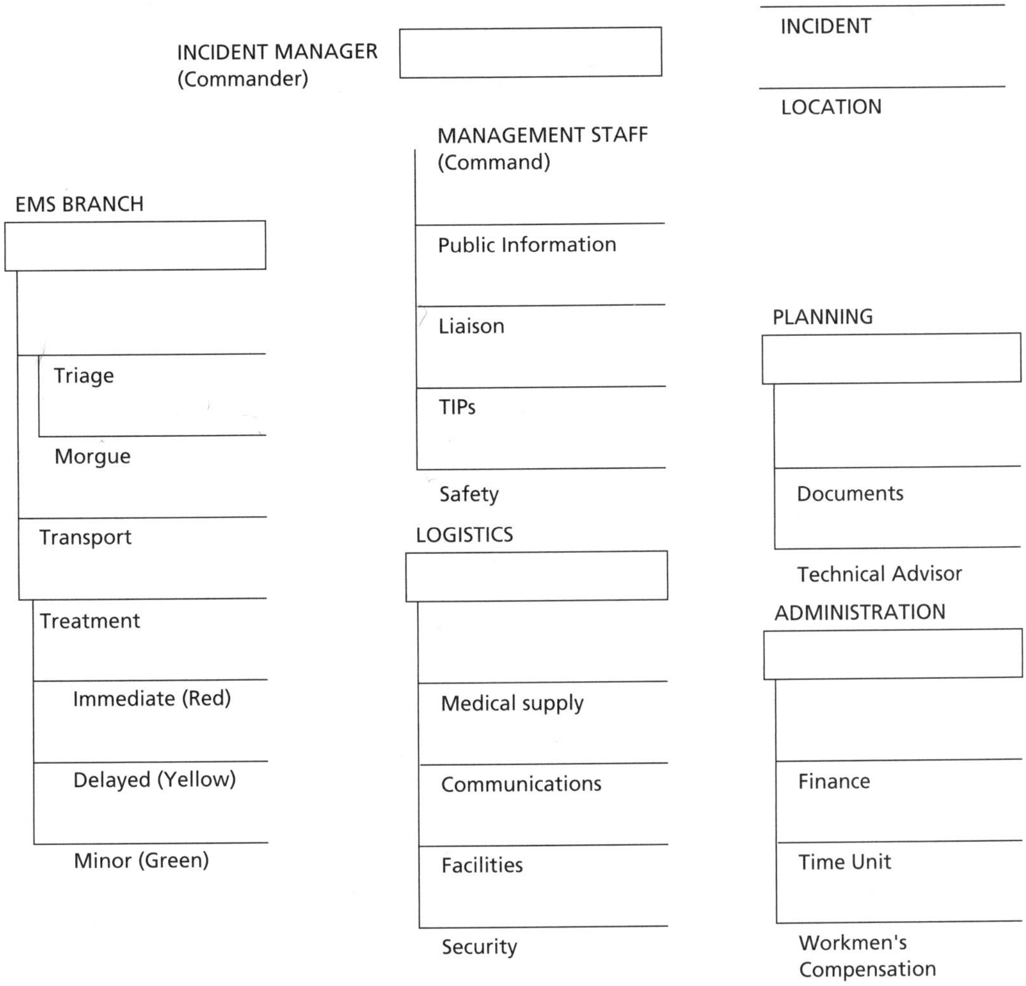

FIGURE 9-4 EMS Incident Management System.

A Planning Section will also be needed. An Incident Action Plan must be developed and coordinated with the Incident Manager in long-term operations. A resources unit will be needed to track ambulances (both air and ground), personnel, and outside agency resources. A medical records (documentation) unit will be needed to keep patient treatment records and records of patient destinations.

A Logistics Section will provide medical supplies, communications, and facilities (including food and water) for the disaster team.

The Operations Section will have to be expanded into an EMS Branch consisting of multiple treatment areas, if the scene dictates. Triage will become a sector function. Transport will become a major sector, coordinating arrival of incoming patients and dispersal of outgoing patients. Staging will be expanded to sector level.

Each section of the EMS Incident Management System is discussed in detail in future chapters and each position in the system is described in Appendix 1.

Where Do the Managers Come From?

So far the EMS Incident Management System looks great on paper. However, the obvious question is, "Where do all of the managers come from?"

Many EMS systems do not have several tiers of mid-level managers or supervisors. In numerous cases, EMS will be working within the Fire Incident Command System. This means the Command Staff and several of the support staff may be fire service personnel. In the school bus accident previously described, some EMS systems would not have the supervisory personnel to staff the required functions. This is why the EMS Management System must be "street smart" instead of being a mere paper plan. Several important concepts must be understood.

- The elements of IMS are functions, not necessarily management positions.
- The Incident Manager assumes all functions not formally delegated. This is the foundation of the system.
- Not all IMS functions are necessary. Only the largest medical disaster requires full implementation.
- Individuals can perform more than one function.
- Section Chiefs and unit leaders do not have to come from the ranks of managers or supervisors. Any qualified person, regardless of rank, can fill a functional position in IMS.
- The system builds from the bottom up. The structure grows as the incident grows.
- The IMS is like a toolbox. You select the tools you need but rarely empty the box.

CHAPTER SUMMARY

The basic management concepts inherent in the EMS Incident Management System date back thousands of years. Military and business management systems are based on unity of command, chain of command, and span of control.

The modern Public Safety Incident Command System evolved from experiences in the urban fire service and from lessons learned during severe wildfire incidents in California (the California Firescope Program). These systems contained operations (line functions) and support functions (staff) and were further refined by the National Fire Service Incident Management Consortium and the National Fire Academy.

The EMS Incident Management System (IMS) is designed to respond to EMS incidents that vary from routine to medical disasters. The IMS concept utilizes a Command Staff, an Operations Section, a Logistics Section, and a Planning Section. Operations include triage, treatment, and transport (and staging in disasters). Logistics includes communications, EMS supplies, facilities, and mobilization. Planning includes an Incident Action Plan, resources status, patient records, and administration.

A mass casualty incident (MCI) has more patients than providers. Patients are triaged and treated with BLS procedures. Rapid transport of critical patients is the goal. A Medical Disaster is an expanded MCI usually caused by a natural event, technical failure, or terrorism. EMS resources are overwhelmed. Regional, state, and federal assistance are needed. The incident is long in duration.

CHAPTER QUESTIONS/EXERCISES

1. What were the main management objectives in the development of the California Firescope Program?
2. Diagram the EMS Incident Management System. Include the functions in the Command Staff, as well as the functions in the Operational and Support Sections.
3. Define the key management functions that would be necessary in the following incidents.
   a. A vehicle roll-over on an expressway during rush hour. Three vehicles are involved, two patients are critical, four patients are serious, two patients have minor injuries.
   b. A major airplane crash, two miles short of the runway in a residential area. There are 52 fatalities, 28 critical, 15 serious, and 10 minor injuries. Your agency has only eight available transport units.
   c. A tornado has struck a major urban area. There are over 200 destroyed structures. Initial reports indicate 75 fatalities and over 200 injuries of varying degree. The only trauma center in the region has been destroyed.
4. Your EMS agency does not have the supervisors or personnel to fully staff the required IMS positions. What people and/or agencies in your community could be utilized to staff the following functional positions:
   a. Logistics
   b. Trauma Intervention Program (TIPs)

    c. Public Information Officer (PIO)

    d. Resources

    e. Safety

    f. Facilities

    g. Communications

5. Examine the management system and operating procedures currently being used by your organization. Also study the area disaster plans. What key elements in Incident Management are present in these plans? What key elements in IMS are not indicated in your present incident management structure?

10
Who's in Charge?

Paul M. Maniscalco
Hank T. Christen

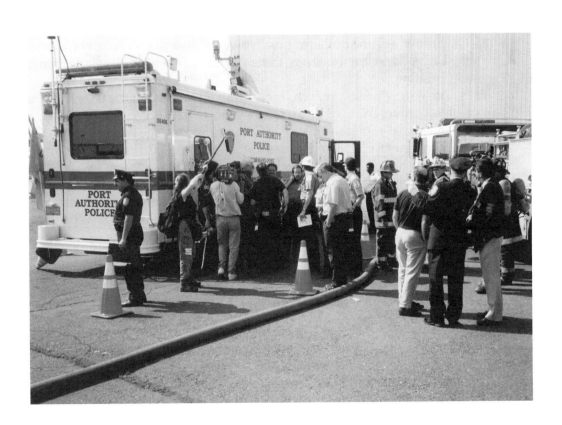

Chapter Objectives

After reading this chapter, you will be able to accomplish the following objectives:

1. Have an awareness of the duties and responsibilities of an Incident Manager.
2. Recognize the political problems and turf problems associated with leadership in an Incident Management System.
3. Understand the relationship between the EMS Branch and the Fire Incident Manager.
4. Understand the concept of Unified Management.

In some incidents, no one is in charge. In others, the wrong person is in charge. In some cases, too many people are in charge. We've all been there.

- No one is in charge—Most of us like that mode. We can operate freely without anyone bothering us. However, in a mass casualty incident (MCI), there are too many things to track. We need someone to run the show.
- The wrong person is in charge—Can you remember the last time you took orders from an Incident Manager with no EMS training? Many of us have experienced police officers running the scene. There's the horror story of EMS administrators, with no street experience, arriving to "help." The right person must be in charge.
- Too many people are in charge—The Fire Chief is in charge, the EMS Commander is in charge, and the Sheriff is in charge, simultaneously. Orders and instructions are coming from all directions. When one commander devises a plan, another commander changes it. One person, or a unified team, must be in charge.

What Determines Who's in Charge?

In a single agency, it's clear who runs the organization. All organizations/ agencies have "Heads of State" that preside over a precise organizational chart. Everyone knows who is the "boss."

When mass casualty incidents occur, many agencies become involved. Suddenly it is not obvious who is in command. This is true when several agency heads arrive, each expecting to manage the incident.

Command authority, when several agencies are involved, is usually determined by state legislation. The legislation specifies who should be in command. In some states, the fire chief of the appropriate jurisdiction is in charge at non-law enforcement emergencies. This includes mass casualty incidents. The approach is logical since fire departments usually have extensive emergency experience, along with communications and organizational command experience.

Most states specify that the ranking EMS professional on the scene is in charge of patient care. He/she determines the order of treatment, the type of treatment, and priority and destination of transport.

Statutes give authority to law enforcement officers to control crime scenes. State law enforcement (Highway Patrol) has operational authority on state highways. In a few states, the Highway Patrol has authority over hazardous materials incidents. Statutes give the sheriff (an elected official) authority over all law enforcement incidents in a county. These laws give a sheriff jurisdiction over incidents that effect the general welfare of the county or its citizens. Most state legislatures give sheriffs far-reaching powers. Federal statutes, e.g., Nunn-Luger legislation, give command authority to the FBI if an incident is caused by terrorism.

Determining the Incident Manager by legislation raises many questions.

1. What about the inexperienced or poorly trained manager? Levels of sophistication vary greatly. Many agencies have no Incident Management System.
2. What happens when non-medical managers try to dictate patient treatment?
3. What happens when there are conflicts of authority? You can have a hazardous materials incident on a state highway with fire/rescue problems and injured patients.

Resolving Turf Problems

You want to give your patients the best medical care possible. But you're constantly at incident scenes that are defined by non-EMS individuals as "their turf." We want the public to think all agencies work together on a scene holding hands and singing "Kumbaya." This is not always the case. If you've been a street EMT or paramedic for more than a week, you've already been an unwilling participant in an inter-agency conflict.

Legislation is not a total solution. However, state and local statutes are a good place to start. Examine the laws that apply to your jurisdiction and determine who is in charge under various scenarios. Next comes the hard part. Identify the players and bring them together for consensus. This process cannot be initiated at the EMT/paramedic level. EMS management must be the facilitator.

The first goal of the committee is to develop a formal Community Disaster Plan. This plan should apply to routine incidents, mass casualty incidents, and disasters. The plan must identify who is in charge.

The Committee should answer the following questions:

1. How do EMS agencies relate to the Fire Incident Command System?
2. How is command shared with law enforcement when there are multiple victims at a crime scene?
3. When does the EMS Commander become the Incident Manager or a member of a Unified Management Team?
4. Who has management authority at transportation accidents?
5. Who is in charge at hazardous materials scenes?
6. What is the formal process for changing management during an incident? (Note: All management changes must be communicated to personnel at an incident scene.)

The answers to these questions depend on state statutes, local procedures, the Fire Incident Management System, historical precedents, and personalities. The answers comprise a formal document called the Community Disaster Plan, signed by all agency managers outlined in the Plan.

The Committee's job is never finished. There should be a review of major incidents and situations where questions of command authority have arisen. Revisions to the agency or Community Disaster Plan should be added as needed. These changes most times will become recognizable due to the results yielded from your Post Incident Analysis (PIA). Changes implemented can range from communication protocols to who has the jurisdiction for supply acquisition for logistics. In any event the inclusion of an objective process which evaluates agency performance and community risk analysis must be a vital component of the planning process.

Critical Factor: The Incident Manager must be identified and specified in a formal Community Disaster Plan.

Qualities of an Incident Manager

An Incident Manager should be qualified. Defining Incident Managers in a Community Disaster Plan does not mean they can do the job.

Texts in the management and public safety fields have identified the characteristics of a good manager. Based on these writings, we can define the ideal manager as:

1. All-knowing.
2. Forceful, yet sensitive.
3. Omnipotent (not impotent).
4. Totally calm under fire.

5. Likes dogs and small children.
6. Free of impure thoughts.
7. Brave, honest, clean, trustworthy.

No one can meet the requirements of this "tongue in cheek" list. But it is important that your leader have the following attributes:

1. In-depth Incident Management training. This especially applies to administrators who do not have the command experiences.
2. A thorough knowledge of the EMS Incident Management System.
3. Be familiar with the Community Disaster Plan and participate in disaster exercises.
4. Stay at a command post and not perform hands-on operations. An Incident Manager's tools are a hand-held radio and a clipboard, not a gun, fire-hose, or bandage scissors.

NOTE: The term "Incident Manager" is gender neutral.

Duties of an Incident Manager

The Incident Manager (IM) does not "command" in the true sense of the word. The IM coordinates the major functions of operations, logistics, and planning. The IM ensures there is a flow of information, personnel, and resources between support functions and operational functions.

The word "commander" is nationally accepted terminology. However, the duties of this position are to lead and manage. Therefore, the term Incident Manager is used in this text.

As an incident increases in size, more diverse agencies play a role. This is why a military style command structure does not work. Agencies do not have to obey the Incident Manager. Therefore, the IM must depend on consensus and coordination rather then coercion (charisma and a sense of humor also help). The agencies and the IM must operate within an agreed upon management system (another plug for EMS/IMS).

The IM is responsible for the outcome of a mass casualty incident. The IM is also a liaison between the outside world and the incident scene. Resources come from outside the system and are inserted into the arena in a planned and effective manner.

The primary duties of the IM are:

1. Establish a command post.
2. Maintain a reasonable span of control by delegating major functions.
3. Delegate responsibilities for the functions of planning, logistics, and operations.
4. Assume responsibility for any functions not delegated.

5. Provide a liaison with outside agencies.
6. Provide for personnel safety (mental and physical).
7. Prioritize the allocation of scarce resources.
8. Receive and disseminate vital information among all sections of the IMS.
9. Ensure effective communications among all system elements.
10. Coordinate the development and implementation of an operational plan.
11. Coordinate accurate release of information to media agencies.
12. Terminate incident operations.
13. Produce a post incident report and critique.
14. Cooperate with post incident investigations.

The list is extensive. No individual can accomplish all these duties. The IM needs help. But the IM must assume final responsibility for the outcome of a mass casualty incident. Harry Truman's favorite expression, "The buck stops here," certainly applies to the IM. (See Figure 10-1.)

Political Realities

Mass casualty incidents can have political implications. First, every incident is on someone's political turf. Second, most of the people involved, including EMS professionals, are government employees. Third, the cause or outcome of an incident can have far-reaching political effects.

The IM has a political challenge. Elected officials will respond to high profile emergency scenes. Political officials may take command or make operational decisions. (This is every Incident Manager's nightmare).

When political officials arrive, direct them to the command post. The IM should give the officials a short and concise briefing. Attempt to link the officials with the Public Information Officer (PIO).

The PIO must get the officials away from the operational scene and into a pristine press briefing area. Since most elected officials are interested in media exposure, this is usually acceptable. This allows officials to make a positive contribution. Because of public recognition and confidence, they are effective in informing and calming the public. That's why it is important for officials to receive updated facts and information about the situation.

If you are in an operational capacity and receive orders from elected officials, notify your supervisor immediately. This information should flow up to the IM. (This process should be done in seconds.) The IM can arrange the proper escorts. Political officials are dedicated. When they respond to a major scene, they have a concern and desire to help. Place them in the media relations mode and out of the operations mode. This can ensure a positive contribution.

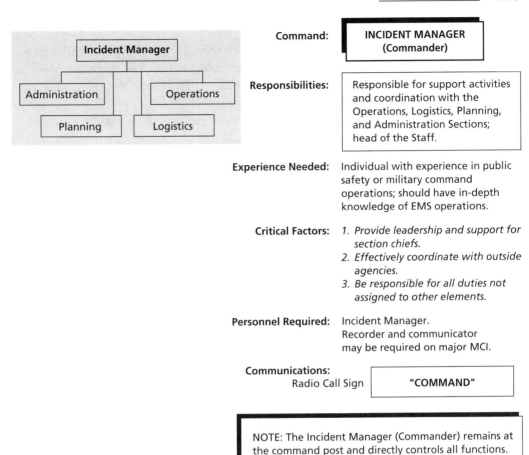

Command:	**INCIDENT MANAGER** (Commander)
Responsibilities:	Responsible for support activities and coordination with the Operations, Logistics, Planning, and Administration Sections; head of the Staff.
Experience Needed:	Individual with experience in public safety or military command operations; should have in-depth knowledge of EMS operations.
Critical Factors:	1. *Provide leadership and support for section chiefs.* 2. *Effectively coordinate with outside agencies.* 3. *Be responsible for all duties not assigned to other elements.*
Personnel Required:	Incident Manager. Recorder and communicator may be required on major MCI.
Communications: Radio Call Sign	"COMMAND"

NOTE: The Incident Manager (Commander) remains at the command post and directly controls all functions.

FIGURE 10-1 Incident Manager (Command).

Unified Management

In the beginning pages of this chapter, we examined the responsibilities of an IM. The demands of such a long list of responsibilities can be insurmountable. In complex incidents, there are several operational objectives. A team may have to manage the incident. This form of incident management is known as Unified Management.

A Unified Management Team is needed in any scenario where operations are shared by two or more diverse organizations.

Consider the following examples:

1. A mass shooting incident where the suspect is still on the scene—operations are shared by law enforcement and Emergency Medical Services—the Unified Management Team would be police and EMS.
2. A building collapse with trapped victims and mass casualties—operations are shared by EMS and fire/rescue—the Unified Management Team would be fire and EMS.
3. A terrorist incident involving the release of a chemical agent with casualties and a large area evacuation—operations are shared by law enforcement, fire/Haz Mat, and EMS—the Unified Management Team would be police, fire, and EMS.

The Unified Management Team avoids operational confusion. Major operational areas are managed by people familiar with these functions.

On paper, the concept of Unified Management looks sound. It works when the following requirements are met:

1. The managers must coordinate and share the management turf.
2. The managers must be adequately trained in Incident Management.
3. The troops at the street level must understand how to work under Unified Management.
4. There cannot be major personality conflicts between the players on the Unified Management Team.

A Unified Management Team may be needed when a large-scale incident occurs in more than one political jurisdiction. This may happen when a city, county, or state boundary bisects the emergency scene. In these cases, managers from both jurisdictions may share management functions.

Critical Factor: Incidents with more than one operational function, or incidents involving multiple jurisdictions, need a Unified Management Team.

Chapter Summary

In emergency management systems, it is important to determine who will take charge. This can be decided by legislation, but ultimately must achieve a consensus of the agencies involved.

Major emergency incidents become political incidents. Elected officials may respond to a mass casualty scene. They should be assigned to the Public Information Officer and kept away from scene operations.

An Incident Manager is directly responsible for coordinating support functions (logistics and planning) with operational functions. The Incident Manager is responsible for liaison with the outside world.

More than one individual may be responsible for incident management. This is called Unified Management and occurs when operational functions are shared, or an incident is in more than one jurisdiction.

CHAPTER QUESTIONS/EXERCISES

1. What statutes in your state determine who is in charge of disaster incidents? What authority is given for patient care responsibility? What are the powers of sheriffs in your state?
2. What disaster plans are in effect in your community? Who is specified as the Incident Manager in the Community Disaster Plan?
3. You are the Incident Manager. A city councilman and county commissioner have entered the operational area. How would you handle this matter? How would you solve this problem if you were an EMT or paramedic on this incident?
4. List the fire chiefs in your area. What is the Incident Management training/experience background for these individuals?
5. List and define at least five duties of an Incident Manager.
6. During a recent MCI in your area, the fire chief was the Incident Manager. The chief was non-medical, but made several decisions that directly affected patient care. When confronted, the chief vehemently defended his sole authority as Incident Manager. How would you solve this problem?
7. Discuss and define the concept of Unified Management. List three scenarios where a Unified Management Team would be effective.

11
The Management Staff

Paul M. Maniscalco
Hank T. Christen

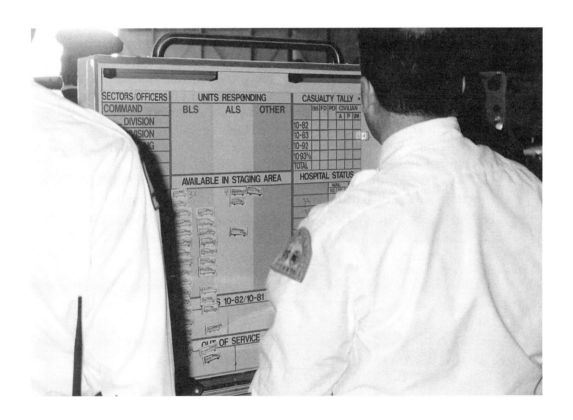

Chapter Objectives

After reading this chapter, you will be able to accomplish the following objectives:

1. Understand the concept of a Management Staff.
2. Diagram the organizational structure of the Management Staff.
3. Understand the relationship between the Incident Manager and members of the Management Staff.
4. Define the duties of the Public Information Officer, Safety Officer, Liaison Officer, and the Trauma Intervention Program (TIPs).

The Management Staff Concept

In Chapter 10 we reached the conclusion that the Incident Manager has a long and demanding list of responsibilities. In a major incident, an Incident Manager cannot perform the required duties without help. This assistance comes from a Management Staff.

The Management Staff concept has proven its effectiveness in business and military management. A manager (or senior officer) has an appointed staff of specialists to provide expertise directly to him or her. You commonly hear about administrative assistants in business or staff officers in the military. In politics, there is continuous reference to congressional staffers or to the White House Staff.

In emergency incident management, the Management Staff handles the functions of safety, liaison, public information, and traumatic stress management. (See Figure 11-1.) The staff has a direct relationship with the

FIGURE 11-1   The Management Staff.

Incident Manager. It is the Management Staff's job to assist the Incident Manager. The Management Staff is unique because it does not directly supervise major command functions (logistics, planning, operations). Staffers do not usually have subordinates, but incident size or complexity may require them.

Most of the staff positions are not physically anchored to the command post. These people move throughout the incident area depending on their duties. They may be working in any of the functional sections or coordinating with outside agencies.

When Do You Appoint a Staff?

Where does the Management Staff come from? This is a valid question since most organizations are understaffed. In an MCI, treatment personnel are overwhelmed. All available people are needed to treat patients. Therefore, a Management Staff may be perceived as a luxury rather than a necessity.

Two critical points serve as guidelines when appointing a Management Staff:

First, remember the cornerstone of Incident Management. Any duties not assigned by the Incident Manager are assumed to be the Incident Manager's responsibility. In minor incidents, the Incident Manager can monitor safety, serve as a liaison to the other agencies, and give brief media statements. As complications arise, or as the incident increases in size, these responsibilities become too demanding and the Incident Manager must assign staff to necessary functions.

Second, Management Staff positions do not require medical professionals when confronted with large-scale or high-impact events. Paramedics and EMTs are needed in the Operations Section for these instances. The liaison, safety, public information, and stress management personnel *can* be professionals in other fields. The Safety Officer can be a fire officer or safety inspector. The Liaison Officer can be a fire officer, Emergency Management director, or EMS administrator. The Public Information Officer should be the jurisdiction's public affairs professional. Stress debriefing should be conducted by a local or regional team.

Critical Factor: The Management Staff should be assigned as needed. Staff functions should be performed by trained specialists, not emergency medical professionals.

Management Staff Scenarios

The following scenarios demonstrate effective use of Management Staffs:

1. Automobile accident with five victims and two fatalities—The Incident Manager serves as a liaison with law enforcement. The Incident Manager monitors safety and is able to give a statement to a media crew. There is no need for stress debriefing on the scene. In this scenario there is no Management Staff. Instead, the Incident Manager has assumed all staff functions.

2. School bus rollover with 10 minor injuries, 8 critical injuries, and 4 fatalities—The Incident Manager performs liaison duties with outside agencies. Since extensive extrication is involved, a fire training officer is selected as a Safety Officer. The city's public relations specialist serves as the PIO. The Incident Manager calls the trauma intervention program to deal with the victim's parents. In this scenario the Management Staff consists of safety, public information, and stress management personnel.

3. Major airline crash in a residential area with 75 fatalities and 50 injuries—From the onset, the Incident Manager realizes this is a mass casualty incident and a full Management Staff will be needed. The Incident Manager assigns a Battalion Chief to coordinate safety functions. The Director of Emergency Management is assigned as the Liaison Officer. The county Public Affairs Officer arrives and establishes a media team with airline and government PIOs. The Trauma Intervention Unit is immediately called. It will assist on the scene and schedule a stress defusing session for the next duty day. Throughout this incident, the Management Staff coordinates with the Incident Manager.

The preceding scenarios provide a varied range of incidents. In the one case in which there is no Management Staff, the Incident Manager assumes the duties. At the other end of the spectrum, there is a full Management Staff that may operate for several days and incorporate multiple agencies or functional areas. When you need a staff, assign the appropriate people. If you don't need a staff, don't waste your most valuable resource—personnel.

The Stress Management Concept

In public safety circles, trauma intervention programs for both acute and long-term treatment of traumatic stress is still a relatively new concept. The emotional toll that emergency services can have on members was not appreciated nor understood until just recently.

The "macho code" governed a predominantly male organization. Emergency services professionals were perceived as emotionally tough.

People were not supposed to be psychologically affected by their work: "Real men and women didn't cry."

We now recognize that emotional reactions to the stresses of our job is quite human. Emergency incidents involve an enormous potential for producing high emotional stress. We see human suffering that can include hideous trauma or dismemberment. We confront the death of children. Unfortunately, we sometimes see serious injury or death of fellow workers.

The concept of trauma intervention is that emotional maintenance is as important as equipment maintenance. We acknowledge equipment has to be inspected, maintained, and repaired, but we dismiss thoughts that people won't operate at 100% capability. The uninformed Incident Manager believes that the members "will deal with it." But this is just not the case. Acute or cumulative events can and do affect members. Therefore, utilization of the trauma intervention process helps to maintain our people.

Trauma Intervention Teams are formal organizations with a Director (usually a mental health professional). Team members have a formal training process. Peer support is essential since many emergency workers trust their colleagues but may not trust doctors, psychologists, etc. Trauma intervention experts caution the use of mental health professionals not familiar with emergency services, not trained or suited for disaster operations.

The job of the Trauma Intervention Team begins before the incident. An effective team will conduct training for all emergency services personnel. This acquaints emergency professionals with the team members and exposes people to the Trauma Intervention Program philosophy. It also teaches stress reducing techniques. Most of all, it demonstrates that emotional reaction is normal and help is available.

During the incident, the Trauma Intervention Team provides on-scene support. The Trauma Intervention Officer advises the Incident Manager about stress-related matters. Reduction of noise, effective scene control, and assisting in the emotional care of victims' families can diminish the stressful atmosphere of an emergency. Other techniques include rest and rotation periods for workers and pre-deployment briefings for arriving personnel. (See Figure 11-2.)

Immediately after the incident, the Trauma Intervention Team conducts a defusing session. This is followed by a debriefing session within 24 to 72 hours. In some cases, individuals may require longer-term counseling with licensed mental health professionals.

An Incident Manager should remember:

1. People are the most important asset in emergency services.
2. A Trauma Intervention Team should be part of the management system.
3. If you think a Trauma Intervention Team may be needed, you should have already called them.

Staff:	**TRAUMA INTERVENTION PROGRAM**
Responsibilities:	Trauma Intervention Program (TIPs); interacts with all members to help reduce and defuse emotional stress; conducts post-incident stress debriefings.
Experience Needed:	Individual with formal TIPs training and working knowledge of EMS operations.
Critical Factors:	1. *Provide emotional support to personnel working under conditions of extreme physical and emotional stress.* 2. *Coordinate with Command in eliminating stress conditions.*
Personnel Required:	TIPs Team members.
Communications: Radio Call Sign	**"TIPs"**

Staff support for Incident Manager (Commander).

NOTE: The TIPs Team operates freely throughout all areas of the incident site.

FIGURE 11-2 Trauma Intervention Program.

Safety

Physical safety of emergency personnel is as important as emotional safety. Disasters are dangerous places to work and operate. The area can be on fire or have hazardous chemicals present. There may be partially collapsed structures, downed wires, and debris. Severe weather and darkness can be threatening. Power tools, equipment, and vehicles are being operated. In terrorist and law enforcement incidents, there may be explosive devices or people with weapons (good guys and bad guys). Disasters are bad places to work.

Another danger factor is the mindset of medical professionals and emergency workers. We are action-oriented people. We recognize positive action. We want to arrive at an incident and control it. We take chances without considering safety, never recognizing ourselves as potential victims.

The Incident Manager is responsible for the safety of everyone on the scene. Considering the conditions at a disaster, coupled with the mindset of the personnel, safety is a difficult task. This makes a Safety Officer essential on major incidents.

Safety Officer Duties

The Safety Officer's job is to monitor all phases of the operations and to advise the Incident Manager of procedures that reduce risk. This includes effective lighting, rest and relaxation schedules, vehicle traffic control, and utility shutdowns.

Safe operations complement scene control safety efforts. This includes proper lifting, patient securing techniques, and safe operations of tools and equipment. Use of protective equipment, such as breathing apparatus, headgear, and protective clothing, is an important factor. Personnel accountability is important in many mass casualty, fire, and law enforcement incidents. Infectious disease control is essential to ensure EMS personnel having direct patient contact are implementing proper precautions to protect themselves.

Safety Officer Operations

The Safety Officer should be an emergency services professional familiar with disaster operations. An individual with this background is well versed in Incident Management and communications procedures. The Safety Officer should also be familiar with nationally accepted safety standards. These standards include, but are not limited to:

1. OSHA Safety Standards—29 CFR, part 1910
2. National Fire Protection Association (NFPA) standard 1500—Fire Department Occupational Health & Safety Programs
3. NFPA 471,472,473—standards for Hazardous Materials Operations
4. NFPA 1521 Fire Department Safety
5. Infectious Disease Control Procedures (OSHA 29 CFR, part 1910.1030)

Safety Officers may be provided by non-medical agencies. Many urban fire departments have a full-time Safety Officer. Fire inspectors and/or training officers are qualified to serve in this capacity. Large EMS organizations may have a training officer with similar qualifications. Local and county governments have safety inspectors and risk management people who can provide safety expertise.

Specialized strike teams often have their own safety position. These safety specialists are not part of the Management Staff and do not have safety responsibility for the overall incident. Their duties are confined to the operations assigned to their team. This includes hazardous materials teams, high angle rescue teams, SWAT teams, confined space rescue teams, bomb disposal teams, heavy rescue teams, and underwater dive teams.

The Safety Officer should report to the Incident Manager upon arrival and receive an initial briefing. The Safety Officer is then responsible for monitoring safety procedures throughout the area and identifying any threats to personnel (scene threat assessment). In major disasters the Safety Officer may need support personnel to monitor several areas.

The Safety Officer should make corrections in procedures through the normal line of authority. Safety violations should be reported to the appropriate supervisors. There may be times when a serious safety violation warrants immediate action. THE SAFETY OFFICER SHOULD HAVE THE AUTHORITY TO STOP ANY OPERATION THAT IS LIFE-THREATENING TO PERSONNEL. Naturally, such action must have the moral support of the Incident Manager.

Critical Factor: The Incident Manager is responsible for the safety of all personnel. In complex operations, a Safety Officer is needed to assist the Incident Manager.

Liaison

One of the brutal lessons learned in the California wildfire experiences of the 1970s was that diverse agencies do not automatically cooperate. In day-to-day operations, each agency does its thing. Coordination is routine. In disasters, agencies that do not normally work together are thrown into a stressful and uncontrolled arena. Coordination is anything but routine. Operational goals differ, personnel do not know each other, terminology varies, and radio frequencies are incompatible. Under these conditions, coordination is a miracle.

These problems occur because many government public safety agencies operate as a closed system. In systems theory, a closed system is an organization that operates internally, with little input from, or exchange with, outside systems. An open system is the opposite. In an open system, the organization is structured to exchange information with other systems. Interaction between systems is sometimes referred to as "boundary spanning." This means that boundaries confining organizations are easily crossed.

It is vital that incident management systems operate as open systems. As an incident escalates, dozens of agencies may become involved. These agencies descend upon the command post with the greeting, "Hi, I'm here to help you" (pun intended).

The most effective means of coordinating with the outside world is through a Liaison Officer. The Liaison Officer serves as a link between the management system and outside systems or agencies. The Liaison Officer ensures "boundary spanning."

Critical Factor: The Medical Incident Management System must coordinate with a myriad of outside agencies (open system). Liaison with outside agencies is a vital management function.

The Liaison Officer works with assisting agencies and cooperating agencies. An assisting agency is one that provides direct support and resources. This can include the EMS or medical agencies, law enforcement, fire departments, and public works. Cooperating agencies provide indirect support or service functions. Examples include utility companies, American Red Cross, advisory agencies (EPA, OSHA, etc.), and technical support agencies.

When an agency arrives at an incident, an agency representative is appointed. The representative must have authority to make decisions, represent the agency, and coordinate directly with the Liaison Officer. An agency representative provides a single point of contact for the Liaison Officer.

The primary function of the Liaison Officer is to funnel outside agency resources into the appropriate section of the EMS/IMS. Usually, assisting agencies function in the Operations Section. Cooperative agencies work in a support category under the Logistics Section or Planning Section. The Liaison Officer may receive requests from incident personnel for contacts with other organizations.

With multiple organizations, there is a potential for organizational conflict. We don't always get along. The Liaison Officer should try to identify possible conflicts between organizations. The Liaison Officer can serve as a mediator between conflicting agencies. Without liaison assistance, the Incident Manager often becomes involved in conflicts that misdirect his or her attention from more vital tasks.

Working with the Media

A mass casualty incident is a newsworthy event. But all too often the words "uh-oh, here comes the media," are uttered by members when operating at the scene. The arrival of media crews can be a major source of stress if you are not prepared to professionally and confidently address the issue.

Today's broadcast, print, or photo journalist is well-educated and informed regarding emergency incidents. Members of the media have to report back to an assignment editor with their story, and very often work under strict deadlines for presses rolling or live shots for the news. They need the story and/or their sound bite, and, if you don't give it to them, they'll get it from somewhere else.

We've all had the shock and dismay of reading the next day about an incident we worked and wondering if the reporter was at the same scene as we were. If a story is wrong, don't blame the reporter. Blame yourself. Ask the questions, "Did we cooperate with the media in every possible way? Did we give them the correct information?" If the answers are "no," an incorrect story is your fault or your organization's fault.

An Incident Manager needs a public information professional for media assistance. It's not possible to maintain the concentration and activity to manage an incident and conduct media briefings simultaneously. The media specialist designated in the Incident Management System is called the Public Information Officer (PIO) and is an integral member of the staff.

The topic of media relations could occupy one or more textbooks due to its specialization. In this text, the subject will be provided in the format of a brief overview.

Critical Factor: Timely and accurate release of information in a professional manner is key to the positive reflection of your organization's action at the MCI. The command staff position of PIO is integral in EMS/IMS.

Public Information Officer Duties

In street language, the PIO's job description could read, "Keep the media off everybody's rear and make sure we look good." The PIO's job begins before the incident. A good PIO has already developed media contacts and a rapport with them that fosters trust, professional respect, and a willingness to attempt to work together. The media contacts get their story and the PIO makes the department look good. Not a bad trade off, eh? Most times in the local arena this goal is achievable. In many instances though, if your incident attracts national or international attention, the rapport with the local outlets may not be enough to get you through. On these occasions you might find yourself confronted with networks and reporters from around the world. In these cases the importance of a PIO on your command staff cannot be over emphasized. (See Figure 11-3.)

Staff:	PUBLIC INFORMATION OFFICER
Responsibilities:	Expedites the effective and accurate dissemination of media information.
Experience Needed:	Public relations professional with writing ability and broadcast interview experience; needs an understanding of EMS operations; may be required to coordinate with national media.
Critical Factors:	1. *Obtain and communicate accurate information in a professional manner.* 2. *Escort media through an incident scene.*
Personnel Required:	Public Information Officer
Communications: Radio Call Sign	"P.I.O."

Staff support for Incident Manager.

FIGURE 11-3 Public Information Officer.

The PIO reports directly to the Incident Manager. The Incident Manager has the overall authority to authorize press briefings and the release of information. At large-scale or criminally related events, the release of information needs to be coordinated by all agencies involved in order to avoid compromise of patient confidential information or a criminal investigation. It is the obligation of the PIO to stay current with all pertinent data at the scene (units operating, present status of the incident, number of patients, types of injuries, hospitals that receive patients).

The PIO should establish a media briefing area separate from operational areas and the command post. Ideally, this area will provide the media with a good vantage point of the incident while ensuring their safety and crowd manageability. PIOs should also be prepared for requests for computer printouts, agency and incident fact sheets, incident maps and diagrams to assist the media. Release of this information is sometimes prohibited, so it is incumbent upon the PIO to be familiar with current departmental policy, governmental laws, and directives to ensure compliance.

The PIO should conduct scheduled incident briefings at predetermined and announced times. In many instances updates may be required between briefings due to major changes that might occur. Updates also facilitate the media contact with the Incident Manager and other staff members that operate at the scene. This control of access to the Incident Manager and responders allows the PIO to arrange interviews without compromising the incident operations.

News teams or reporters should not be permitted to roam freely throughout the operational area. This creates a safety hazard for them and an operational distraction to the working staff. All staff operating on the incident site should refer unescorted members of the media to the PIO and refrain from entertaining questions while they are engaged in patient care or rescue activities.

Broadcast crews go to great lengths to get close-up shots of scenes. As previously stated this can present great danger to them due to their lack of training and understanding of the dynamics of the particular scene. Some departments have embarked on a unique training program where members of the media are permitted to go through training programs that familiarize them with emergency operations, EMS patient care, firefighting, and rescue activities. This training program, permits the media participants to have controlled contact and experience with the tasks that we are exposed to everyday. Upon successful completion of this program, they are issued protective gear and a different colored press pass that allows closer access to the incident scene. This program has yielded a number of positive results for the department and the media.

1. The media now have hands-on experience with what they're covering and can report the actions of the scene more accurately, providing the sponsoring department with better coverage.
2. The media outlet obtains better positioning at the scene to get its story, while making the department look great.
3. An enhanced relationship between the department and the media is fostered, allowing the PIO and the department to hopefully obtain coverage when needed. The arrangement has been found to be a public administrative and media win-win.
4. Media tape footage can be accessed for operational critique and training purposes. In the event that your local laws do not permit this type of program and access, the PIO should arrange for the crews to be escorted through the safe and secure scene to assist them getting their shot.

Helping the media is helping your department. It gives you control, and helps to guarantee that the story is portrayed accurately. But most importantly, never lie or misrepresent the facts. Don't be afraid to say, "I don't know but I'll check that out and get back to you." Many years of work and rapport can be destroyed in a moment. The better coordination between public safety agencies and media, the better and more accurately informed the community will be during the emergency.

CHAPTER SUMMARY

The Management Staff consists of a Safety Officer, Public Information Officer, Liaison Officer, and Stress Management Team. As an incident escalates, the Incident Manager can appoint staff to assist command duties.

The Management Staff does not consist of medical professionals. Staff members are safety inspectors, public affairs professionals, liaison specialists, and stress management team members.

The job of the Management Staff is to assist the Incident Manager. The Liaison Officer interfaces with assisting agencies and cooperating agencies. Liaison keeps Incident Management an open system. The Safety Officer operates in all areas of the incident to ensure operations are conducted safely. The Trauma Intervention Team assists in maintaining the mental health and emotional well-being of incident workers. The Public Information Officer coordinates with the media and ensures the release of information.

CHAPTER QUESTIONS/EXERCISES

1. List several non-medical professionals in your area that could assist as members of a Management Staff.
2. Diagram the organizational structure of the Management Staff.
3. What are the functions of the Liaison Officer? What is a cooperating agency? Assisting Agency?
4. What are the duties of the Public Information Officer?
5. What is the Trauma Intervention Program concept? What type of individuals should participate on a Trauma Intervention Team?
6. What media relations programs are now in effect with public safety agencies in your area? How can these people be integrated into the IMS?

12
EMS Operations

Paul M. Maniscalco
Hank T. Christen

Chapter Objectives

After reading this chapter, you will be able to accomplish the following objectives:

1. Understand the concept of EMS operations.
2. Understand the relationship of operational functions to support functions.
3. Define the operations units in the EMS Incident Management System.
4. Define and discuss the effective use of medical strike teams and task forces.

What Are Operations?

Operations are direct, hands-on functions conducted by an organization to accomplish its mission. Most organizations are defined by their operational capabilities. For example, General Motors builds cars or Gateway makes computers. Both companies have extensive accounting systems and large research and development divisions. But you don't think of them in those terms. Their operations are the essence of the organization.

In the EMS Incident Management System, the treatment of patients is the mission. All the functions exist to support treatment operations. The Command Staff, the Logistics Section, and the Planning Section function to assist the Operations Section. (See Figure 12-1.)

Medical treatment operations involve triaging patients, treating them in logical order, and transporting them to a medical facility. To accomplish these treatment objectives, medical operations is divided into the following sectors:

1. Triage
2. Treatment (red, yellow, green)
3. Transport

EMS Branch Director

The EMS Branch Director commands all operations units and serves directly under the Incident Manager. The EMS Director does not remain at a command post like the other section chiefs. The Branch Director is in the middle of the operational area. He/she has a moving position in the heat of the battle. (See Figure 12-2.)

The EMS Director has one of the busiest jobs on the incident scene. The Director is continually working with logistics and the staff to get scarce resources and support for EMS operations units.

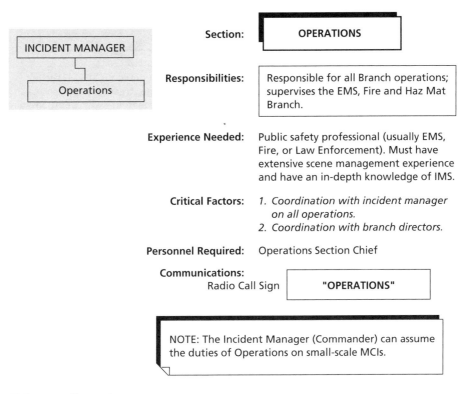

FIGURE 12-1   Operations.

It's extremely important to understand that the EMS Branch Director is a manager, and does not treat patients. It's hard for medical professionals to operate in treatment areas without "reaching out and touching someone." When a Director starts treating people, he/she is in big trouble, for no one is managing the bigger operational picture. In the operations area, good management ultimately leads to the saving of lives and limiting of suffering because it ensures that treatment personnel are adequately supported.

The EMS Branch usually has inadequate personnel and limited resources. A balancing act has to take place. Personnel must be rotated to where they are needed. If one treatment area gets real busy, people must be shifted.

The EMS Branch is also in close contact with the Logistics Section. Operations, at the early stages, will consume more supplies and equipment than Logistics can generate. Therefore, prioritizing supplies is as important as prioritizing personnel.

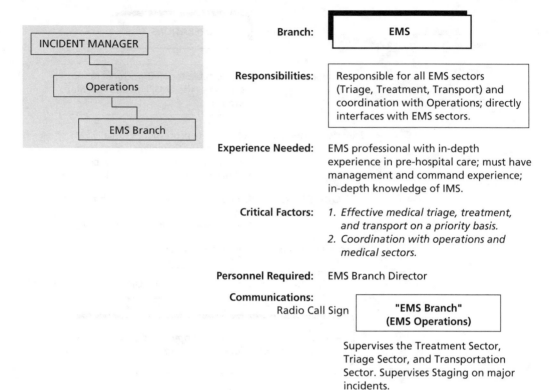

Branch:	EMS
Responsibilities:	Responsible for all EMS sectors (Triage, Treatment, Transport) and coordination with Operations; directly interfaces with EMS sectors.
Experience Needed:	EMS professional with in-depth experience in pre-hospital care; must have management and command experience; in-depth knowledge of IMS.
Critical Factors:	1. Effective medical triage, treatment, and transport on a priority basis. 2. Coordination with operations and medical sectors.
Personnel Required:	EMS Branch Director
Communications: Radio Call Sign	"EMS Branch" (EMS Operations)

Supervises the Treatment Sector, Triage Sector, and Transportation Sector. Supervises Staging on major incidents.

FIGURE 12-2 EMS Branch.

Operations/Command Relationships

One of the most confusing aspects of any command system is the distinction between the Incident Manager and the Operational Branches. (See Figure 12-3.)

There is a tendency for Incident Managers to control operations and command responsibilities. This is especially true when the Incident Manager has an in-depth background in operations. As an example, a medical professional, as Incident Manager, is tempted to command/control treatment operations. The same situation occurs in fire operations, when the fire commander attempts to control fire operations along with command responsibilities.

At routine incidents, command and operations are combined. Combining command and operations at major incidents is a mistake. As the incident escalates, operational demands begin to separate from management responsibilities. If the incident requires a command staff or other sections, such as Logistics or Planning, Management and Operations should be separated.

EMS Branch Director

Sector (Group/Division) Supervisor

Unit Leader
(ambulances/special units)

FIGURE 12-3   Operations Levels.

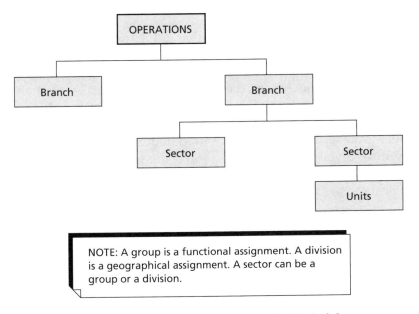

NOTE: A group is a functional assignment. A division is a geographical assignment. A sector can be a group or a division.

FIGURE 12-4   Branch Separation—National IMS Model.

Critical Factor: In an MCI, patient treatment operations should be separated from management responsibilities.

The Sector Concept

Throughout this book there is emphasis on the flexibility of EMS/IMS. A Section can be separated into a Branch, such as the EMS Branch. The EMS Branch can be further divided into divisions or groups. (See Figure 12-4.)

A division is an element that operates in a specific geographical area. A group is a functional assignment that is not restricted to a specific area. Divisions relate to geography; groups relate to functions.

As an example, in a New York subway crash, New York EMS divided the Medical Branch into three divisions. There was a train division, which consisted of initial triage treatment, and extrication at the actual wreck. A platform division was established several hundred feet from the train. On the platform, patients were retriaged, treated, and prepared for transport to the street level. A street division was formed at the station entrance (street level) for transport.

In many areas, groups/divisions are called sectors. The term "sector" began in urban fire ICS. Examples are a roof sector, an interior sector, or a basement sector. Many EMS systems also refer to sectors, such as treatment sector, triage sector, etc.

A disadvantage of sector terminology is that it does not distinguish between a geographical assignment and a functional assignment. The advantage of sector nomenclature is that it's simple; everything is a sector, instead of a group or division. In most cases, the term describing a sector is the important element. If you are assigned to a triage sector, you don't really care if it is a group or a division. (See Figure 12-5.)

For simplicity, the term "sector" will be used in this text. Where you see the words "group/division" in other literature, the term "sector" can be substituted.

Geographical sector assignments are usually made when the incident is separated into two or more areas. (Remember the example of the subway accident.) By assigning sectors, the EMS Branch Director effectively manages a complex incident. Let's consider more examples:

1. A bus accident with multiple injuries. Several casualties are in the bus, and several patients are outside the bus. Treatment operations may be divided into a bus sector and a street sector.
2. A high-rise fire (Floor 24). Casualties are on the 23rd floor. Treatment could be divided into sector 23 (to denote the floor), a lobby sector, and a street sector.

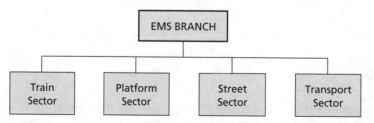

FIGURE 12-5   Dividing an Incident—Geographical Sectors.

3. An airplane crash. The aircraft has broken into two sections, with patients on the runway. Treatment could be divided into a nose sector, a tail sector, and a runway sector.

Remember the toolbox analogy. Simple problems require few tools. When a problem becomes complex, the Incident Manager can dig into the toolbox and use whatever tools are necessary. Sectors are examples of these tools. Strike teams and task forces are also effective tools.

Strike Teams and Task Forces

A strike team is a group of similar personnel or units under a single leader with common communications. Ambulances assembled for transport or five engine companies assembled for fire fighting are examples of strike teams. In each case, the units are assembled as a functional team. The team has communications, with the team leader reporting to the appropriate branch.

The task force is a group of dissimilar people or units temporarily assembled for a specific mission. A task force has a leader and common communications. Task force examples include an ambulance and two police units (medical/law enforcement), or a fire/rescue team working with an EMS Team.

Strike teams and task forces give the Operations Section Chief flexibility to accomplish any mission. It is impossible for planners to predetermine every type of operational problem that may confront incident managers. By forming strike teams or task forces, problems can be solved according to needs.

Some task forces and strike teams are formed before an incident. This is common in the fire service with engine strike teams, or task forces consisting of two engines and a ladder company. Strike teams are not usually preestablished in EMS agencies. Most EMS teams remain as units and are assigned to sectors as appropriate.

Throughout an incident, strike teams and task forces can be formed and disbanded. Units and personnel can be assembled whenever they are needed. Their mission can last the duration of the incident or be completed in minutes. When a mission is finished, the strike team/task force personnel can be reassigned to their units to perform normal operations.

Actual examples demonstrate effective use of strike teams and task forces by operations commanders:

1. A military aircraft has crashed with munitions on board; there are numerous victims. An Explosive Ordinance Disposal (EOD) unit is combined with a medical unit to form a triage task force.

2. A mass shooting incident with numerous victims; the suspect's location is unknown. A SWAT unit is combined with a medical unit to form a treatment task force.
3. A tornado strike with major damage in three separate areas. EMS units are combined into strike teams and assigned to each area.
4. A building collapse with a critically injured trapped victim. A fire/rescue team is combined with an EMS team to form a rescue task force.

Critical Factor: Personnel and equipment resources can be assembled into strike teams or task forces to accomplish specific missions. The task force/strike team concept gives managers flexibility to build operation teams as needs dictate.

CHAPTER SUMMARY

Operations are the identity of any organization. In a mass casualty incident, medical operations consist of triage, transport, and treatment.

Medical operations are under the command of the EMS Branch Director. This branch serves directly under the Operations Section Chief.

The EMS Branch Director is one of the busiest people at the incident. The EMS manager must move throughout patient treatment areas. His/her job is to ensure that adequate resources/supplies are available and that patients receive effective treatment. The Branch Director must coordinate resources needs with the Incident Manager.

A strike team is a group of similar units. A task force is a group of dissimilar units. Strike teams and task forces are operational groups that can be assembled to handle specific mission needs. This concept gives operational commanders flexibility. The most common element of EMS organization is the unit.

CHAPTER QUESTIONS/EXERCISES

1. Define the concept of operations in the EMS/IMS. What are the EMS operations units in the EMS Operations Branch?
2. What are the duties of the EMS Branch Director?
3. Briefly describe several cases where a medical professional should be the Operations Section Chief.
4. Define the terms "strike team" and "task forces."

13
The Chemical Environment

Paul M. Maniscalco
Hank T. Christen

Chapter Objectives

After reading this chapter, you will be able to accomplish the following objectives:

1. Understand the principle of mechanism of injury and how it relates to hazardous chemical exposure.
2. List and discuss the function of the decon unit, including the unit's relationship to triage.
3. Describe the principles of effective decontamination.
4. List and discuss the supplies and equipment needed in a decon kit.
5. Understand the concept of a Technical Advisor and how it relates to Haz Mat operations.
6. Discuss reference materials and sources of reference information for Haz Mat incidents.
7. Discuss the requirements of a hospital decon protocol.
8. Discuss the functions of a medical unit in the hazardous materials ICS.
9. Recognize the importance of detection and mass decontamination in a chemical-biological terrorism incident.

The Chemical Environment

We live in a chemical society. Although exact numbers are debatable, chemical experts agree there are over one hundred thousand hazardous materials in our society. Chemicals are also effective terrorist weapons. These materials can be solids, liquids, or gases. They produce acute trauma such as radiation burns, pulmonary edema, respiratory arrest, explosion injuries, and neurological damage. Chronic effects include gradual organ dysfunction, infertility, birth defects, and cancer.

Chemicals that produce harmful vapors can spread over a large area. With railroad or maritime quantities, or a chemical-biological attack, there is potential for hundreds of patients.

An effective management system anticipates the need for decontaminating and treating chemically exposed patients. Medical treatment protocols for chemical emergencies change as our knowledge of toxicology progresses. Exact protocols will not be discussed. However, reference sources will be covered in a later section.

Mechanism of Injury

A key concept in emergency medical care is mechanism of injury. Mechanism of injury is a sudden intense energy that is transmitted to the body and causes trauma. The chest hitting the steering wheel in an MVA, a bullet entering the body, or the sudden stop after a fall are all mechanisms of injury. In each case, the mechanism lasts a second or less and is depleted by the time first responders arrive.

Normal mechanism of injury concepts do not apply with hazardous materials exposure or chemical weapons. If the patient is touching, ingesting, or breathing the material, the mechanism of injury persists. If EMS responders become exposed to the chemical source, they will be affected by the mechanism of injury. If the patient is not decontaminated, the situation gets worse, because transporting the patient brings the mechanism of injury to the hospital. Chemical fumes can be circulated in the hospital air conditioning system and can injure medical personnel and patients.

Critical Factor: In chemical exposures, the mechanism of injury can last for an extended period and expose treatment personnel and patients to chemical trauma.

The objective, in any hazardous materials or terrorist chemical attack incident, is to remove the mechanism of injury quickly. Remember, the mechanism affects everyone, including John Wayne type rescuers.

Case Histories

Several recent incidents demonstrate the seriousness of chemical injuries in disasters and the danger of a lingering mechanism of injury.

CASE 1: A helicopter air ambulance crew assisted in extrication operations at a vehicle rollover. The truck was not placarded and had no shipping papers. Its cargo was organic pesticides. The helicopter crew showed minor signs of chemical exposure. After several days, exposure symptoms worsened. It was discovered that the leather flight boots were contaminated. The mechanism of injury had been removed from the patients, but stayed with the rescuers.

CASE 2: Two laborers were exposed to a chlorine leak. They were treated on the scene for respiratory exposure and transported to the hospital in their work clothes. They were examined and released, only to return to the scene still reeking of chlorine. The injury mechanism left the scene and came back.

CASE 3: An explosion and fire in an office complex resulted in several patients being transported. ER personnel noted that the patients smelled like chemicals, and their hair was melting. Doctors and nurses began to cough. Other staff members and patients smelled chemical fumes coming from air conditioning ducts. The ER had to be evacuated and decontaminated by a fire department hazardous materials team. It was discovered that patients had been exposed to corrosive chemicals used in photocopying. In this case, the mechanism of injury visited the hospital and decided to roam around.

CASE 4: In Tokyo, Japan, a fanatical religious group intentionally released Sarin (nerve gas) in the subway system. There were multiple casualties. There were additional casualties to paramedics, firefighters, and police officers due to chemical exposure.

In each case, the Incident Management System failed to properly respond to the chemical problem. In the EMS Incident Management System, a decontamination (decon) unit must be established whenever chemical or hazardous materials exposure is confirmed or suspected. (See Figure 13-1.)

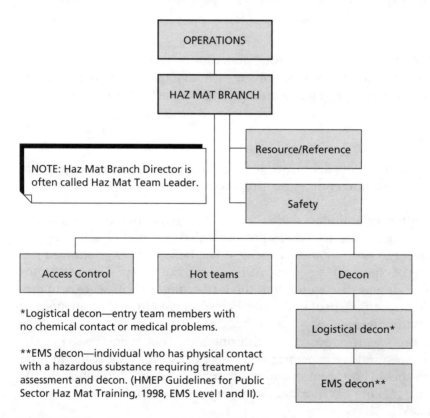

FIGURE 13-1   Hazardous Materials Branch.

The Decon Unit

When hazardous materials are present at an emergency incident or disaster, patients must be decontaminated before or during medical treatment. In the EMS Incident Management System, a decon unit is a team assigned to decontaminate chemically exposed patients. Contaminated patients are usually discovered during triage. The patients must be removed from the source of the exposure and decontaminated, before routing to a treatment area in order to protect rescuers and expedite patient care.

The decon unit is supervised by the Haz Mat Branch Director. If patients are in a known chemical hot zone, they are removed by rescuers and pass through a decontamination corridor operated by the decon unit. These patients are routed through the EMS Branch for triage, treatment, and transport.

Many disasters are not actual chemical incidents, but involve large numbers of chemically exposed patients. Examples are natural disasters and transportation accidents. Most of the victims are trauma patients, mixed with chemically contaminated patients. In these situations, victims are dispersed over a wide area. Contamination is discovered by EMS teams during triage. The decon unit has to be mobile and decontaminate patients in place, or move them to a decon area. Affected patients must be decontaminated before they are moved to a treatment area. Remember, the chemical mechanism of injury will continually harm the patient, rescuers, EMS personnel, and other patients.

Critical Factor: Chemically contaminated patients must be decontaminated before medical treatment.

The decon unit/sector should be staffed by appropriately trained and equipped rescuers. The proper personal protection equipment (PPE) is essential when hazards are present, as is having the experience and knowledge to properly execute decisions relative to the selection of the type of PPE. No decision that the decon unit leader will make is more important than the determination of level of protection for both the respiratory protection or suit selection. There is a real big difference in the level of protection afforded between, let's say, a self-contained breathing apparatus and an air purifying respirator. The personnel assigned to perform decon duties need to have not only a high level of medical training, but also a high skill level in Haz Mat operations.

Principles of Decontamination

In the 1980s, decontamination procedures were complex. There were five decon solutions (A to E) recommended, depending on the chemical. Some of the solutions were weak acids or alkali agents, designed to neutralize acid/base chemicals and could cause harm.

Today, the decontamination process is simplified. The patient, after clothing removal, is washed with water or a light detergent, or wiped with dry cloths, depending on the chemical. Warning: *Water is suitable for most chemicals, but may be harmful in some cases; use an adequate reference source to determine the decon protocol.*

The basic principles of decon are not "rocket scientist" concepts. Removing the patient from the hot zone and removing the patient's clothing are the basics. (If possible, bag the clothing and leave it in the hot zone for disposal. Jewelry and personal effects can be separately bagged for reclaiming.)

The principles of patient decon are summarized as:

1. Move the patient away from further exposure.
2. Remove the patient's clothing and jewelry.
3. Wash the patient, or use dry wiping for water reactive materials.

Remember the decon saying is: "Move 'em, strip 'em, and clean 'em."

Decon Equipment

Basic equipment for decontamination includes the following categories:

1. Personal Protective Equipment (PPE)
2. Washing equipment
3. Containment equipment

PPE is necessary to protect the decon unit. Respiratory equipment and protective suits and gloves are required. Reference materials will indicate minimum suit requirements appropriate for a given chemical. In many cases, a Tyvek disposable suit (Saranex coated), with a hood and booties, will be adequate. Firefighting turnout gear or work uniforms will absorb chemicals, become permanently contaminated, and serve as a mechanism of injury.

Washing equipment consists of soft bristle brushes (dish mops will work), sponges, a soft detergent, towels, and water.

Containment equipment prevents chemical runoff from causing environmental damage. This consists of a roll of plastic, or a vinyl fire salvage cover, and an inexpensive children's inflatable pool. Water that runs off the patient is contained by the pool or plastic sheeting. A disposal bag is used to store contaminated clothing or clean-up equipment.

Emergency operations can result in the uniforms of EMS personnel being contaminated. Shoes are famous for absorbing liquid chemicals; all contaminated clothing must be immediately removed and bagged. EMS units should carry inexpensive disposable coveralls that can be donned after uniform removal. This provides your members with a garment until they return to the station.

Mass Decontamination

With the advent of chemical-biological terrorism, there is a possibility that hundreds of patients must be decontaminated. The military considers mass decon of trained soldiers a major problem. With civilian children and the elderly, the problem is monumental.

Traditional decon, utilizing inflatable pools, is not practical. Fixed spray systems, with lines of ambulatory patients, are a possible solution. The patients must be de-clothed before the decon process. After decon, disposable suits (Tyvek for example) will be needed for privacy and environmental exposure.

Non-ambulatory patients present a more serious problem. Each patient needs individual attention; contaminated litters will not be able to enter the clean area, but must be rotated back into the hot zone. This means litter changes at the clean end of the decon corridor.

A national protocol for civilian mass decontamination is not available at the time of publication of this text. However, such protocols are being drafted, with assistance from military experts.

Technical Advisor

The Technical Advisor, in the IMS model, is any individual with specialized expertise. The Technical Advisor is an important component in the IMS toolbox when hazardous materials or military chemicals are involved. Toxicologists, military specialists, and industrial hygienists can provide expert advice on decontamination and treatment procedures. A Poison Control Center is another source of technical advice, especially in the absence of local expertise. Since most physicians do not have the in-depth toxicology background necessary to give adequate support, it is important to include a Technical Advisor in disaster pre-planning.

Reference Materials

With over one hundred thousand known hazardous chemicals, it is impossible to memorize even a fraction of them. One of the most important medical tools is chemical reference books.

The first step in using reference materials is to identify the chemical. Correct spelling is important, as one incorrect letter can change the name of a chemical to a different substance. If the name of the chemical cannot be obtained, try to determine the general classification from a shipping label. General classifications are explosives, combustible liquids, corrosive materials, flammable liquids, flammable gases, nonflammable gases, flammable solids, organic peroxides, oxidizers, poisons, etiologic agents, and radioactive materials.

EMS providers need, as a minimum, the *DOT North American Emergency Response Guide.* The book is written in plain language and serves as a quick reference source. The guide describes BLS treatment for the chemicals listed. ALS units need reference books with ALS procedures and decon protocols.

The local hazardous materials team needs extensive reference materials. In the hazardous materials IMS, there is a Resource/Reference Officer (Figure 13-1). This position is responsible for obtaining all possible data on given chemicals. The Resource/Reference Officer may also access on-line computer databases, Material Safety Data Sheets (MSDS), and faxed information by cellular telephone.

Another important reference source is CHEMTREC. This is a chemical information center established as public service by the Chemical Manufacturers Association. CHEMTREC is accessible 24 hours a day at 800-424-9300.

Hospital Decontamination

Joint accreditation standards require that hospital emergency departments have a plan for chemically contaminated patients. Contaminated patients are an infrequent hospital occurrence and present an unpleasant surprise to the ED staff. Hospitals cannot assume the EMS system will deliver a clean patient. Patients also arrive by private vehicle, making the hospital the first step in the decon process, instead of the last. A hospital needs a decontamination plan that specifies which personnel perform decon operations, define a decon area, and list decon procedures and equipment.

Personal Protective Equipment and Training

Hospital emergency department personnel may be called upon to perform patient care and decontamination within the hospital. These personnel may be exposed to a significant risk of secondary contamination from their patients. In addition, these personnel may be called upon to assist prehospital personnel requiring technical assistance in patient decontamination.

Consistent with the demands of rendering care to a contaminated patient, hospital and ED administrators must review the legislative and professional mandates for training and equipping staff members. (Refer to JCAHO and HMTUSA guidelines.) "At a minimum, hospital personnel must be able to analyze the situation, assess patient conditions and problems, take the necessary steps to assure medical provider safety, attempt identification of the offending chemical substance, and initiate the decontamination and medical care process." (HMTUSA 1997 Guideline For Public Sector Hazardous Materials Training–Hospital Personnel.)

An important element in a hospital decon protocol is the identification of an emergency decontamination area. This area should be an outside location, separate from return air intakes to the hospital air conditioning/ventilation system. A water spigot should be accessible for washdown purposes. A loading dock (if it is close to the ED), or a covered entrance-way, provides a good decon area. Many hospitals are designing state-of-the-art decon facilities, and building them into new ERs. Plastic sheeting and/or a water recovery pool prevents floor or ground contamination. It is important to cover floor drains to isolate the drainage system from chemical runoff. A decon area exposes a patient to the weather and does not provide privacy. However, outside decon is necessary in extreme cases to avoid the dire consequences of chemical liquids or vapors penetrating treatment rooms or entering the air conditioning system.

All decon materials can be kept in a kit and stored near the decontamination area. The kit is inexpensive and includes:

1. A decon checklist
2. A copy of the hospital decontamination protocol
3. Reference materials and telephone numbers
4. Disposable coveralls and chemical gloves
5. Washing materials, decon solution, and towels
6. Plastic sheeting, inflatable pools, and collection/containment equipment, if required
7. Garden hose, spray nozzle, and water source

Hazardous Materials Team Support

An EMS unit is an important team in the hazardous materials team's Incident Management System (Figure 13-1). The EMS unit coordinates with the Decontamination Officer and Safety Officer, and is commanded by the Haz Mat team leader (NOTE: The EMS unit is not assigned to an EMS Branch, but works with the Fire/Rescue Branch).

The primary function of the EMS unit is to conduct medical surveillance of hazardous materials team members before entry and after exiting the decontamination area. The medical unit is positioned near the cold (clean) side of the decontamination corridor. The most common medical problems of Haz Mat team members are fatigue and heat stress from working in chemical suits. Members with high BP or heart rates, or high body temperatures, cannot report to a staging area for re-suiting. Chemical exposure or trauma can occur to a Haz Mat team, but it is not common.

The key functions of the EMS unit supporting a hazardous materials team are:

1. The EMS unit is a component of the Haz Mat team IMS and assigned to the Haz Mat team leader.
2. The EMS unit coordinates with the Haz Mat Safety Officer and decon unit.
3. The EMS unit is vulnerable to chemical injury and must remain in the "cold zone."
4. The EMS unit's mission is to evaluate and/or treat team members or victims after decontamination.
5. The EMS unit may utilize the Resource/Reference Officer for chemical information.

Chapter Summary

Hazardous materials exposures and chemical terrorism present an unusual mechanism of injury. This mechanism can continue to expose a patient and/or harm medical personnel. If a patient is not decontaminated, the hospital emergency department and other patients can be exposed.

Patients exposed to hazardous materials must be decontaminated before the triage. The decon unit is an element in the IMS and is assigned decon responsibilities. The decon unit is staffed by rescuers with breathing apparatus and appropriate personal protective equipment (PPE). The decon unit is responsible for removing patients from the chemical hot zone and decontaminating the patient. The patient is then routed to the triage unit.

The principles of patient decontamination are the removal of contaminated clothing and shoes, and rinsing/washing chemicals from the patient's hair and skin. Water reactive chemicals must be removed by dry towels. Decontamination equipment includes washing supplies and containment material to confine runoff.

A Technical Advisor is any individual with specialized expertise. Industrial hygienists, military specialists, and toxicologists are technical experts who can assist physicians in providing treatment advice for chemical injuries. Reference materials that contain ALS treatment protocols and decontamination procedures are sources of information. Computer databases, Material Safety Data Sheets, military manuals, and CHEMTREC provide additional assistance.

Hospitals are required to have a procedure for on-site chemical decontamination. Hospital personnel, usually emergency department staff, need PPE, washing materials, containment material, and reference sources. These supplies are carried in a decon kit. A decon area, separate from the building's air conditioning system, must be established.

An EMS unit provides support to the hazardous materials ICS. The EMS unit is managed by the Haz Mat team leader, and coordinates with the Safety Officer and decon unit. The EMS unit evaluates the Haz Mat team members or patients after they exit the decon corridor. The tasks and knowledge required of a Haz Mat team member exceed that of a basic emergency responder. The intent of this chapter is to allow the basic responder to develop a fundamental understanding of the complexities involved with a hazardous materials emergency response. A variety of standards exist that the responder or organization must consult regarding training and operations. Some such standards are 29 CFR 1910.120, EPA 311, NFPA 471, 472, and 473, and the Hazardous Materials Uniform Transportation Safety Act's *Guidelines for Public Sector Hazardous Materials Training,* to name a few. The reader is strongly encouraged to consult these and other guidelines and to successfully complete a certified hazardous material training program prior to executing hazardous materials response actions. Successful completion of the program exceeds the responders' current sanctioned certification level.

CHAPTER QUESTIONS/EXERCISES

1. What is "mechanism of injury"? Why is the chemical mechanism of injury unique compared to trauma?
2. At the next training meeting, discuss several local case histories where chemical contamination was a factor. What decon procedures were used? What protocols or equipment are needed to control future chemical exposure incidents?
3. What is the decon unit? Diagram the decon unit in the IMS.
4. What are the principles of decontamination?
5. What equipment, supplies, and materials should be carried in a decon kit?
6. What is a Technical Advisor? How does this position relate to hazardous materials? What Technical Advisors are in the local and regional area?

7. What reference materials should be available to the decon unit? What are other sources of chemical reference material?
8. What are the essential steps in a hospital decon protocol? What materials should be contained in the hospital decon kit?
9. What is the function of the EMS unit in the support of an operating hazardous materials team?

14
Response Agency Management Systems

Paul M. Maniscalco
Hank T. Christen

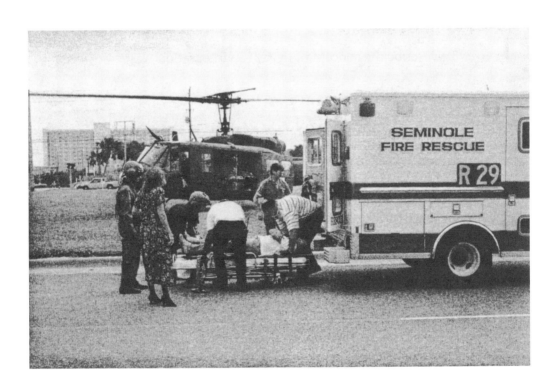

Chapter Objectives

After reading this chapter, you will be able to accomplish the following objectives:

1. Understand the integration of response agency management systems into the Medical Incident Management System.
2. Describe the relationship of an EMS unit to various incident management systems.
3. Diagram the Public Works ICS and discuss its major components.
4. Diagram the Fire ICS and discuss its major components.
5. Diagram the Law Enforcement ICS and discuss its major components.
6. Diagram the Hospital Emergency ICS and discuss its major components.
7. Understand how a medical unit can evolve into an IMS operations structure.
8. Describe the concept of EOC/ICS integration.

Response Agency Management Systems

The EMS/IMS is structured for mass casualty incidents. However, there are many emergency incidents that do not involve multiple patient injuries, but they always exist. These incidents include industrial disasters, public works operations, law enforcement incidents, and firefighting. There is also an incident management system that provides an organization for hospital disasters.

All of the Incident Management Systems (still referred to as the Incident Command System, ICS, in some agencies) have the same principles discussed in Chapter 9. These principles include unity of command, span of control, an incident action plan, common terminology, effective coordination, and logistical support. In each system, the basic structure is a Management Staff that supervises an Operations Section, Logistics Section, Planning Section, and Administration Section. These systems also have a common management structure that provides division into branches (branch director), sectors (group/division), strike teams or task forces (strike team leader), and finally units (unit leader).

EMS Units in Other Systems

The agency-specific management systems (hospital IMS is an exception) all have an EMS unit assigned to the Logistics Section, Support Branch. The purpose of the medical unit is to treat operations personnel or civilian victims. The medical unit was first structured in the wildland fire ICS, where the EMS unit is used to evaluate, treat, and transport injured fire-fighters. In the structural fire ICS, EMS units are in the standby mode at fire scenes. Similar support is utilized at law enforcement, public works, or industrial incidents.

If the incident escalates to the MCI level, additional EMS units or EMS strike teams are utilized. When the incident escalates to a long-term MCI level, a major change must occur. Medical concerns no longer remain a support function in the Logistics Section. Medical care becomes an operations function. This requires the establishment of an EMS Branch in the Operations Section. The change reflects the evolving nature of the incident. Instead of the problem being purely fire, law enforcement, or public works, the EMS aspects now have equal footing.

The EMS unit leader has the burden of initiating escalation of EMS functions to an Operations Section (branch level status.) The system builds from the ground up. When the medical unit or EMS strike team leaders get overwhelmed, they must notify the Incident Manager, via their Logistics Section Chief, of the need for a change. (It's time to dig deeper into the IMS toolbox.)

The EMS unit leader is elevated to a Branch Director, or other people in the EMS chain of command are called to assume this position. The EMS Branch Director, in coordination with the Operations Section Chief and the Incident Manager, will then establish a treatment sector, a triage sector, and a transportation sector (see Figure 14-1).

EMS units do not form a separate management system. Instead, they integrate with the established IMS. Because of the common rules and common terminology in IMS, this integration is quick and effective.

The EMS function is downsized in a similar manner. Patient care may be under control, but other operational units may need to function for some time. Where there is no need for an EMS Branch, the EMS system is reduced back to an EMS unit.

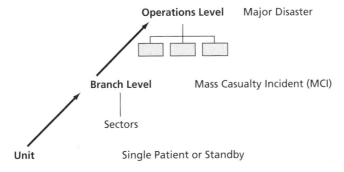

FIGURE 14-1 Expansion of EMS/IMS.

The two important concepts discussed are:

1. Medical functions integrate into the IMS structure: EMS units form an EMS Incident Management System, under an EMS Branch, not a separate system.
2. EMS functions escalate from unit level to branch level, or vice versa, as the incident evolves.

An urban structural fire demonstrates the changing incident management structure. When a working fire is declared, an EMS unit responds for standby purposes. The EMS team reports to the Logistics Section. Initially, two victims are treated for smoke inhalation and transported. A secondary search uncovers four patients. More EMS units respond, with a supervisor to lead an EMS strike team. There is fire extension into an occupied exposure, and a structural collapse. There are now six injured firefighters and ten civilian victims. The EMS strike team leader declares an MCI. The EMS Director responds and becomes the EMS Branch Director. He/she then establishes the appropriate IMS structure.

Later, the fire is controlled. All patients have been transported, and fire overhaul is underway. The IMS is demobilized with a single EMS unit remaining on the scene in a standby mode.

The Fire Incident Command System (ICS)

The IMS model for all agencies was derived from the wildland fire ICS. The operations objective in the fire ICS is fire suppression. The Operations Section is divided into a Ground Operations Branch and Air Operations Branch.

The Ground Operations Branch consists of engines, tenders, and fire teams that are organized as single resources, task forces, or strike teams.

Air Operations are very intricate on wildland fires, and are organized as a branch level status. This branch is further divided into an air support group and an air attack group. On major fires, there is a combination of fixed wing aircraft and helicopters dropping water at precise locations. This requires water pickup locations, helibases, heliports, and fixed wing bases, all coordinated by an air traffic control system.

Since wildland fires usually occur in remote locations, the Logistics Section uses a fully staffed Service Branch and Support Branch. These branches provide a food unit and facilities unit. A medical unit is also assigned to the Service Branch.

The structural firefighting system is called the National Fire Service Incident Management System (Fire IMS). (See Figure 14-2.) It uses the same boilerplate as the wildland system, but operations branches are divided differently. The Fire Branch consists of divisions/groups of units, strike teams,

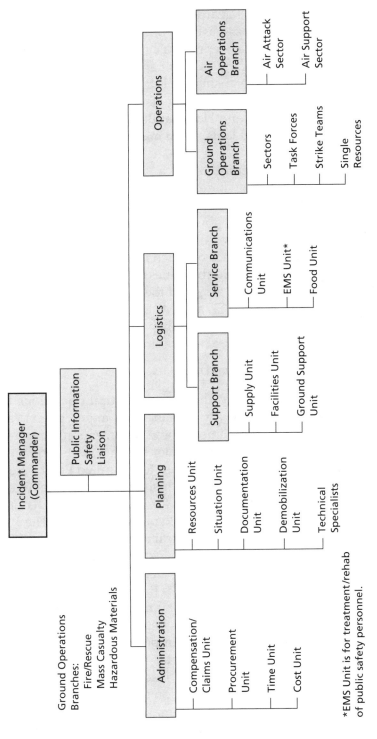

Ground Operations
Branches:
   Fire/Rescue
   Mass Casualty
   Hazardous Materials

*EMS Unit is for treatment/rehab
of public safety personnel.

FIGURE 14-2 National Fire Service IMS—Major Incident.

and task forces. This is the most commonly used branch. The Haz Mat Branch is initiated for hazardous materials problems or chemical/biological terrorism. A Mass Casualty Branch is initiated if the incident becomes an MCI. In this case (as previously discussed), medical treatment is elevated to branch status and is commanded by an EMS Fire Chief, or a third service EMS manager, using the IMS.

Communications needs are met by using several tactical channels. The Fire Branch, EMS Branch, and Haz Mat Branch are assigned separate tactical channels. In major incidents, there may be logistics and air operations tactical channels.

In the Fire IMS, the medical unit is assigned to firefighter rehabilitation (rehab) during operations where mass casualties are not a factor. Treating firefighters is a challenge because they have a "testosterone moral code," which means you fight until you drop. Female firefighters have a similar "estrogen code." In summary, good luck when treating firefighters.

The most common interface between Fire and EMS is during motor vehicle accidents. Fire is assigned the duties of rescue/extrication and control of fuel spills and fire. EMS is assigned the duties of patient care and transport. If the incident is an MCI, an EMS Branch Director will supervise a treatment sector, triage sector, and transportation sector.

Management of Industrial Disasters

In many areas of the country, there are industrial operations that rival a small city in size and complexity. This includes mines, plants, factories, refineries, and chemical companies. These organizations are vulnerable to natural disasters, explosions, fires, major haz mat spills, and terrorism.

Industry maintains private response teams called Plant Emergency Organizations (PEOs). (They were previously called Industrial Fire Brigades.) PEOs have trained emergency teams for fire suppression, confined space rescue, elevated rescue, and chemical spill suppression. The PEO coordinates with in-plant security and medical teams. (See Figure 14-3.)

In the Industrial IMS, the Operations Section is divided into the PEO, Medical, and Plant Maintenance Branches. The Plant Maintenance Branch has functions similar to a Public Works Branch in a government structure. Security is usually a support function. If the incident requires law enforcement, security moves to branch status in the Operations Section.

In industrial disasters, it is very important for the PEO and other industrial segments to effectively integrate with local government agencies. Industrial companies rarely have the resources to handle a plant disaster without mutual aid. Effective integration is assured when agencies on both sides of the fence use the IMS structure. Because of common organization and common terminology, the IMS becomes a valuable asset.

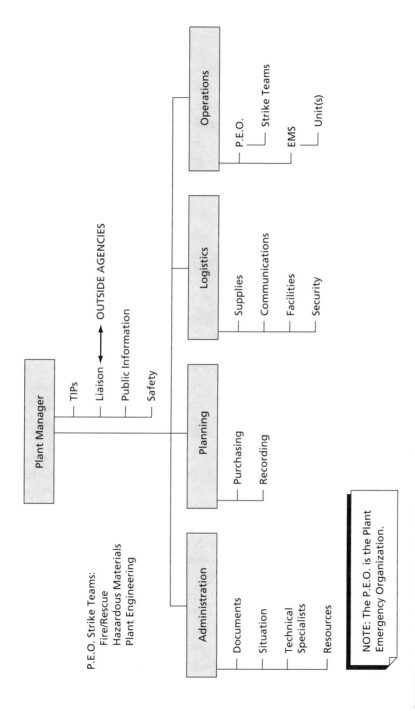

FIGURE 14-3 Industrial Incident Command System.

P.E.O. Strike Teams:
Fire/Rescue
Hazardous Materials
Plant Engineering

NOTE: The P.E.O. is the Plant Emergency Organization.

223

Industrial accidents present serious medical challenges to EMS units or strike teams. There may be burn cases and chemical injuries, along with multisystem trauma. Patients may be in hot zones and require rescue by the PEO or firefighters before triage and treatment. Patient decon may be necessary. (See Chapter 13.)

Technical advisors are an important asset in industrial emergencies. Patients can be injured by industrial processes or special chemicals unfamiliar to paramedics. Industrial hygienists, chemists, engineers, and safety inspectors, available from the industrial staff, can provide life-saving technical assistance.

Trauma intervention is another important asset to the EMS Branch. Industrial MCIs generate a flood of relatives and friends responding to the scene. These people are directed to an area distant from treatment and transportation areas. TIPs personnel have a calming affect on family members awaiting news about casualties.

Law Enforcement Incident Command

The Law Enforcement Incident Command System (LEICS), like other systems, is an extension of the IMS. Progression of a LEICS has been slower than the fire service or emergency medical services command system because of the nature of law enforcement operations. Normally, police/security incidents involve one or two units. In the past, law enforcement agencies had limited experience in large-scale operations involving large numbers of personnel, vehicles, and multi-faceted mission objectives. Recent history has required law enforcement agencies to prepare for large-scale incidents.

Major incidents include natural disasters, transportation accidents, mass shooting incidents, bombings, hostage situations, and terrorism. Many of these incidents result in prolonged operations, military in nature.

LEICS divides mission assignments into groups/divisions. (See Figure 14-4.) These assignments include units and/or tactical teams. The primary groups/divisions are SERT (Special Emergency Response Team), hostage negotiation, bomb disposal, traffic control, and evacuation. The structure discussed is oriented to ground operations. Law enforcement agencies that have air assets assign an Air Operations Branch, similar to the fire organization.

The Logistics Section is divided into three groups. The service group has a communications unit, a food unit, and a medical unit. The supplies group has a ground support unit, a staging unit, and a supply unit. The personnel group has a volunteer services unit and a mutual aid unit (Figure 14-4).

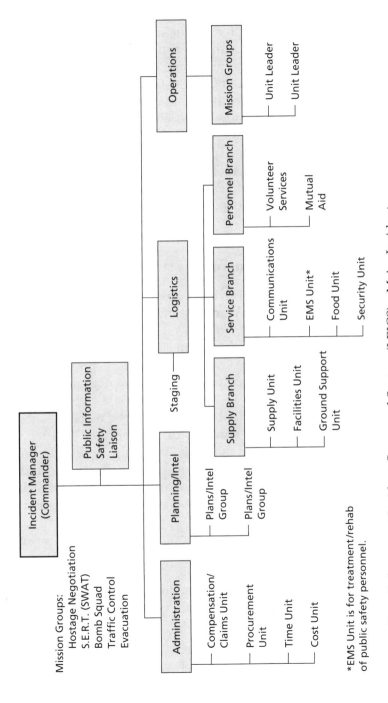

FIGURE 14-4 Law Enforcement Incident Command System (LEICS)—Major Incident.

*EMS Unit is for treatment/rehab of public safety personnel.

Mission Groups:
Hostage Negotiation
S.E.R.T. (SWAT)
Bomb Squad
Traffic Control
Evacuation

The Planning Section in LEICS is called a Plan/Intel Section. Intel means intelligence and is responsible for intelligence information on hostages, suspects, terrorists, or other aspects of an incident.

EMS is at risk in law enforcement scenarios. EMS units, arriving with first response officers, may be threatened with gunfire. The EMS unit leader must determine the hot zone, and stage in a safe area, secured by a law enforcement perimeter. EMS units have to be prepared to move quickly if their staging area comes under fire. It is emotionally difficult for EMS units to remain staged when they know there are patients. But the temptation to "charge" must be resisted to ensure safety. In many areas, EMS maintains "SWAT Medic" teams that are specially trained to support law enforcement.

The trauma from law enforcement incidents can be hideous. Victims may be severely injured from explosives and military type weapons. There may also be a need to decontaminate officers exposed to chem-bio weapons.

Public Works Incident Command

After the experience with Hurricane Hugo, and scores of other natural disasters, the American Public Works Association adopted the IMS model. The end product was the Public Works IMS. (See Figure 14-5.) This system was implemented with a training program and mailed to public works agencies throughout the United States. The objective of the program was to adopt a system that was operationally efficient and integrated with emergency agencies.

The primary operational objectives of public works agencies are sanding, road clearance, debris removal, diking, bridge/road repair, snow removal, confined space entry, shoring, trenching, and traffic control. These functions are carried out by personnel, units, strike teams, and task forces. For example, a debris-clearing task force might include three dump trucks, a front loader, and a team leader. All functions are assigned as groups/divisions in the Operations Section.

Public works may be a branch supporting other response agencies. This could include Haz Mat diking, clearing debris in a rescue operation, or building a road to an inaccessible site.

Routine public works operations do not require an EMS unit. During emergency operations, EMS units are usually on-scene supporting other operations.

Emergency Operations Center Interface

Major incidents require the coordination of multiple response agencies and many support agencies. In a natural disaster, all sixteen ESFs may have to

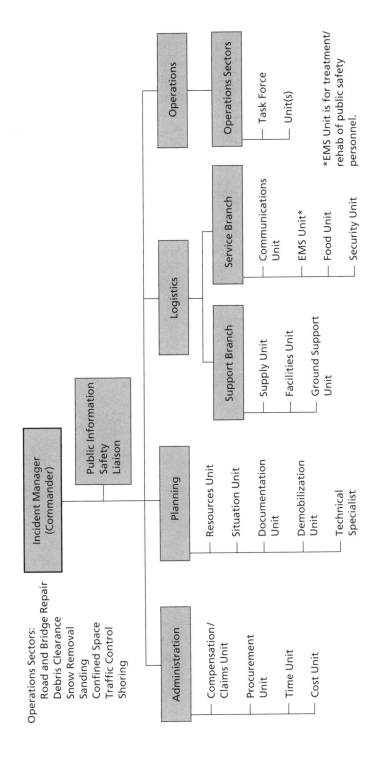

FIGURE 14-5 Public Works Incident Management System.

Operations Sectors:
Road and Bridge Repair
Debris Clearance
Snow Removal
Sanding
Confined Space
Traffic Control
Shoring

*EMS Unit is for treatment/
rehab of public safety
personnel.

227

function in a coordinated manner. This coordination is the responsibility of the Director of Emergency Management, and takes place at the local or county government level. Major incident operations are coordinated at an Emergency Operation Center (EOC). The EOC, also called a Multi-Agency Coordination Center (MAC), is a central command center, staffed by representatives from all sixteen ESFs (Figure 14-6).

The Operations Section consists of the following branches:

1. Medical
2. Fire/Rescue
3. Law Enforcement
4. Public Works
5. Human Services

EMS resources are coordinated at the EOC or MAC level by a senior EMS manager and the county Public Health Director. In a medical disaster, the state health department or the U.S. Public Health Service (USPHS) may respond to the region to direct all ESF 8 (Health and Medical) operations. This is accomplished by a medical support unit (MSU). The MSU is not a "unit" in incident management terminology. It is a branch level team, structured to manage ESF 8 functions. The MSU may operate in the EOC or locate in another building, if there are space limitations.

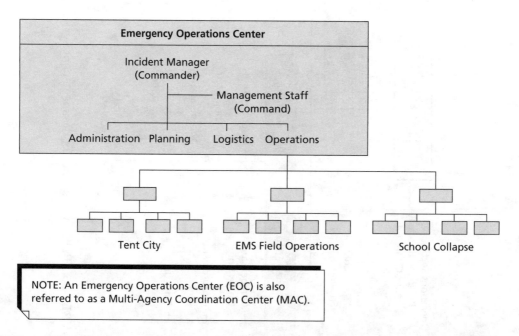

FIGURE 14-6 Emergency Operations Center Interface with Emergency Medical Services.

In this book, discussion has focused on emergency medical operations. In a medical disaster, functions expand to include community health issues such as:

1. Assessment of health/medical needs
2. Health surveillance
3. Medical care personnel
4. Health/medical equipment and supplies
5. Patient evacuation
6. In-hospital care
7. Food/drug medical service safety
8. Worker health/safety
9. Radiological hazards
10. Chemical hazards
11. Biological hazards
12. Mental health
13. Public health information
14. Vector control (control of disease-carrying organisms, usually rodents)
15. Potable water/waste water and solid waste disposal
16. Victim identification/mortuary services.

All of these functions are assigned as a branch, group/division, or unit in the IMS.

In a medical disaster, all ESF 8 functions are not at one location. Each geographic area where medical functions are conducted is a separate "incident," related to the "big incident." Each incident has an Incident Manager and an IMS. These Incident Managers report to the EOC or MSU. The EOC or MSU maintains the big picture and coordinates ESF functions coming from state or federal sources.

An earthquake serves as an example. The disaster is a medical disaster. Medical problems include:

1. A school collapse with trapped students.
2. A severely damaged hospital.
3. A large volume of emergency calls.
4. A large tent city of homeless victims.

The school collapse has a Fire Chief Incident Manager. EMS is an Operations Branch. The hospital operates as a clinic in a nearby undamaged building staffed by a DMAT. The emergency calls are managed by the EMS Director at the EOC. The tent city is managed by a Public Health Officer.

Each "incident" in this scenario has its own IMS structure. Any medical support requests are channelled to the MSU. These requests are routed to the MSU Operations, Logistics, Planning, or Administration Section, or the

Management Staff. The appropriate ESF then receives the mission request and reacts accordingly. If an ESF has inadequate resources (a likely situation), the applicable state or federal ESFs are tasked.

This process develops from a simple structure; functions are conducted at the lowest level. Additional needs channel upward from a unit all the way to an MSU controlling federal resources. *The critical factor is that the IMS structure is maintained at all levels in a medical disaster.*

Hospital Emergency Incident Command System (HEICS)

In 1991, the Orange County Health Care Agency Emergency Medical Services received a grant from the California Emergency Medical Services Authority to develop the Hospital Emergency Incident Command System (HEICS). Orange County EMS produced a document that includes an organizational chart and job action sheets (position descriptions). (See Figure 14-7.)

The HEICS uses the national IMS structure, common terminology, and standard procedures. The HEICS is designed for any hospital emergency. This includes external emergencies such as terrorism, MCIs or medical disasters, or internal emergencies such as fires, explosions, Haz Mat, mass shootings, or natural disasters.

The organizational chart for the HEICS appears complex, but close examination reveals a familiar pattern. There is a Management Staff supervising the four major IMS sections. The Operations Section has three branches. A reminder: The functions and units in the HEICS are tools. Full use of this chart would require the staff of a large hospital; the incident would be a "once in a career" event. Each tool is used as needed, and discarded after utilization. Remember that one person can also be responsible for two or more functional assignments.

At the management level, the Liaison Officer is an important position. A scenario large enough to cause the HEICS to be implemented is a scenario requiring outside agencies. In a medical disaster, the Liaison Officer interacts with the county EOC and/or a state/federal MSU. (See Chapter 15, Hurricane Andrew.)

The Operations Branches are Medical Care, Ancillary Services, and Human Services. Medical Care is the largest branch and is divided into an inpatient services group and a treatment area group. The inpatient services has units as follows:

1. Surgical services unit
2. Maternal-child unit
3. Critical care unit
4. General nursing care unit
5. Outpatient services unit

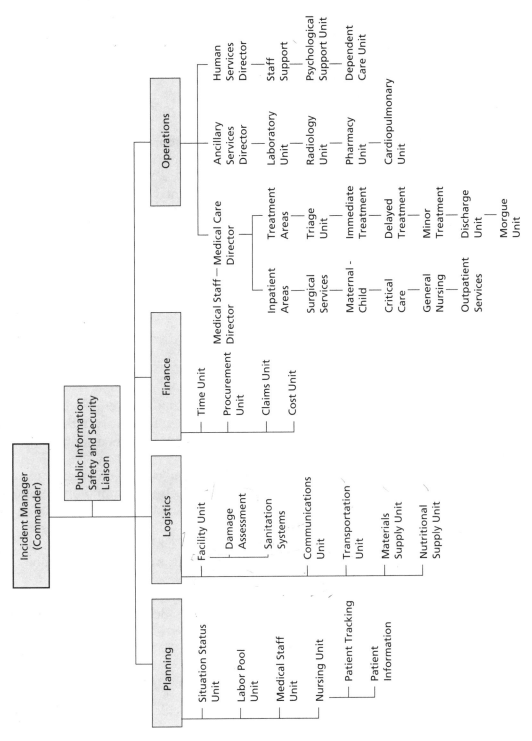

FIGURE 14-7 Hospital Emergency Incident Command System (HEICS)—County of Orange, Emergency Medical Services.

The treatment group is organized using the IMS structure as follows:

1. Triage unit
2. Immediate treatment unit
3. Delayed treatment unit
4. Minor treatment unit
5. Discharge unit
6. Morgue unit

The Ancillary Services Branch has radiology, laboratory, pharmacy, and cardiopulmonary units. The Human Services Branch has staff support, psychological support, and dependent care units.

In the HEICS, the transportation unit is assigned to the Logistics Section. The transportation unit coordinates internal transportation of patients and transport of discharged patients. In an internal disaster, the hospital is the source of victims and may have to transport patients to other hospitals.

The HEICS is an important planning and emergency response guide for medical facilities. The HEICS provides effective liaison with outside agencies that are trained in the Incident Management System. Further, the HEICS is a combination of hospital positions with the IMS that provides an efficient organization for managing a hospital disaster.

Military Liaison

In many communities, there are military bases that have emergency response agencies. These agencies are frequently used for mutual aid by the civilian community. Vice versa, civilian agencies are used as resources for on-base incidents.

In past years, coordination between military and civilian emergency response agencies was ineffective. Command structure, terminology, and procedures were incompatible. This unfortunate situation has changed. In the early 1990s, the U.S. Air Force mandated that all response agencies in the Air Force implement IMS (U.S. Air Force Ops Plan 355.1). The Air Force Fire Service was the first agency to complete the transition. Coordination problems have been reduced or eliminated because agencies on both sides of the military fence are wearing the same command vests, speaking an identical language, and using common procedures. Because of IMS, people are working together.

CHAPTER SUMMARY

The original fire service ICS has evolved into an Incident Management System (IMS) used by all types of response agencies. There is the Fire IMS (wildland and structural), Industrial IMS, Law Enforcement ICS (LEICS), Public Works ICS, and the Emergency Operations Center (EOC) interface.

In each system, there is a medical unit for rehab and patient treatment. As the number of patients increase, the medical function moves upward in the IMS, increasing in size to a strike team/task force, group/division, branch, and section.

In all of the systems, there is a Management Staff and an Administration, Planning, and Logistics Section. These sections, and their related units, support the operations mission.

The Hospital Emergency Incident Command System (HEICS) is a specialized IMS for hospital disasters (internal or external). Hospital services are divided into a Medical Care Branch, Ancillary Services Branch, and Human Services Branch. This system provides effective disaster planning, disaster response, and coordination with outside agencies that use an IMS structure.

The military has mandated the IMS for emergency response agencies. Civilian and military agencies, especially fire services, are now coordinating effectively because they are using similar incident management systems.

CHAPTER QUESTIONS/EXERCISES

1. List and describe at least three incident management systems other than the EMS IMS.
2. What is the function of the medical unit in the systems discussed in question 1?
3. What precautions must be taken by an EMS unit or EMS strike team in Law Enforcement Operations (LEICS)?
4. Define and discuss the functions of the EOC.
5. Define and discuss the functions of the MSU.
6. Obtain an organizational chart from a medical facility in your community or region. Design a hospital disaster response system using the HEICS model.
7. What are the functions of Health and Medical (ESF 8) in a medical catastrophe?

15
EMS Incident Management in the Real World

Paul M. Maniscalco
Hank T. Christen

It's time to kick back after fourteen chapters of academic material. This chapter is a "war story." It describes how well the IMS worked under fire, in Miami during emergency operations after Hurricane Andrew and at the 1993 New York World Trade Center bombing.

This chapter is a summary. It demonstrates how academic concepts work in the real world.

Medical Operations During Hurricane Andrew

Prepared by Hank Christen, Team Leader, Gulf Coast DMAT

Introduction

On August 29, 1992, the Gulf Coast Disaster Medical Assistance Team (DMAT) boarded the C-130 at Hurlburt Field, Florida. We were a motivated group of paramedics, nurses, doctors, firefighters, and amateur radio operators from northwest Florida. Hurricane Andrew hit Miami; it was the real thing.

The Management System

The IMS had been implemented by trial and error two years before Andrew. The basic fire ICS model was used and modified for medical operations. The teams had plenty of practice at two weekend training exercises at Keesler Air Force Base, a staged airplane crash at Pensacola Airport, and a simulated earthquake exercise at Walnut Ridge, Arkansas.

Exercises proved the management system had to be implemented as a first step. Before takeoff, critical command positions were assigned. This included issuing command vests, checklists, and handheld radios.

Experience proved to be a good teacher. We landed at Opa Locka (north Miami), approximately thirty miles north of the disaster site in Cutler Ridge (south Miami). The ground movement, with thirty-two people and all their equipment, taxed the team management system before the first patient was even treated.

The Logistics Section, commanded by Firefighter Charlie Barber, was the driving force at this point. A Mobilization Unit, formed by Firefighter Rick Moak, directed the movement of personnel and supplies. Upon arrival at Cutler Ridge, a grassy section in front of Government Center was assigned as a team home.

The mobilization unit became a facilities unit and directed the erection of tents and storing of equipment. (Capt. Richard Pitts was a great help as an electrician.) Doctors and nurses worked beside paramedics and firefighters, driving tent stakes and making beds.

We got our first lesson in flexibility upon landing. Our equipment was secured to large aluminum pallets. (They're called a 463.) The pallets are designed for Air Force transports, but are two inches too wide for Army Chinook Helicopters. We had to unload the pallets and hand load the helicopters, instead of an easy fork-lift load. When I asked an Army Sergeant about this, he replied, "That's what you get for usin' the Air Force."

Communications

We landed with radios issued to vital management units. Since MED 8 was a national mutual aid channel, radios for inter-team tactical use were set on MED 8. It was discovered that Metro-Dade Fire Rescue was using MED 8 as a dispatch channel. The communications unit carried a laptop computer with software for programming the radios. New channels were established and used throughout the incident for tactical communications.

Regional communications were another problem. The medical support unit (MSU) directed the DMATS from Government Center. When teams deployed to remote locations, problems developed. Telephones were out, and the cellular system was intermittent at best. The local public safety network was destroyed. (Metro-Dade Fire Rescue used an extended aerial ladder with a makeshift antenna attached to the tip.)

The regional problem was solved by using radio caches from the U.S. Forest Service. These VHF radios, with portable repeaters, were issued to each team and worked well.

Contacting home and the NDMS headquarters in Rockwell, Maryland, was easy. Ham operators R. W. Stancliff and Dale Sewell established a national network. This system used voice and computer packet transmissions. These channels were used for contacting families with welfare messages and for issuing press releases to Pensacola and Fort Walton Beach media.

The Incident Management System

The team received all mission assignments from the medical support unit (MSU). The MSU was headed by the overall USPHS medical commander. The MSU's job was to coordinate all ESF 8 activities. This included receiving all medical assistance requests, conducting patient needs assessment, determining medical missions, and assigning DMATs. The MSU was also responsible for logistical support of DMATs in the field.

The MSU staff was organized with an IMS structure similar to the field DMATs. There were personnel assigned to Operations, Logistics, Planning, and Administration. Military liaison was also an important MSU function. (NOTE: In IMS nomenclature, the management team is called an overhead team. The USPHS calls the overhead team an MSU.)

The mission assigned to the Gulf Coast DMAT was to relieve the Fort Wayne DMAT. Fort Wayne team leader Lynn Patton, RN, was operating an emergency room (ER) at Government Center. Two hospitals in the area were closed because of severe damage. The ER served an area of two hundred and fifty thousand people.

The change of command was not simple. It was important to interface with counterparts at every level, yet not affect patient care. This was complicated by the Fort Wayne team being physically and emotionally exhausted. Lynn and I decided to phase in the new team over a twenty-four hour period. We were assisted by EMS Director Bruce Yelverton, Assistant Team Leader.

Hurricane Andrew was the largest DMAT deployment in history. (Similar deployments would later occur for Hurricane Inniki, the Northridge Earthquake, and Hurricane Marilyn.) Other teams operating on our arrival (along with Ft. Wayne) were Albuquerque, New Mexico; Fort Thomas, Kentucky; Boston/Worcester, Massachusetts (Dr. Susan Briggs); and Winston Salem, North Carolina (Dr. Lew Stringer). Later teams that deployed into Miami were our sister team from Port Charlotte, Florida (lead by Capt. Gary Lindbergh and Connie Bowles, RN) and Toledo, Ohio, under Dr. Paul Rega, Kelly Burkholder-Allen, MPH, and Churton Budd, RN. A final DMAT deployment included DMAT stress teams From Baltimore, Maryland, and Kahului, Maui, Hawaii, along with the Tulsa, Oklahoma DMAT (Dr. Art Malone, Tim Walton.) We would later work with the Tulsa team in the Virgin Islands.

Because of the IMS, coordinating with personnel at Metro-Dade Fire Rescue was easy. When the DMAT donned identification vests for the various positions, Metro-Dade Chief Carlos Perez and his people, familiar with IMS, knew how to coordinate. Because of common terminology, people could understand communications and functions. The IMS worked just like the old wildland fire ICS. Within minutes, people from diverse agencies who had never met were efficiently doing business.

Patients were routed to a triage desk operated by Lynn McDaniels. A simple patient form included name, address, telephone number, age, sex, and a brief description of the medical complaint. The patient's triage level was indicated by a red, yellow, or green slash mark across the form with a magic marker.

There was a red, yellow, and green treatment section, with a treatment unit leader for each section. Drs. Craig Broome and Charles Neal directed the red area, nurses Patty Heath and Kay Brooks ran the yellow area, and a paramedic supervised the green section. Patients who required hospitalization were routed to a transportation unit for air or ground transport. (More about transportation later.)

We were assigned twenty-four-hour operations for nine days. I divided the team into a blue team and a gold team; each team worked a twelve-hour shift. Fatigue was a major problem. The sleep and rest area was next to the treatment area. Because of helicopter noise and emotional stress, sleep was almost impossible.

The regional medical community provided much needed support. Physicians and nurses from unaffected counties provided invaluable assistance. Pediatricians and pharmacists were especially welcomed.

The large number of medical volunteers resulted in a need for credentialing and license verification. A volunteer unit (ESF 15) was established to serve as a check-in station before volunteers were assigned to the treatment unit. Licenses were verified before patient assignments. In one case, two medical students worked for two days before it was discovered they were not physicians. (They wore scrubs and spoke the lingo.) A volunteer unit stopped the problem.

Media coverage was unrelenting. Because of personnel shortages, I doubled as the PIO. The media was escorted through treatment areas and given free access, providing patient care was not compromised. To the media's credit, this access was not abused. The coverage made the team look good to the folks back home. The highlight of the media barrage was a national feed on NBC's Today Show. I was quoted as saying,

> One afternoon, a clean cut guy in a suit entered the treatment area and identified himself as a Secret Service Agent (he fit the mold). He told me Marilyn Quayle, wife of the Vice President would be arriving in thirty minutes. She arrived on cue, without an entourage. She was at ease with the surroundings and got the grand tour. This had a calming effect on our patients, and boosted team morale. She was a gracious lady.

Logistics

Logistics was a major lesson. Team members did not appreciate the number of logistics people required to support treatment personnel. Since people were scarce, off-duty medical personnel were used to support the working staff. The Logistics Section Chief was a busy man.

The team was advised to arrive with enough supplies and equipment to be self-sufficient for three days. This was good advice, especially for the first arriving teams.

A need for an efficient "push" logistics system was one of the major points at the post-Andrew debriefing session. In the future, a standardized cache of medical supplies, medications, and equipment will be "pushed" to the scene from regional supply depots.

DMATs ran out of cardiac monitors, monitoring pads, tetanus, insulin, suture sets, Dilantin I.V., and batteries. Local pharmacists were an enormous help. Medications were supplied by private donors and regional Veterans' Administration hospitals. There was also a need for portable refrigerators to keep insulin cold. This problem was solved by procurement from local vendors.

In remote medical areas, we were supplied by Chinook helicopters carrying sling loads. The loads included tents, blankets, cots, and non-perishable medical supplies.

Facilities were installed and maintained by the DMATs (another drain on logistics personnel). Our DMAT raised three tents in a windy rainstorm, and had an ALS treatment center operating within forty-five minutes.

Enterprising team members used plywood to construct a makeshift shower. A length of firehose, a nozzle, a hydrant wrench, and duct tape completed the project. The original shower had no roof, but a roof was built after helicopters kept flying low to watch the nurses take showers.

Water supply was another problem. The team deployed with only one day of drinking water. Fortunately, water was flowing at Government Center. The non-potable water was suitable for patient washing and irrigation. Stainless steel milk tankers supplied drinking water. In outlying areas, teams were supplied by military water buffalos (water tanks on trailers).

Patient Care

In the first three days, trauma care from storm-related injuries was the norm. Later, primary care, preventive medicine, and treatment for chronic conditions became the norm.

The most common trauma was from falls and foot injuries, as people attempted to fix their homes. Podiatrists were a big help in the suture areas. MVAs were also a constant source of trauma. Traffic was heavy, and stop lights were not functioning. There were many severe accidents caused by drivers hitting the expressway toll booths. The booths were closed, and people were not used to driving through them at high speed.

The burn cases were usually critical. Most of the burn patients were injured attempting to fill portable generators while they were running. These burns were second- and third-degree, below the waist. Most of these incidents also caused working structural fires.

Gunshot and knife trauma was down, but it didn't stop. In one case, a patient had been shot in the buttocks with a nine-millimeter pistol. He was exiting a home with a television in his hands when he was shot by the homeowner. One teenage gang member we treated had scars from eight previous gunshot wounds.

After three to four days, chronic medical problems began to surface. They included seizures, pediatric asthma, brittle diabetes, hypertension, and respiratory problems (COPD).

When large numbers of oxygen-dependent patients began to seek treatment, the yellow treatment unit was modified to include an oxygen therapy area. Large oxygen cylinders (H Cylinders) were laid on the floor, with a single hose to a manifold. The manifold supplied up to six nasal cannulas or rebreather masks. Cardboard boxes were cut on an angle and duct taped to cots to provide a means of elevating COPD patients.

Humans were not the only patients. Many homeless animals, especially dogs, wandered through the devastated areas. The dogs had lacerations from fighting, or suffered from dehydration. In a severe dehydration case, Dr. Lew Stringer started an I.V. of normal saline on a dog. Obviously, animal treatment did not compromise patient care or deplete patient supplies. Treatment of animals was well-received by the public and extended our philosophy of preservation of all forms of life.

I often think about some of the people I met during this MCI:

Eddie Miranda   He owned an oxygen therapy company in Miami. He delivered some badly needed oxygen cylinders to our team and stayed for five days. Eddie was bilingual, and provided Spanish translation for our patients. He helped run an oxygen therapy area, second to none. When we left we gave Eddie a team tee shirt, and made him our honorary member. He was speechless, but with tears in his eyes managed to say, "I'll never forget any of you; thank you very much."

Matilda Brown   I saw her from across the room. She was a patient in the oxygen therapy unit. She wore a Panama hat, her best Sunday dress, and white shoes. "Come over here and talk to me and hold my hand, young man," she said. For a minute, I quit playing Incident Manager. We talked. She said, "Whenever I'm down, I put on my best clothes, hold my head high, and deal with life." I've thought of her many times since then.

Outreach Medicine

In a normal situation, the patient initiates access to the emergency medical system, usually via 9-1-1. In Miami, communications were malfunctioning or non-existent. It was difficult to find out who needed help, and where.

After the storm dissipated, Metro-Dade Fire Rescue had two hundred and fifty critical 9-1-1 calls holding. Fire stations in the storm area had hundreds of people reporting for medical treatment or assistance.

Each emergency run generated three more incidents. Victims were flagging down emergency vehicles responding through their neighborhood.

Police units were encountering similar problems. Transit buses were also picking up patients and transporting them to treatment areas.

The public's ingenious method of accessing the medical system was breaking curfew. The dusk-to-dawn curfew was rigidly enforced by the 82nd Airborne Division and law enforcement. Any person stepping outside immediately encountered patrol units that could get medical help.

There were many freelance aid stations and treatment areas established by private medical practitioners. These units operated out of cars, tents, and motor homes. One treatment station, unknown to officials, was operated by two LPNs and a veterinarian.

When the 82nd Airborne arrived, they set up BLS aid stations at schools and parks. These areas were marked by large red balloons that were on a one-hundred-foot tether.

We were concerned that elderly patients with chronic conditions were not being treated. A similar concern existed for migrant workers in Homestead, Florida. 82nd Airborne vehicles, with DMAT members, began a house-to-house search. Many patients were found. Some were treated on site and given food, water, and essential supplies. Others were transported to a hospital, when required.

The Army used Humvees with powerful public address systems, that slowly cruised the streets and notified citizens about the location of treatment areas, supply and food areas, and information on preventive measures. The messages were broadcasted in English, Spanish, and Creole (the Haitian language).

Home health nurses played a major role. In many cases, the nurses had lost their homes and their offices. With sparse records, they attempted patient contact with personal vehicles. Many patients had left damaged homes and had to be tracked.

Patient assessment teams were sent by the MSU to survey areas and determine what care was needed. Public shelters were also assessed. As needs were uncovered, DMATs or 82nd Airborne Units were given mission assignments. The objective was to distribute medical resources in zones where they were most needed. Preventive health measures were also addressed.

Transportation

The Transportation Unit in the DMAT structure was always busy. Since emergency treatment areas could not admit patients, serious cases had to be transported to hospitals in greater Miami. Jackson Memorial Hospital (JMH), in northwest Miami, was the only operating trauma center.

A Metro-Dade firefighter was assigned to each DMAT transportation unit. When transport was required, the requests were coordinated by radio, via the firefighter.

Ground ambulances were the main transportation mode. These vehicles were Metro-Dade units, private ambulances, and ambulances from mutual aid fire departments from south and central Florida. Severe trauma cases were air evacuated to JMH. Metro-Dade's two air medical helicopters were destroyed. The flight paramedics were re-assigned to Army Black Hawk helicopters. These combined teams performed admirably. Whenever a transportation unit called for air evac, a helicopter was there within five minutes.

Response

Responding to incidents in a distant city is a strange experience. In Miami, street signs were down along with expressway exit signs. Landmarks were destroyed, making it difficult for even local units to find their way around. I am a Miami native, but still got lost.

Medical assessment teams needed maps to find their assigned areas. Helicopters had difficulty finding landing zones. In one case, helicopters couldn't find the Homestead High School football field. The field was debris littered, and did not look like a football field from the air.

Local road maps were at a premium. Government agencies quickly ran out of maps, as mutual aid and regional/national support agencies consumed the supply. The 82nd Airborne went to convenience stores to buy all the maps available. A logistics function planned for future disasters is appropriation of maps. Emergency management agencies should have at least one hundred excess maps as part of a Disaster Plan.

High technology helped solve response problems. Geo Positioning Satellite (GPS) technology was a solution. Most aircraft now have GPS navigation systems. A medical team, with an inexpensive ($500), handheld GPS receiver, can obtain exact grid coordinates and direct incoming aircraft. This is especially important at night. GPS can also be used for ground units. The course and distance to a set of coordinates can be obtained by handheld units. We did not have GPS in Miami, but GPS receivers are now required equipment. (GPS has many practical applications in day-to-day operations, especially when coordinating with helicopter air ambulances.)

Following is a vivid example of the scarcity of maps: A huge Army Chinook helicopter landed at Cutler Ridge Mall with our re-supply order. The pilot had landed at two other malls, and asked startled shoppers for directions to our site. He was relieved to finally find us. A young lieutenant remarked, "We can give you grid coordinates for the darkest back alley in Thailand, but we don't have any maps for Miami."

Geobased Information Systems (GIS) produces computer-drawn maps. The Metro-Dade County GIS Department used this effective tool to produce real-time maps of the damaged area. These maps included locations of DMATs, aid stations, water supplies, food distribution, and FEMA

Disaster Assistance Centers. New maps were produced daily, giving an accurate depiction of the "big picture."

Stress Management

The trauma intervention program (TIPs) was an ongoing process. The patient care activity was like another day at the office, the environment was not. There was destruction everywhere, with no greenery. At night, the darkness was total. There were no night sounds, no crickets. Helicopter noise and sirens were all that could be heard. This environment, coupled with little or no sleep, took its toll on our patients.

The patients were in a daze, emotionally numb. The "thousand-yard stare" was common in treatment areas. People lost their homes and were suffering from injuries. Although the TIPs unit was originally slated to treat team members, their efforts were soon concentrated on patients.

Patients with injured children were devastated. In many cases, they went from numbness to hysteria without warning. The behavior affected the children and other patients. Mental health professionals became a vital facet of patient care.

Local public safety personnel reacted stoically after suffering personal losses. Firefighters, paramedics, and police officers lost their homes, yet worked long hours in the line of duty. Professionals from throughout the country conducted stress debriefings for hundreds of public safety professionals.

Our team conducted an informal debriefing after each twelve-hour shift. Team members shared feelings, talked about patients, complained about the supply bureaucracy, and bolstered each other. At the end of the session, we held hands in a moment of silence. Our intervention unit included Larry Rappe, Pat Ross, Terry Watkins, and Bill and Sandy Hartley.

Going back to the real world, post de-mobilization required an adjustment period. An arrival session was conducted at the home airport. Several weeks later we had a homecoming party where we shared pictures, jokes, and war stories. There was a comraderie that comes from dependence on others under the strain of combat.

Experience from Hurricane Andrew revealed that the mental health needs of an affected community are as serious as the trauma care needs. Mental health DMATs now exist to provide the high level of emotional care needed in a disaster area. The TIPS unit continues to be an important element in the team level management structure.

We knew that someday we might have to apply our Andrew experience at home in Florida's Panhandle. Unfortunately, 1995 was the year we were hit by Hurricane Erin. Soon after, we deployed to St. Thomas, Virgin Islands, and operated a tent emergency room for ten days. Forty-eight hours after coming home, we were hit by Hurricane Opal. We called it "Sixty Days in 95."

Summary

The IMS got a severe test in Miami, and it passed with flying colors. Patient care was effective; triage, treatment, and transport were accomplished. Interagency coordination was effective. Communications and logistics operations were strained to capacity, but remained adequate.

We had to dig deep into the IMS toolbox. For every problem, there was a solution. Most importantly, a great team of dedicated men and women, with excellent U.S.P.H.S. and VA support, performed above and beyond the call of duty.

Medical Operations at the World Trade Center Bombing © March, 1993

Prepared by D/C Paul M. Maniscalco, B.S., EMT/P, Chief of Special Operations, NYC EMS

Introduction

Terrorist acts occur worldwide, almost daily. Whether the origins are Narco-Terrorism or religious/political, we have become all too familiar with these events and the results that are perpetrated by cowardly individuals and/or organizations. As the result of a terrorist bomb on Friday, February 26, 1993, at approximately 12:18 hours, the New York City Emergency Medical Service was called upon to respond to the largest patient-generating incident up to that time. No one ever imagined the scope of this incident when we commenced our response, and many people, EMS members and patients, soon had their lives changed forever.

Response

While conducting normal administrative duties at the quarters of the Special Operations Division (SOD) with Capt. Jeffrey Armstrong, SOD. Executive Officer, our meeting was interrupted by Lt. Robert Browne, who advised us that there was a report of a transformer explosion at the World Trade Center in lower Manhattan. We also learned that there were at least three additional calls into the 9-1-1 system corroborating the first report of an explosion.

Based on the available information, I commenced my response with Capt. Armstrong, Lt. Browne, Lt. Fenton, and the SOD. Emergency Response Squad (ERS). It should be noted that our (SOD) response at this juncture was predicated on the initial report of a transformer explosion. We thought the potential for a haz/mat decon was high due to the use of PCBs as transformer coolant in some locations. The Special Operations Division of NYC*EMS is responsible for patient and rescuer Haz Mat decon.

As we neared the Brooklyn Battery Tunnel, the scope of the incident started its upward growth. At this point, Lt. Juan Torres gave his preliminary report of many patients and requested numerous resources to respond. Early unconfirmed reports of a bomb began to surface. The Brooklyn Battery Tunnel was closed to all traffic except emergency vehicles, which greatly assisted the multiple responding emergency units attempting to get into lower Manhattan from the outer boroughs.

The Incident Site

To fully grasp the scope of this incident, let me digress for a moment and describe the structures and surrounding campus of the WTC complex. The World Trade Center consisted of two 110-story office towers (One and Two World Trade Center), a 47-story office building (Seven World Trade Center), two nine-story office buildings (Four and Five World Trade Center), an eight-story U.S. Customhouse (Six World Trade Center), and a 22-story hotel (Vista International New York, Three World Trade Center), all of which were constructed around a five-acre plaza. All seven buildings have entrances onto the plaza, as well as on to the surrounding city streets. The Trade Center's Concourse, located immediately below the plaza, houses the largest enclosed shopping mall in Manhattan. The two office towers, each rising 1,350 feet, are the tallest buildings in New York City and the second tallest buildings in the world. The center is located on a 16-acre site in lower Manhattan, stretching from Church Street on the east to West Street on the west, and from Liberty Street on the south to Barclay and Vesey Streets on the north. The campus also has a six-level, below-grade area that accommodates over 2,000 cars for parking and provides a station and track area for the PATH (Port Authority Trans Hudson) train system. If you were to plot out the entire property horizontally, it would encompass greater than 2,000 acres. The Port Authority of New York and New Jersey reports that "some 60,000 people work in the World Trade Center, with another 90,000 business and leisure visitors coming to the center daily." The property size and numbers of people associated with the WTC Complex have qualified it for its own zip code from the U.S. Postal Service.

The Explosion, Damage, and Terrorist Group

Upon examination of the wreckage left by this bomb, FBI Special Agent David R. Williams, of the FBI Headquarters Explosives Unit, was quoted at the first press conference as saying, "This explosive device that we've seen here today is the largest by weight and by damage of any improvised explosive device since the inception of forensic explosive identification, and that's since 1925." The blast occurred on the B-2 level of the sub-basement in the underground parking structure of Three World Trade Center. The blast tore a 130-ft. × 120-ft. hole, involving 16 bays, surrounded by 20 bays of damaged eleven-inch thick, reinforced concrete slab that is "sloping up to four feet in a very precipitous state," said Leslie E. Robertson. Ms. Robertson, a World Trade Center designer, believes that the bomber was not aiming just for a parking garage and five or six people, but to take down an entire building and 25,000 workers. "It [the van] was parked right next to the outside wall of the north tower," she continued. "If you wanted to take down the towers, that would be one of the places you would try to bomb." The blast pattern extended vertically two floors through the B-1 level upward into a restaurant area of the Vista International Hotel and downward three stories to the B-5 level. The blast concussion vented itself horizontally with a massive displacement of air through the parking garage and ramps located throughout the sub-grade structure. A significant level of damage is associated with this air displacement. Numerous vehicles were picked up and tossed as they were caught in the violent air drafts. Debris flew through the air literally sandblasting items down to their bare metal. Additional damage occurred in the B-6 level that houses the PATH train station. Other emerging issues that complicated the rescue efforts were that reportedly 1.8 million gallons of water had collected in the sub-basement levels from ruptured pipes and would need to be pumped out, and the presence of asbestos throughout the building in areas that had yet to undergo the abatement process.

Within hours of the blast, over fifty groups had telephoned authorities to claim responsibility for the terrorist bombing. We would learn, as it was confirmed several days later, that an Islamic extremist group, allegedly headed by Sheik Omar Abdul Rahman, was responsible for this heinous crime. Three members of the group, Mohammed Salameh, Nidal Ayyad, and Mahmud Abouhalima, have since been arrested by the FBI and NYPD and charged with various crimes associated with the World Trade Center bombing. U.S. and international law enforcement officials continue the investigation and pursuit of others who might have participated. A note of interest in this case is that "Sheik Omar Abdul Rahman, a fundamentalist extremist who hates Western values and is an avowed enemy of the United States, Israel, and the notions of secular governments in the Islamic world, has been tied to the assassinations of Egyptian President Anwar el-Sadat and Rabbi Meir Kahane (founder of the Jewish Defense League), as well as to other acts of violence both in Egypt and in the United States." (*The New York Post*, "The Reality of Terrorism," March 9, 1993.) In the Sadat incident, Rahman was acquitted for lack of evidence, and he was never charged in the Kahane murder. "The suspects appear to be tied spiritually to Rahman . . . Before arriving here, Sheik Omar was better known as the man

who issued the fatwa (religious orders) calling for the assassination of Anwar Sadat. Some 107 of his followers were convicted for their roles in the
uprising surrounding that killing." (*The New York Post*, "The Reality of Terrorism," March 9, 1993.)

Structuring and Managing the Incident

Upon arrival I conducted a face-to-face meeting with Lts. Torres, Browne,
and Fenton, and Capts. Armstrong and Olsen to begin implementation of
the EMS Incident Management System (IMS). Capt. Armstrong was designated the Safety Officer, Capt. Olsen was assigned to assess the situation in
One WTC, Lt. Browne was to assess the Winter Garden Theater, Lt. Torres
was to assess the Triage Sector for One WTC, and Lt. Fenton was to assess
Two World Trade Center.

The EMS IMS is clearly delineated within the *NYC*EMS Operating
Guide* under our Emergency Medical Action Plan (EMAP). It is the constant
use of IMS at each and every incident to which NYC*EMS responds that
permitted the fluid management of this massive incident, and it is one of
the crucial reasons that this incident was managed with success. All members of NYC*EMS undergo training with the EMS IMS, from trainees in the
academy right on up to ranking officers.

As I assumed command of the signal 10–30 (Explosion), the initial incident presented us with a myriad of complex issues: thick acrid smoke pour-
ing from the West Street entrance ramps to the underground parking
facility and the WTC Towers, numerous people evacuating the affected
buildings throughout the WTC campus and seeking EMS assistance, thick
shards of glass raining down on the civilians and rescuers from One World
Trade Center and the Vista Hotel, and the inclement weather elements of
snow, ice, and rain.

After receiving the initial updates from each of the officers detailed to
assess proximal locations to the blast area, it was determined that at least
three divisions would be needed to effectively manage this incident. These
divisions were: One WTC Operations under the command of D/C Edward
Gabriel, Vista Hotel Operations under the command of Captain Robert
Iannarelli, and Two WTC Operations under the command of D/C Michael
Rice. As each operational division was implemented, the requisite sectors
were also established to support those operations, i.e., triage, treatment,
and transport. This would permit the necessary allocation of resources, allowing for tracking of units, personnel, and patients in each specific area as
best as possible considering the huge scope of the event.

A central staging sector was established at West Street and Vesey Street,
with Lt. John Perruggia as the Sector Officer to coordinate and control all
vehicle/unit distribution. In addition, Capt. Joseph Apuzzo, Lt. Richard
Garcia, and Lt. Steven Sammis were detailed to be the control/access offi-

cers to keep units from being pulled into the site unnecessarily and to limit freelancing of units. This strategy was extremely effective, providing us with greater accountability of the units that were requested into the site from Staging and a passport system to track unit movement in and out of the incident site. I cannot overemphasize the importance that these roles played in the management of resources. Another key asset was the utilization of the EMS Field Communications Unit. Upon the arrival of this unit, D/C James Basile assumed the responsibility for coordinating communications from the incident site as the Communications Sector Officer.

Shortly after the primary deployment of resources, Lt. Browne reported back to me that he had an estimated 200 patients in the Winter Garden Theater who would require assessment and possible treatment. The creation of a fourth division, Winter Garden Operations, under the command of Lt. Robert Browne, was now necessary to better manage this area.

Early in the incident, several strategic requests would prove to help maintain operations at the incident site as well as assist with the maintenance of normal 9-1-1 responses. First, with the response of senior EMS management to the site, I had immediate access to Chief David L. Diggs, NYC*EMS Executive Director; Mr. Vincent Clark, Deputy Executive Director; Dr. Lorraine Giordano, Medical Director; Chief MacNeil C. Cross, Chief of Operations; and Ms. Lynn Schulman, Associate Executive Director for Public Information. On-site access to these officials permitted quick implementation of decisions regarding issues such as holding over an entire NYC*EMS tour from the day shift and redeployment of members of the service in reserve ambulances to support the citywide operation, as well as the transportation of spare members to the site for relief purposes. The canceling of training classes at the EMS Academy and redeployment of members to the site also proved beneficial. Activation of the NYC*EMS Mutual Aid Radio System (MARS) helped to muster assistance from the volunteer ambulance corps within NYC. An unprecedented formal request for mutual aid from units in New Jersey and from commercial ambulances in New York City proved to be key in the overall success of the operation.

A/C Pedro Carrasquillo was assigned to the role of Liaison Officer to help expedite requests for interagency assistance to support the EMS operation. Chiefs Walter Drivet and Keith McCabe of University of Medicine and Dentistry of New Jersey EMS arrived at the scene and were immediately assigned to coordinate the New Jersey mutual aid resources that were responding to the incident. Upon the arrival of a field communications unit from the Ridgefield Park, New Jersey First Aid Squad, we were able to position this unit parallel to the NYC*EMS Field Communications, coordinating New Jersey unit access and movement to and from the site. In addition, Chief Joseph Cali of Jersey City Medical Center EMS established a staging location on the New Jersey side of the Holland Tunnel for all NYC-bound units. This permitted the resources to be organized into task forces that could be escorted to the incident site as they were needed.

Expanded Operations

As incident operations continued, the need to redeploy arriving resources to other areas to support the ever-growing patient numbers became evident. A/C Zachary Goldfarb was assigned to assume responsibility for Two WTC operations and D/C Rice for coordinating interior operations at Two WTC. As the numbers of patients continued to rise in the previously established divisions, repeated calls for EMS were being received at two additional locations. Upon assessment of conditions on the Vesey Street side of the WTC, it was determined that another division would be required. Capt. Michael Garufi assumed responsibility for the Vesey Street Operations. At the same time. Capt. Andrew Tychnowitz reported that numerous patients had congregated at the Five WTC site and were in need of EMS assistance. Capt. Tychnowitz was assigned as the Five WTC Operations Officer.

One of the more effective tactics that was employed at the division level was a forward triage station located on the upper floors of the towers. In each instance as victims were being evacuated through darkened, smoke-filled stairwells, EMS crews were enabled to conduct a cursory triage. In an incident of this origin and magnitude, one would expect trauma to be the prevalent injury. This was not the case. We experienced numerous minor trauma patients, but the overwhelming number of patients were those with smoke inhalation, exhaustion, and aggravation of pre-existing medical conditions, i.e., C.O.P.D., asthma, cardiac, hypertensive crisis, etc. Also encountered at the site was a high number of pregnant patients who had been exposed to the above-listed elements.

Another tactic employed that assisted greatly was the utilization of transit buses with EMS personnel and equipment on them and police escorts to transport numerous patients with minor injuries to area hospitals. This permitted us to conserve the use of ambulances for the more serious patients requiring transport to designated hospitals.

Another element that was handled through the coordination of the Field Communications and EMS Communications Divisions was monitoring the available bed status in New York City and surrounding communities. In addition to the standard bed status, the availability of trauma, burn, and hyperbaric beds was assessed frequently to avoid overloading any one facility. This information was provided to the EMS Incident Commander and Division Transport Officers to guide transportation destination decisions.

Consistent with the growing numbers of patients and the anticipated extended operations, the development of several other support sectors was imperative to ensure the effectiveness of overall incident management.

With a significant media presence on-site, the need for a public information liaison is self-explanatory. Under the direction of Ms. Schulman (AED/Public Information), a public information sector was established, EMTs Sandra Mackay and Robert Leonard helped to balance the plethoric demands for information and access to EMS operations and officers on-site. At EMS headquarters, Inspector Charles DeGaetano provided support by managing the non-stop telephone inquiries for information and updates.

Assessment of long-term needs regarding the maintenance of normal 9-1-1 operations and those associated with the WTC incident was of significant importance. Chief MacNeil Cross, Chief of Operations, requested that this assignment be given a high priority. Based upon the fact that the incident was in Manhattan, the task was assigned to A/C Pedro Carrasquillo, Manhattan Borough Commander. With the assistance of D/C Steven Kuhr, fundamental strategies were developed to conduct on-site relief and assignment of units to provide WTC coverage for the 12 hours after the "acute" event had been secured so that we could assume a long-term operation posture. This area was designated as the planning sector. A/C Ulysses Grant replaced A/C Carrasquillo as the Liaison Sector Officer at the Interagency Command Post.

Earlier in the incident, D/C Jerry Gombo had activated the NYC*EMS Emergency Operations Center at EMS headquarters. At this location the coordination of all EMS resources—with the goal of maintenance of full system effectiveness—took place. This difficult task was accomplished with the assistance of the staff from the Office of the Chief of Operations (OCO) and Chief John Lazzaro, D/C Mark Steffens, and D/C Thomas Ryan of the Communications Division. These individuals were confronted with a relentless task that became very complicated at times. What needs to be understood is that, as unbelievable as this might sound, the World Trade Center incident was only one of over 3,100 calls for help that the NYC*EMS system would be called upon to respond to on this date. Constant juggling and redeployment of available resources would need to be accomplished over a twelve-hour period in order to ensure proper response to all who requested EMS assistance. Additionally, OCO was required to send a representative to the NYC Mayor's Office of Emergency Management, Command and Control Center, to help with the overall citywide impact coordination and the role that NYC*EMS would need to provide.

Consistent with the highly specialized operations that were being conducted on-site, and in addition to the roles already mentioned in which the NYC*EMS Special Operations Division (SOD) was engaged, there existed the need for several other sectors. The utilization of NYPD aviation helicopters to evacuate patients through the airlifting of rescuers to the roofs of the World Trade Center Towers necessitated the establishment of a Med E Vac Operations Sector. Lt. Roy David of SOD was assigned this task.

Lt. Kevin Haugh of SOD was assigned to the SOD tactical support sector. With the assistance of the Emergency Response Squad, a group of highly trained EMTs in SOD, all support functions were executed, from electrical power supply and scene lighting to being poised to conduct hazardous materials decontamination in the event it became necessary (the latter under the direction of Lt. JoAnn Mack as the Haz Mat Sector Officer).

In order to maintain an adequate supply of equipment at the incident, five logistical support units and two Quartermaster Response Trucks responded to the site, and a formal logistics sector was established under the direction of Capt. Jace Pinkus. In addition to ensuring access and distribution of the supplies, Capt. Pinkus was also required to institute a system for tracking and recovery of equipment that was issued.

Ensuring the physical and mental health needs of rescuers at an incident of this magnitude is no small task. Capt. Fran Pascale was assigned to establish the rehab sector. By using NYC MTA transit buses for shelter, the EMS members of the service were afforded a rest area temporarily away from the elements of the weather and the demands of the scene. Food was available through the generosity of the American Red Cross, Salvation Army, and cafeteria facilities of Merrill Lynch and American Express. I extend my sincere thanks and appreciation to these organizations for their assistance and generosity to all the rescuers. All too often the care givers forget to give themselves or their brothers and sisters care at these incidents. Thankfully this was not the case at the WTC incident. On the mental health side, the NYC*EMS CISD team was activated and under the supervision of Ms. Lori Sullivan and Ms. Susan Sabor. On-site evaluations, assistance, and long-term evaluation strategies were quickly developed to aid all EMS MOS.

The final sector that was established was a morgue sector. This area received four of the five DOAs that were recovered that day. The fifth DOA was pronounced at the hospital after a unit transported him as a traumatic arrest. At this location the proper tracking and identification documentation was completed and a constant interface with officials from various agencies (PAPD, NYPD, FBI, and Chief Medical Examiner's Office) took place. Eventually the bodies were transported to the Chief Medical Examiner's Officer for further forensic investigation. The sixth DOA would be recovered weeks later.

Securement of the "Acute" Event

More than twelve-and-a-half hours into the incident the scene was secured, with more than 1,043 patients generated by the bombing of the World Trade Center. Of these numbers, 632 patients had EMS contact, 450 of whom were transported to 17 hospitals in three boroughs. A total of 176 were treated and released on the scene and six deaths were attributed to the event. The aggregate of patients above the 632 sought treatment at hospitals on their own.

The decision to secure the scene was made in order to start the incident reconstruction activities for the "acute" event and capture all associated activities for the WTC bombing on a single NYC*EMS Computer Aided Dispatch (CAD) call number. "Acute event" is defined as the activities and injuries that immediately surrounded the bombing itself. The long-term activities would encompass a separate accounting and reconstruction process, utilizing separate CAD numbers each day the operation was in existence.

Long-Term Operations and Support

After numerous on-site interagency meetings throughout the day, it was quickly determined that Operations would need to make the transition from reactionary to extended. The initial reports by the Port Authority of New York and New Jersey structural engineers was that it would be at least several weeks before they could complete shoring operations. The primary concern was for the B-5 level, which was presently supporting the rubble of the blast and the fear of secondary collapses. The blast produced damage that created almost 2,700 cubic tons of debris that would need removal from the sub-grade level. This activity would be an ongoing process while the search teams and investigators operated in the area termed "ground zero," the epicenter of the blast.

In order to properly support EMS operations during this stage of the incident, a request to activate the NYC*EMS collapse medic component of the NYC Interagency FEMA USAR Team was made and approved. Although this program is still in its implementation phase, I was able to access members of the service who had previously volunteered to participate in this program. In most cases they already had some training in operating in this type of environment and would be able to quickly interface with the other rescue workers, should a secondary collapse occur and rescuers become injured or trapped. By temporarily reassigning these members from their present commands to the WTC detail, we were able to decrease some of the mounting costs of the operation.

Although we initially operated under the pretense that there was only one person unaccounted for, the prevailing feeling among most rescuers was, if that was truly the case, we were very lucky. The day of the blast was wet, snowy, and windy. Based upon the weather, even if there was no one else present in the garage blast area at the time (lunch time) of the explosion, the possibility of homeless people seeking refuge from the elements was a plausible concern. We would later find out that, although we had valid fears, they were unfounded, with the last missing victim of the blast being recovered on the B-5 level under several feet of rubble seventeen days after the explosion. The consensus of all parties involved was that we were extremely fortunate that we were not forced to confront a greater number of trapped patients.

More immediate concerns that emerged were the logistical issues that surround an extended operation such as this. Through the courtesy of the Port Authority of New York and New Jersey, the owners of the WTC Complex, a 10 ft. × 40 ft. trailer was brought to the site for use as an EMS temporary headquarters vehicle (THV). In order to enhance the effectiveness of the extended operations, the following equipment was requested and brought to the scene: EMS Radio Services delivered a full radio complement including 400 MHz and 800 MHz bases, portable radio rack chargers, and spare batteries installed in the trailer; EMS Information Technology Division delivered a 486 computer and laser printer with full software support and a CAD dispatch terminal and modem permitting us to compartmentalize the operation, control the dispatch and assignment of units on-site, and support the lower Manhattan 9-1-1 operation because of the impact that traffic closures in the area were having on travel times; Consolidated Edison provided full power to the trailer; New York Telephone provided on request five voice lines and three data lines; and Bell South Communication Systems provided all the telephone instruments and a facsimile machine necessary to ensure the consistency of the EMS continued operations.

The EMS resources that were assigned to the extended WTC detail consisted of:

One (1)	Chief Officer Tour 2 and 3
One (1)	Captain All Tours
Two (2)	Lieutenants 1 - Staging/Triage; 1 - Safety Officer [SOD]
One (1)	Dispatcher
Two (2)	ALS Units 1 - On-site; 1 - Collapse Medic Unit
Two (2)	BLS Units 1 - On-site; 1 - Haz/Tac
One (1)	SOD Emergency Response Squad

Implementation of twelve-hour tours instead of the standard eight proved to be beneficial to both EMS and to the members who would be operating at the incident. The utilization of these resources were assessed on a daily and weekly basis in meetings that were held between Chief Robert McCracken, Chief of Field Services, and myself. Our meetings were convened after the two daily on-site interagency meetings. Risk assessment, structural stability, call volume, patients generated at the site, and the numbers of people operating in the "hole" were taken into consideration.

While we were still operating at this incident and at the over 3,000 calls a day we normally respond to, the City of New York was hit with the worst blizzard of the decade. The winds at the WTC site were clocked at 78.4 mph at one point, and required us to install additional shoring to the EMS THV because of the potential for it shifting and/or flipping over. Additional safety precautions were taken with EMS vehicle positioning and taping of windows for fear of breaking glass. After the storm passed, another safety concern arose from large chunks of ice, some as large as 6 ft. long, 3 ft. wide and 3 in. thick, that were falling off the towers and causing damage to vehicles, surrounding structures, and a high hazard to public safety personnel working in the area. Constant monitoring of this condition and declaring a hard-hat (helmets worn) operation was necessary until the Port Authority maintenance personnel were able to mitigate this condition.

Further considerations that were addressed included the ability to feed the EMS members of the service who were assigned to the extended operation and unable to leave the scene to procure meals. This concern was not unique to NYC*EMS but was shared by the multitudes of agencies that were operating on the scene. The Port Authority secured a location within One World Trade Center to serve food six times a day. The "disaster diner," as it was dubbed, provided a small haven for my members and gave them a break from the rigors of this scene, along with the opportunity to meet with other rescuers and officials who were operating at the incident.

The presence of U.S. Department of Labor, Occupational Health and Safety and the N.Y.S. Public Employee Safety Health Officers provided some interesting issues for all agencies to address on scene. First, all members were closely scrutinized for proper personal protective equipment and its applications. Next, a decision was made that all personnel who could operate in the sub-grade levels would be required to undergo pulmonary function tests, be fit-tested, and taught the use of APRs because of the dust levels and the potential of asbestos. This had little effect on the members of EMS SOD because of the stringent medical standards that they must adhere to during the Haz Mat physical assessment process, but it did require us to have the officers and line units assigned to the detail complete this process prior to going on-site. The testing process and equipment was provided, once again, by the Port Authority.

Because of the need to enhance security and limit access to the affected sixteen-acre campus, all persons, regardless of whether in uniform or not, were required to secure credentials for access to the site. These credentials, similar to concert backstage passes, established what level of access clearance an individual was granted. EMS personnel who were assigned to the incident for the long term were issued All Area Access, while the transient overtime units were given escorts to areas when required. Due to the crime scene and the ongoing investigation, access to the area was kept to an "as required" basis.

As the risks lessened, the level of EMS presence was gradually decreased, until the operation was finally secured on 3/20/93 Tour 2, with over 90 more patients being treated by EMS at the WTC site. The decision to secure the EMS operation was based upon the site becoming a "pure" reconstruction site, rather then a rescue/recovery/crime scene.

Summary

In retrospect, I find that some extraordinary tasks were accomplished by extraordinary people. To the members of New York City Emergency Medical Service, Volunteer Ambulance Corps of NYC, the New Jersey Mutual Units, and the commercial ambulance personnel who jumped in to assist with this unprecedented event, I salute you and thank you for your dedication and commitment to pre-hospital care.

Down the line we have learned many lessons that will be shared with the profession and future generations of EMTs and paramedics to come. Many of these lessons will be incorporated immediately in the way we respond to mass casualty incidents and disasters. We were confronted with a monumental challenge, never faced before in the history of the New York City Emergency Medical Service, and we were able to effectively respond to it consistent with the highest traditions of Emergency Medical Services. This incident is truly a story of teamwork, because, without it, many more people would have been injured or possibly died. To the hundreds of EMS professionals who responded, all I can say is, I'm proud to call you my peers and extend my heartfelt thanks for your assistance.

Appendix I

Additional Accounts of EMS Incident Management in the Real World

When the Mighty Mississippi Lived Up to Its Name

By Gary G. Ludwig, MS, EMT-P, Chief Paramedic, St. Louis Fire Department, St. Louis, MO

> I do not know much about gods, but I think that the river is a strong brown god—sullen, untamed and intractable. Patient to some degree, at first recognized as a frontier; useful, untrustworthy, as a conveyer of commerce; Then only a problem confronting the builder of bridges. The problem once solved, the brown god is almost forgotten by the dwellers in the cities—ever, however, implacable, keeping his seasons and rages, unpropitiated by worshipers of the machine, but waiting, watching and waiting.
>
> T. S. Elliott, *The Dry Salvages*

The Mississippi River, 2,348 miles long, is the second longest river, after the Missouri River, in the United States. Unfortunately for St. Louis, both rivers meet in a confluence with the Illinois River just north of the city of St. Louis, before flowing by the Gateway Arch. The Mississippi River provides a drainage area for about 40% of the country, and runs through or touches all or part of 31 states in the west. The Mississippi is a friend to many with irrigation for crops, transportation of commerce by barge from city to city, and provision of recreation. Because of unusually heavy rains in the upper midwest during the months of April and May of 1993, the Mississippi River became a foe to many who depend upon it. The first warning for St. Louis was on June 25, 1993, when the Army Corps of Engineers warned that rain

in the north would cause substantial flooding in St. Louis. By June 27th the river rose above what is considered the flood stage mark of 30 feet.

St. Louis, approximately 63 square miles, is a port city on the Mississippi River. The city of St. Louis is a county within itself, with its eastern border the Mississippi River. The population in St. Louis is approximately 400,000, but it swells to approximately one million during the business day.

Emergency medical services and all 9-1-1 medical calls are handled by St. Louis EMS, a "third service" operation. (The operation is now a part of the St. Louis Fire Department.) Consisting of some 172 personnel, the system handles roughly 65,000 emergency calls a year. St. Louis EMS has a fleet of 30 ambulances, numerous support and administrative vehicles, including a 42-seat-passenger bus that was converted into a mobile command post.

In July and August of 1993 the Emergency Medical Service for the city of St. Louis was tested in not only resources, but manpower and fortitude. Unlike most disasters, floods lend themselves to prediction and precision. Tornadoes skip and veer, hurricanes seem to wallow at whim, and large fires with multiple patients can come and go before you can even get to the scene. But a flood has only one way to go, and it usually follows a schedule. Each morning the 0800 staff meeting, which consisted of managers of the involved city, federal, and private agencies would meet in the Emergency Operations Center of the City's Emergency Management Agency (CEMA). Each meeting would include a report from each agency, including the Army Corps of Engineers. The Army Corps of Engineers would start off with a report from the hydrologist. Hand a hydrologist a contour map and form numbers on upstream rainfall and river readings, and you'll get back with great accuracy figures on which basements and streets will go under water and when.

The trouble is that this year's numbers refused to sit still. Upriver from St. Louis, the rain kept falling and the rivers kept rising. The longer the rain continued, the longer water-soaked levees strained to hold back the water. Eventually many levees broke and flooded farmlands, destroying 1993 crops. St. Louis is not farmland. It is a densely populated urban city, whose economy and residents are protected by a flood wall running for an 11-mile stretch adjacent to most parts of the city's waterfront. The rest of the city's riverfront is protected by high bluffs and earthen levees. However, some areas are unprotected. One area that particularly plagued emergency personnel in St. Louis was the River des Peres. River des Peres is a watershed basin that conveys most storm water from the central part of St. Louis County, through the south part of the city, finally emptying in the Mississippi River. The problem was not storm water, but backup of river water from the Mississippi River. As the Mississippi rose, so did the River des Peres. The flood stage in St. Louis is at the 30-foot mark. As of this writing, the river has crested three times, with the highest crest being at 49.4 feet on August 3rd, 19.4 feet over flood stage. In parts of the country, the Mississippi River was described as 8–10 miles out of its banks.

Mitigation

The first stage of any disaster is the mitigation stage. EMS providers are generally not involved in the mitigation phase of a flood disaster. In mitigation, the attempt should be made to control or reduce the disaster, long before the emergency occurs. A prime example of this was the construction of the flood wall on the St. Louis riverfront. The flood was designed to handle a flood up to the 54-foot mark. Unfortunately, it became apparent that the force and power of water can overcome anything manmade. Flood gates were closed along the wall to provide a continuous wall. The second month of the flood emergency, St. Louis officials were concerned about possible breaches in the levee wall. Breaches can occur not only at the flood gates, but under the wall, as well. On July 23 a 20-foot hole was created on the dry pavement side of the flood wall when water forced a path under a 24-foot wide, six-foot-deep footing of concrete supporting the flood wall. If a breach of any of the gates or wall were to occur at the highest point of the flood, which was 49.4 feet, an entire, densely populated, commercial and residential area stretching some 8 miles long and 1 mile wide would have been saturated with water.

Preparedness

The first warnings from the Army Corps of Engineers triggered the City's Emergency Management Agency (CEMA) into action. Often disasters will occur regardless of the efficiency of mitigation efforts. The preparedness phase of any disaster involves putting actions and plans into play that would minimize the impact of a disaster. The optimum preparedness phase involves planning for the most efficient and effective response to minimize injury and loss of life. The preparedness phase involved all vital city agencies meeting to develop a plan of attack if flooding were to occur. This involved looking at contour maps to determine what would be flooded at the 40-foot level versus the 48-foot level. Early in the planning stages, officials had no idea that water would reach the magnitude of the 49.4-foot mark. It was determined that the 43-foot mark would be the key indicator for the response phase of city agencies.

The preparedness phase for St. Louis EMS involved the establishment of staging areas, a check of resources and supplies, rescheduling employees to optimize human resources, and coordination with other city agencies responsible for the response phase of the flooding disaster. On July 11, the Army Corps of Engineers notified the city of St. Louis that on July 16 the flood stage along the River des Peres would reach the 43-foot mark. It was at this point that the city agencies switched from a preparedness phase into the response phase.

Response

The response phase of this flooding disaster was a prolonged and challenging chain of events that would test the St. Louis EMS system repeatedly with one misfortune after another. Up to the time of this writing, the St. Louis EMS system was tested with three record crests, levee breaks, one optional evacuation, two mandatory evacuations, sudden and severe thunderstorms with flash flooding, tornadoes, two fires in a propane tank farm, three break-away riverboat attractions on the St. Louis riverfront, and dignitary visits.

As with any disaster, each agency plays a vital role in supporting a disaster operation. In St. Louis, EMS supported the flood operations in a variety of ways. One of the first decisions in the preparedness phase was the establishment of a forward command post for police, fire, and EMS, near the flood-affected areas. Carondelet Park, a large city park, was chosen for the established command site. The site provided an opportunity to keep curiosity seekers and press away, while still providing easy access to the flood-affected areas. A press center was established near the command post, in order to allow senior staff to field press inquiries in the vicinity of the affected flood area.

The establishment of any EMS command post for a long-term operation in St. Louis involves activating the EMS mobile command post. The mobile command post is a converted 42-passenger bus donated to EMS by the public transportation authority for the St. Louis area. Conversion included painting and decaling the outside of the bus, removal of some seats, and the installation of workstations and tables with radios and computers for communications with all city agencies, plus fire/EMS districts in St. Louis County. Once on site, telephone lines were installed for voice and data communications. Computers were hooked up and connected directly to the CAD system at the EMS communications center for instantaneous information pertaining to street unit availability, as well as to the disaster. The computers' fax capability allowed reports to be generated on site to be immediately faxed into the Emergency Operations Center of CEMA. The fax capability was also important for receiving instantaneous information from a contracted weather service, which would fax hourly updates on weather reports for the south St. Louis area. In several cases, the unstable air over the midwest suddenly produced violent thunderstorms and flash flooding near the flood-affected areas. Flash flooding occurred several times over the course of the two-month operation, and on July 31 tornado warnings were issued for the city of St. Louis when multiple tornadoes were spotted aloft throughout the metropolitan area.

Sudden and violent thunderstorms can and did produce over 2–4 inches of rain within an hour. The effect of flash flooding played havoc on the levee walls. During and after the storm, levee walls gave way and caused immediate flooding of the nearby areas. The electric utility company provided a power drop to the bus, and tied it into a circuit breaker box already configured on the bus. A large air conditioner was then powered, providing the cooling necessary for St. Louis summers, while still providing power for lights, radios, and computer equipment. Also staged at the command post site was St. Louis EMS's disaster response vehicle (DRV). The DRV is a converted ambulance whose interior has been removed and replaced with metal shelving. Inside this vehicle is all required equipment for dealing with any multi-casualty event, such as 25 backboards, 14 jump kits, and multi-port oxygen tanks.

Once the command post was established, a detailed map was drawn of the flood-affected areas. The most flood-prone areas in south St. Louis included over 1,500 homes and businesses, running some three miles back from the mouth of where the River des Peres empties into the Mississippi. Contour maps provided by the sewer district gave indications of what would flood at different river stage levels. The detailed map was divided into sectors based on geography and ease of access. As the situation deteriorated, the entire St. Louis riverfront from one end of the city to the other was divided into labeled sectors and preplanned with staging areas and command posts in the event one of the flood gates or levee walls gave way.

Early in the response phase of the flooding emergency, the Office of Public Safety for the city of St. Louis initiated an evacuation and cut power and gas to those homes and businesses that were located in the contours of the flood-prone areas. The evacuation was optional. Many people chose to stay without electricity and gas. One of the many roles that EMS played was to perform daily checks on residents on a "critical list." This list was developed with the help of the power utility company and a door-to-door survey of residents in the area. Residents on this "critical list" were people whose lives were dependent upon electricity or had some type of medical condition that might be aggravated by the lack of electricity. The survey and medical list produced people who were on home ventilators, used electric wheel chairs, and had a multitude of other medical conditions. Each day St. Louis paramedics would visit the homes of these people to check on their current condition and determine if any further assistance would be required from the city. In some cases, the residents were evaluated and taken to the hospital when it was determined that their health was deteriorating. EMS paramedics also assisted disabled individuals who chose to evacuate to a friend or relative's home. At times an ambulance was required, but on most occasions, a specially equipped van, working under the auspices of a St. Louis service that cared for disabled people, was utilized.

Sandbagging Operations

One of the most critical operations of the flooding was to raise the levees with sandbags. A request for volunteers was disseminated by the St. Louis Streets and Forestry Departments three weekends in succession resulted in a phenomenal response. As the rivers would rise, the levee walls would have to go higher. Volunteers were asked to report to a staging area several miles away from the sandbagging operations. From there they were bused into the sandbag production site or to the levee where sandbags were needed. On any given day, there were approximately 2,000–2,500 people sandbagging. Sandbagging operations were hampered by the typical St. Louis weather in July and August with its high heat and humidity. Heat indexes (the combination of heat and humidity to produce what the temperature really feels like) went well over 100 degrees on several days, prompting the St. Louis Health Department to issue heat alerts.

One of EMS's most important roles was to support the sandbagging by providing heat relief and minor first aid to the volunteer sandbaggers. The heat relief was the primary concern. At each sandbagging site, EMS crews established cooling stations on large passenger buses and provided icewater-soaked towels. Water sprays were set up by the St. Louis Fire Department, and the Red Cross and Salvation Army provided cool drinks and food. Paramedics patrolled the sandbagging operations, looking for volunteers who might be yielding to the heat. Band-aids and aspirin would be used during the entire operation. In all, six volunteers were transported to the hospital suffering from heat exhaustion.

Levee Breaks

At any given time, and at any place, a water-soaked earthen and sandbag levee could and did break. Immediately, all EMS crews assigned to the flood detail were told to report to a level-one staging area near the incident. Four additional paramedic units and a field supervisor redirected from street operations were also dispatched to a level-two staging area at the command post in Carondelet Park. After conferring with the sewer district officials and reviewing the contoured maps, it would be immediately known what area would flood. Paramedics would converge on what would be the affected areas to notify any residents, who had not voluntarily evacuated, to evacuate immediately due to the impending rushing water. Sometimes this was done on foot, if time allowed. Other times, PA systems on the ambulance were used to make the notifications. Other paramedic crews from the level-two staging area would support Street and Forestry

Department crews who would converge on the breach with strike teams of front end loaders and over 50 loaded dump trucks of sandbags. Working in rushing water up to their chests was extremely dangerous. In many cases, the breach would be "plugged," but on several occasions strike teams and EMS crews were pulled out because the water level was just too unsafe. These areas, along with the homes and businesses, would be completely inundated with water within a short period of time. Another danger to the flood emergency was "sand boils." Sand boils are areas on the dry side of the levee walls that are saturated with water underground. The water attempts to force its way up out of the ground to equalize with the water on the flooded side of the levee walls. In some cases, it was not uncommon to see a city street rise three feet in the course of ten minutes.

A Pivotal Time

The days of July 30, 31, August 1 and 2 would become a true test of the St. Louis EMS system. On July 30 a flooded Phillips Petroleum propane tank farm, near where the River des Peres empties into the Mississippi, reached a critical point. A total of 51 tanks, each containing 30,000 gallons of liquified propane, began shifting and floating in the flooded waters. As the tanks began to float and shift, stress was placed on the valves under each tank. Leaks were detected, prompting St. Louis officials and Phillips Petroleum personnel to make decisions on how to resolve this critical situation. While experts were flying in from all parts of the nation to help remedy the situation, the determination was made to initiate a mandatory evacuation of a half-mile radius of the tank farm. On July 30th that evacuation took place. St. Louis police and firefighters went door-to-door notifying residents. St. Louis EMS set up a forward command post in the back of the deputy chief's van in the affected area utilizing the incident command structure. This command post was known as "Boniface Command," since the command post was established in a small park outside the St. Boniface Catholic Church. A staging area was established with ambulances, transportation buses, and specifically equipped vans for the disabled in another part of the affected area. As a request would be received for someone who required medical evaluation or was in need of special assistance, a triage officer was sent to the scene to evaluate the needs of the individual. The triage officer would then contact the staging officer and request manpower and equipment.

After evaluation by the experts, the decision was made to slowly bleed the tanks, creating a slow release of propane into the air with eventual dissipation. All ignition sources were eliminated because all electric and gas was cut within the half-mile affected evacuation area. On August 1 at around 7 P.M., the radios at the Carondelet Park command post began cracking that there was a flash fire in the propane tank farm and one of the tanks was on fire. Immediately, all EMS crews in the flood affected area were told to report to the level-two staging area, with additional crews and field supervisors dispatched to support the operation. The level-two staging area was in the cold zone, since it pertains to a hazardous material incident. A roll call of bed availability was immediately initiated by the St. Louis EMS communications center over a computerized network. Two alarms were struck by the St. Louis Fire Department to supplement their already established task force for the propane tank farm operation. The fire was extinguished, but not without extensive damage to a one-story brick building on the propane tank farm. Evidently vapor from the propane found an ignition source, creating the fire. As of this writing, the source of the ignition has not been determined. Five tanks containing eight-inch pipes were of particular concern. Computer modeling and further evaluation showed a release of all five simultaneously would produce a 4000 ft. × 4000 ft., twelve-foot-high cloud of propane gas.

With the new computer model predictions, the half-mile radius was not sufficient. Therefore, the decision was made to expand the mandatory evacuation area to a one-mile radius. Starting at 6 A.M. on August 2, the evacuation of 1,300 homes and 11,800 people began. EMS would play the same role as before, providing assistance to those infirmed and to those individuals with medical needs. Since the area was larger than the first evacuation, three sectors were set up. These sectors corresponded with the maps already sectored when the command post was established. Each sector was assigned a field supervisor. Hence, under the incident command system, call letters were known as "Sector G, H, or I Command." A staging area was established outside the affected area with ambulances, buses, and specialty vans for the disabled. The command post in Carondelet Park coordinated the evacuation. A major challenge of the evacuation was moving the residents of a nursing home. Within three hours, the entire evacuation was completed.

The propane tank quandary has yet to be resolved. In the history of the United States, no incident of this type has ever been encountered. Officials of Phillips Petroleum told the media, "We are writing the book on this one." In preparation for any cataclysmic event, an explosion at the propane tank farm was pre-planned. Staging areas for ambulances from other EMS/fire districts were established, and treatment sites for the injured were organized in a cold zone outside the one-mile radius. Medical equipment, along with multi-casualty provisions were pre-staged for days in the treatment area in the event something tragic were to occur.

Hazardous Materials

With the rise of the river, many commercial and industrial complexes besides the propane tank farm were affected. It was not uncommon to see railroad tank cars and large chemical holding tanks sitting in water. On one particular site, holding tanks containing 750,000 gallons of benzene were submerged in river water. At another site, a railroad tank car containing PCBs was completely submerged. In preparation for any major release that might occur, all sites were pre-planned in regard to what type of chemical(s) was on-site, what the health hazards would be, and the necessary treatment if contact was made with the product by rescue personnel or civilians. All information was logged into computers in the command post, and, if necessary, could be instantly recalled and printed out by sector.

Recovery

The fourth stage of any disaster is recovery. The recovery phase of any flood emergency can be just as intensive and far-reaching as the response phase. Besides the health hazards of mosquitos and contamination of the water from chemicals, the prospects are great for someone cleaning a flooded home to encounter river snakes, rats, and leeches. Part of the recovery phase for St. Louis EMS included employees who worked the flood detail to be debriefed by critical incident stress debriefing teams. The concern for the employees relates to the stress of working long periods without rest and little time off. Although briefings were available during the flood emergency, employees were encouraged, once the flood waters had receded, to take advantage of this service.

Stretching Resources

Unlike a fire, plane crash, or train accident, floods are not quite so dramatic. However, high-intensity scenarios, as previously mentioned, are of much shorter duration than the flood experienced in St. Louis in 1993. Of particular concern to the administration of St. Louis EMS were fatigue factors of personnel and the stretching of resources over prolonged periods of time. Overtime personnel were necessary to maintain the staffing levels needed for the flood operations. EMS crews assigned to the flood emergency were often held over based upon the predictions of the river stage. During prolonged flooding, rivers tend to lower and rise. The Mississippi River in St. Louis had crested three times. In other words, the river has gone down, but then rose again to a new height due to rainfall from the north. Therefore, the need to have the maximum amount of personnel assigned to the emergency was not as significant when the river stage lowered. Minimum staffing was necessary for the maintenance of assignments required to be performed by EMS. Usually one week ahead of time, EMS administration knew if flooding or levees would break based upon predictions made by the Army Corps of Engineers. It was at these critical times that additional EMS crews were placed on duty for the flood emergency. Sudden and powerful thunderstorms occurred during the flood emergency that created flash flooding. The flash flooding would cause levees to give and break. However, thanks to the hourly fax updates from the contracted weather agency, EMS administration was able to make staffing adjustments hours ahead of time.

A major concern to the administration during the flood emergency was still the primary role of EMS: expedient response times on the streets. July and August are traditionally the busiest time of the year for St. Louis EMS. It is not uncommon to receive over 250 calls per day, resulting in 175 transports to a hospital. Therefore, the administration could not lose focus of normal street operations. An operational "Status 5" was declared by the Chief. This was the first time that St. Louis EMS invoked a "Status 5." This meant:

1. sick leave and emergency vacation requests were denied,
2. mandatory overtime could be utilized,
3. 9-1-1 calls for minor emergencies were referred to other agencies,
4. patients were transported to the closest, most appropriate emergency receiving facility and not to the hospital of their choice,
5. hospital diversion requests were not honored, and
6. EMS personnel were subject to emergency recall on their off days.

"Status 5" proved successful. July response times averaged 6.8 minutes from the receipt of the call. In July EMS ran 6,083 9-1-1 calls and transported 3,773 patients, including flood patients. "Status 5" resulted in approximately a 20% reduction in responses and patients.

Dignitary Visits

As with any calamity, dignitary visits from elected officials and VIPs are inevitable. During the flood emergency, St. Louis received visits from such individuals as the Reverend Jesse Jackson, Bishop Desmond Tutu, numerous elected officials, and Vice President Albert Gore. It was not necessary for EMS to provide medical coverage to the dignitaries except for the Vice President in response to a request by the Secret Service. Vice President Albert Gore visited the St. Louis area in mid-July to view the devastation and efforts to control the destruction. To cover the event, a special operations tactical unit was assigned to the visit of the Vice President.

Documentation

On July 25, the city of St. Louis was declared a disaster area by President Clinton. With the declaration, federal funding would become available for reimbursement of expenses from the Federal Emergency Management Agency (FEMA). Therefore, it became necessary to maintain detailed records on all employee hours, mileage, and fuel used for all vehicles, supplies that needed to be purchased, or any other operational or administrative expense. The basic rule was to document when in doubt.

Conclusion

The flood throughout the midwest and St. Louis is described as a "once every three hundred year" flood. Over 45 people died as a result of the flooding throughout the midwest. Thankfully, no one died and no serious injuries resulted in St. Louis as a result of the flood. The lack of serious injuries or deaths can be attributed to good pre-planning, the predictability of the flood, the capability of dealing with most situations that arose—and luck. Being a paramedic in a large urban city can bring out cynicism when observing deaths from violence and crime. However, the reaffirmation in humanity was apparent when countless volunteers responded to the call for help. Those who could not sandbag donated food, money, clothes, and their time in shelters. The desire and longing to help a person in need was extraordinary.

When the "Great Flood of 1993" is over and done, critiques will show St. Louis EMS's shortcomings. But those critiques will also show that man took on nature and survived. At the time of this article, Gary Ludwig was the Deputy Chief of EMS for the city of St. Louis. He was the incident commander responsible for the entire flood operation in St. Louis. Several months after the completion of flood operations in St. Louis, he accepted a position as the Chief Paramedic for the St. Louis Fire Department. In April of 1997, St. Louis EMS was merged into the St. Louis Fire Department, and Gary now serves as the EMS Bureau Chief.

Gary is also an elected EMS Executive Board member of the International Association of Fire Chiefs. He has a total of 20 years EMS and fire experience in the city of St. Louis. Gary sits on several state and national emergency service boards, editorial advisory boards of several professional trade journals, the faculty of several colleges, and the adjunct faculty of the National Fire Academy. He lectures frequently at EMS and fire conferences nationally, has a Master's Degree in Management, and is a licensed paramedic in the State of Missouri.

On the Job in Colonial Heights, Virginia

By Dennis L. Rubin, Battalion Chief, Chesterfield Fire Department, Chesterfield, VA

On August 6, 1993, the central Virginia region was assaulted by a killer tornado. The class III tornado developed out of the west at about 1338 hours, without any warning (See Table A1-1 for categories of tornadoes.) Only after receiving damage and eyewitness reports, did area officials realize that a path of death and destruction was cut along the James and Appomattox River basins. In its wake, four people lay dead, hundreds were injured, and over 65 million dollars of property was damaged. The cities of Colonial Heights and Petersburg took direct hits, causing tremendous destruction. Two other communities, Chesterfield and Hopewell, were smacked by glancing blows. The public safety response to this disaster is probably unparalleled in the history of the Commonwealth of Virginia. Over 1,000 responders from some 60 plus agencies would be used to restore order and begin the recovery process. This article will take a detailed look at the incident management structure, strategy, and tactics that were implemented to make sense out of total chaos.

Emergency calls for assistance spiked as soon as the tornado touched down. The alarms ranged from wires down to automobile accidents to building collapses. Due to the high volume of alarm activity, emergency response resources were spread thin. Because of this resource situation, only one engine, two ambulances, and one command officer were dispatched to the Wal-Mart building collapse. The initial size-up indicated that it was a

Table A1-1 Tornado F-Scale*

Category	Winds/Speed	Damaged
CLASS I	72–112mph	Moderate damage. Roofs peeled off; windows broken; trees snapped; trailers moved or overturned.
CLASS II	113–157mph	Considerable damage. Roofs torn off; weak structures and trailers demolished; trees uprooted; cars blown off road.
CLASS III	158–206mph	Roofs and some walls torn off well-constructed houses; some rural buildings demolished; car-lifted and crumbled.
CLASS IV	207–260mph	Houses leveled leaving piles of debris; cars thrown some distance.
CLASS V	261–318mph	Well-built houses lifted clear off foundation and carried a considerable distance and disintegrated.

*Fujita Scale

major incident. The Wal-Mart collapse turned out to be the most serious incident of many that the tornado caused. Deputy Chief Edward Snyder of Colonial Heights Fire Department assumed incident command and implemented the initial action plan (See Table A1-2 for more about the Colonial Heights Department.) The first two objectives were to assess the situation and request mutual aid assistance.

The first scenes at this collapse were hard to comprehend. About 40% of the building lay in total ruins. There were some 150 to 200 people inside the store just prior to the collapse. The building's electrical power went out and occupants indicated that sales associates and shoppers had only a few seconds' notice to brace for the impending disaster. Instantly the store occupants became victims and most needed emergency medical care. Included in this group of unlucky souls was an off-duty Chesterfield firefighter, Kenny Aliceburg. Kenny clung to one of the roof support columns for his life. The noise was deafening and the confusion tremendous, as the structure crumbled. Firefighter Aliceburg, being uninjured, helped with the evacuation and medical treatment process. Miraculously the lion's share of injuries were priority 2s and 3s. There were two priority 4 patients and

Table A1-2 About the Department

Colonial Heights, Virginia. Chief A. G. Moore, Jr.	
Personnel	12 career and 80 volunteer members
Apparatus	2 engine companies
Population	16,500
Area Served	8 square miles

less than ten priority 1 victims. One of the priority 1 patients would expire at the hospital shortly after transport.

The building was a typically large discount store. It was type II construction, noncombustible, primarily steel frame with brick veneer. The occupancy measured 385 feet (across) by 295 feet (deep) for a total of 113,000 square feet of floor space. The building was classified one story, however the ceiling height was 30 feet to allow for high-pile storage. The building consisted of 72 bays (the span from one load-bearing column to another). Twenty-seven of them were missing or destroyed after the tornado hit. The winds ripped a wide path from the front of the store by the main entrance to the rear of the building. Further, there was another area of collapse toward side "D" of the structure that was not connected to the primary damage area. The belief is that the tornado spawned "baby" tornados, and one of these caused the separate pancake collapse.

The parking lot was a small-scaled disaster on its own. Over 100 vehicles were tossed about like so much confetti. The glass from almost all the vehicles now lay in the parking lot. Access to the building was severely limited due to the numbers of wrecked and piled-up vehicles. Early into the incident, a fleet of tow trucks was required to move the wreckage so that apparatus and heavy equipment would have access. The tornado's energy lifted forty-foot trailers and smashed them into the loading dock bays. The resemblance was more warzone like, rather than new suburban shopping mall.

As help arrived, the command structure was expanded to manage the operating resources. The unified command process would be aggressively exercised to coordinate the many jurisdictions that work together under one action plan. Due to the volume of resources from the Chesterfield Fire Department (see Table A1-3), Senior Battalion Chief Paul Shorter was appointed Deputy Incident Command. The next tactical objective was to gain scene control and support emergency medical operations. There were scores of people (sales associates, shoppers, and passers-by) who were working adamantly to remove as much debris as possible to locate trapped

Table A1-3   Resources Deployed

• 12 Engines	• 6 Special Units
• 4 Ladders	• 2 Haz Mat Units
• 4 Heavy Rescues	• 1 Mobile Surgical
• 700 Fire/Rescue Personnel	• 4 Track Hoes
• 29 Ambulances	• 100 Wreckers
• 4 Helicopters	• 11 Dump Trucks
• 8 Command Officers	• 5 Ten-Ton Cranes
• 250 Soldiers	• 3 Back Loaders

victims. These people reacted like an "ant pile" on a fresh piece of bread. They worked feverishly, in a disjointed and uncoordinated fashion. This freelance action was initiated in the collapse zone (of course) without any regard for personal safety. Live electrical equipment, leaking natural gas pipelines, releases of hazardous materials (pesticides), and secondary collapse were of great concern. The well-meaning citizens had to be removed and checked for injuries. Next, the building utilities had to be secured from street disconnects. The hazardous materials were identified by pre-plans and evaluated by the regional level III Haz Mat response team from Henrico County Fire Department. The team leader, Captain Floyd Greene, indicated that the dangerous commodities were in one of the few areas of the building that was left intact, posing no threat.

Once the scene and hazards were controlled, a primary search was organized and implemented. The building was divided into three sectors. Two companies (eight firefighters) were assigned to each rescue sector under the direction of Lt. John Crosby of the Chesterfield Fire Department. The objectives for the rescue sectors were to perform a primary search (mostly visual), identify any additional hazards, and mark locations of the facilities. This was a slow, difficult job. Upon completion, the rescue sectors located two facilities and were able to search about 70% of the building. The remaining 30% of the floor space was not accessible to the rescuers. The request for specialized resources was generated by the rescue sectors. Seven search dog teams were deployed to support the effort. The dog teams from Dogs East were able to arrive early into the situation. They conducted three or four building searches, confirming the primary "all clear."

Simultaneously the emergency medical care plan was now in full swing. Triage, treatment, and transportation sectors were established. Many of the injured left the scene after medical treatment was received and, in some cases, without even being checked by emergency medical care providers. A large number of these folks transported themselves to area hospitals. This self-transportation added to the confusion of tracking patient information. In one case, a person drove himself to one of the local emergency rooms. Upon his arrival, he realized that his automobile had been significantly damaged, causing the doors to be jammed. The hospital emergency room personnel had to call for the Fire Department to respond to the parking lot and extricate the gentleman. Because of the rapid treatment and movement of patients (planned and unplanned), triage tags could not be effectively used.

Fortunately many ambulances and other emergency medical resources were readily available. Due to the level of response and minimal number of seriously injured patients, the bulk of the emergency medical care was over within the first hour. Some 185 people were transported to only two local hospitals. The disproportionate distribution of patients from this incident was of some concern to local hospital officials. However, after investigation, it was learned that a significant number of the injured drove themselves to the hospitals. Also, the major highway (Interstate 95) was backed up for miles. This traffic jam eliminated all hospitals north of the incident as transport alternatives. The ability to treat, package, and transport this volume of customers within sixty minutes stands as a tremendous tribute to the regional effort and response to this disaster. The emergency medical care providers distinguished themselves as outstanding that day.

With the primary search and patient care complete, the incident action plan was updated. The focus now shifted to long-term operations, including removal of the two fatalities, searching the remaining 30% of the building with shoring techniques, removing valuables (weapons, drugs, money, and computer records), and scene security. While the Federal Emergency Management Agency's Urban Search and Rescue Task Force was in transit, manual debris removal got underway. Heavy equipment that was called for about one hour into the incident was now pressed into service.

The heavy equipment would remove the large slabs of falling building components. Once lifted outside the collapse zone, the materials were loaded into a fleet of waiting dump trucks for removal. Once the large items were taken away, hand crews would clear the topical debris, ensuring that no victims remained. This was difficult and primitive work. There was a high degree of danger working in this environment. The heavy equipment was noisy and vibrated significantly. Because of these factors, the remaining walls and roof assemblies had to be constantly evaluated for movement. The movement would be a sign of impending secondary collapse.

In order to perform the tremendous amount of detailed work, the military was called. Soldiers from the Fort Lee Army Post, under the command of the Lieutenant General Samuel Wakefield, were activated early and remained throughout the incident. To maintain communications, crew integrity, and personal safety, the soldiers were divided into crews of five and assigned to a qualified firefighter. Further, the military set up a "tent city" to support their operation. They were completely self-contained from food to sanitary facilities to sleeping quarters. As midnight approached, the FEMA Urban Search and Rescue Task Force arrived. Interestingly, this call made several "firsts" with the Virginia Beach USAR team. It was their "maiden voyage" as well as the first ground activation, the first in-state response, and the first time a federal USAR team was requested by the state government. The USAR team began to provide initial technical support. The task force leader, District Chief Melvin Mathias of Virginia Beach Fire Department, concurred with our incident action plan. The USAR team started their operation by shoring the collapsed area. Once shored, these areas were searched for victims. To ensure accuracy, the search dogs were sent into the now accessed areas. Fortunately there were no additional victims remaining in the building.

It took about eighteen hours to completely search the building. With the life safety priority met, emphasis was placed on debris removal, with great concern for the potential Haz Mat release. The Wal-Mart organization took an active role in the decision-making process at this point. In fact, throughout the operation the Wal-Mart management team was extremely helpful.

In summary, there were several major operational highlights that I would like to mention

- No Firefighter Injuries
- The Organization and Unification of the Command Structure
- The EMS Operations
- The Search/Extrication Operations
- The Logistical Support
- The Federal Emergency Management Agency USAR Task Force
- The Disaster Plan Implementation and EOC Operations

Finally, I would like to point out the lessons that were learned or reinforced at this incident:

1. **Staging**—The initial staging area was established too close to the incident, with many people attempting to self-deploy and "visit" the Operations section area. Once the staging function was moved and better organized, the dangerous practice of self-deployment was resolved. The need for a separate staging area was never more present.
2. **ICS Training**—Some of the agencies that attended the incident were unfamiliar with the incident command system process. The lack of knowledge negatively impacted the effectiveness of the resources on location. On many occasions, "on the spot" ICS training was conducted to be able to deploy resources.
3. **Urban Search and Rescue**—The Federal Emergency Management Agency's Urban Search and Rescue Task Force provided invaluable help. They were able to safely and efficiently conduct a primary search of the building that was not accessible to us. However, two areas presented themselves that could have been improved. When the USAR team arrived, there was a delay in their deployment. The reason for this delay was the request for assistance from the Old Towne Petersburg incident. The best way to have resolved this conflict would have been to request the USAR team from Fairfax County, as well. One team should have been dispatched to each jurisdiction. The other area for improvement is understanding the

USAR team's capability, resources, and needs. Not much, if any, information has been provided about how the team operates.

4. **Control Air Space**—Due to this newsworthy incident, a great number of media agencies covered the story. As part of the media operations, a large volume of aircraft was dispatched to the Wal-Mart scene. At various points, as many as ten aircraft were spotted in close proximity. The number of air operations around the incident increased the risk to the ground forces. As well, they added to the confusion and noise problems.

5. **Media Relations**—The appointment of a Public Information Officer was somewhat late in the process. With local and national media arriving quickly at this incident, we should have placed more emphasis on a media release strategy. Regular media briefings should have been held throughout the incident. The lack of early press releases frustrated the media. Several media representatives contacted me at the Operations area for information. I expressed the need for them to stand behind the barrier line and PIO would contact them. The media perceive that they have a "right to know" and therefore nearly demand information. This stress factor could have been relieved, and we could have utilized the media coverage to our advantage. Once established and supported, the media plan went very smoothly. At one point, the media were taken on guided tours of the destruction area.

This was a highly publicized and scrutinized event. Local, state, and national elected officials attended and reviewed our operation in detail. Only through the implementation and utilization of the incident command system could this massive amount of resources have been managed properly. The responders worked incredibly hard and ICS was successful.

Some of the Agencies Operating at This Incident

Colonial Heights Fire Department
Chesterfield Fire Department
Chesterfield County EMS
Richmond Fire Department
Henrico Fire Department
Henrico County EMS
Prince County Fire Department
Dinwiddie County Fire Department
U.S. Army—Ft. Lee
A & B Ambulance Service
Hanover Volunteer EMS
Virginia Beach Fire Department

High-Rise Fire in Wilmington, Delaware

By Deputy Chief Lawrence Tan, New Castle County EMS Division, Department of Public Safety, New Castle, DE

System Overview

The New Castle County EMS Division is a county, municipal-based agency. The agency is responsible for the delivery of out-of-hospital care to the 437 square miles of the county, including the incorporated and unincorporated areas, serving a population of approximately 468,000.

New Castle County EMS Division has an authorized staff of 97 personnel, which includes 5 EMS supervisors, 72 paramedics, and 14 emergency medical technicians. The executive staff includes a chief and 2 deputy chiefs of EMS. The division usually fields 7 paramedic units and one BLS ambulance on a 24-hour basis, and two additional BLS ambulances on a scheduled, Monday through Friday basis.

Emergency medical services are currently provided in a tiered response configuration with the county volunteer fire service, which provides basic life support ambulance capabilities. American Medical Response provides a contracted, basic life support service to the city of Wilmington, in conjunction with the New Castle County EMS paramedic services.

The city of Wilmington has a career fire department consisting of approximately 130 personnel that staff 6 engine companies, 2 ladder companies, and a heavy rescue squad.

Incident Overview

On Thursday, April 2, 1997, the county emergency communications center received a report of a building fire in the Delaware Trust Building at

902 North Market Street. The caller, a security guard for the facility, reported smoke on the 14th floor. The initial Wilmington Fire Department apparatus reported smoke conditions on the upper floors. New Castle County Medic 1 responded to the incident after the initial reports of a possible "working" alarm, and established an EMS staging area at 10th and Market Streets.

Wilmington Fire Department, crews continued to report heavy smoke and heat conditions on multiple floors of the 22-floor building, prompting the deputy chief of operations to declare a "general alarm" for the incident at approximately 2139 hours. The general alarm recalls all off-duty Wilmington Fire Department personnel, places all reserve apparatus in service, and brings in the volunteer fire service from the county to cover the vacant city fire stations.

At 2151 hours the incident commander requested an EMS assignment of 2 paramedic units, 4 basic life support ambulances, and an EMS supervisor for medical support. The on-duty EMS shift commander and EMS staff duty officer, a deputy chief of EMS, were notified to respond to the scene. All EMS units responded to the designated staging area at 10th and Market Streets. An exterior EMS triage/treatment area was established in a pedestrian walkway in the front of the structure. The triage area was placed in a manner that would not impede access or egress to the building by firefighters, but was in direct proximity to the main entry and exit point to the building. A perimeter was established by the Wilmington Police Department, essentially closing the pedestrian walkway for the duration of the incident. The EMS shift commander was originally assigned as the staging officer, but was later relocated and assigned as the interior EMS triage/rehab sector officer.

On arrival, the EMS deputy chief assumed responsibility for EMS group operations, while the EMS shift commander obtained a detailed accounting of all EMS personnel assigned to the incident. The deputy chief proceeded to the incident command post at 9th and Market Streets and obtained a briefing from the incident commander. The IC advised that units operating on the interior were reporting heavy fire and smoke conditions on the 13th through 16th floors, with smoke conditions on the 17th through 22nd floors. Further, he advised that the interior firefighting personnel were reporting no progress on the interior operations.

The IC requested that EMS personnel be assigned to the 12th floor staging area of the operation as a "forward" triage and rehab area. One paramedic crew (2 paramedics) and two BLS crews (2 EMTs each) were assigned to the interior triage. Paramedics used bottled spring water in the building to rehydrate firefighters, and provided medical support to firefighting units taken off line for a break. Progress reports to the EMS group commander were established at 30–45 minute intervals. Initially

A short time later, the paramedics in the interior of the building reported a "light haze" of smoke on the 12th floor. The IC was immediately notified, and interior EMS operations were relocated to the 10th floor, along with the interior firefighter staging area. Additionally, a patient evacuation and EMS supply route was established using the only functional elevator in the building. The patient evacuation plan enabled EMS group personnel to effect a timely removal of any firefighters who needed to be transported to a medical facility, and provided a coordinated transfer of care to exterior EMS personnel.

The Wilmington Fire Department had committed all of its resources to this operation, and had requested the following additional apparatus from the county volunteer fire service: 8 engines, with an additional 5 engines for cover-up in vacant Wilmington stations, 2 additional ladder companies, 6 additional rescues for air support, and 3 additional BLS ambulances. Later 4 of the cover-up engines would be assigned to the incident, resulting in 4 additional engines being requested from the county volunteer fire service for station coverage (17 total engines brought to the city of Wilmington).

On April 5, 1997, the Delaware Emergency Management Agency issued an "advisory" regarding the potential for asbestos and polychlorinated biphenyls (PCBs) at this incident. Subsequent testing for PCBs proved negative; however, asbestos was found to be present. The detailed accounting of all EMS units and personnel assigned to the incident permitted the EMS Division to document the potential exposure to asbestos and take the necessary post-exposure action. The EMS Division also forwarded copies of all available information to any outside agencies that participated in EMS group operations at this incident.

Results

The EMS Division was providing medical support to an estimated 250 firefighters during an extended firefighting operation that lasted approximately 8 hours. The medical support operation included continuous hydration of the firefighting force and other routine care such as eye irrigation. The EMS group treated seven firefighters and transported five to area hospitals, including a firefighter with chest pain who was admitted to the intensive care unit.

Additional EMS Division personnel and another EMS shift commander were activated to handle the continued demand for 9-1-1 system EMS requests.

Some Lessons Learned

The designation of an EMS staging area by the first arriving paramedics unit was of great assistance in coordinating the response of additional EMS units to the incident, and enabled us to maintain continuous accountability and tracking of EMS personnel assigned to the incident. This information proved to be valuable when the issue of potential exposure to hazardous materials was presented several days after the incident. The use of a "joint command post" facilitated the transmission of information to the EMS group and enabled us to provide immediate notification of any firefighting personnel who were being transported from the scene.

The designation of a single EMS group commander permitted the co-ordination of supply and/or personnel requests. Additional supplies, such as oxygen administration equipment, towels, blankets, etc., could be re-quested and coordinated with area hospitals. In fact, two local hospitals provided after-hour access to their laundry facilities in order to provide ad-ditional towels and blankets to the scene. The EMS group commander was also able to verify that the requesting persons had received the items. It would have been helpful for an aide to be assigned to the EMS group com-mander at the incident command post. The aide would have been helpful in tracking the status of EMS units and personnel, monitoring communica-tions, and maintaining documentation of the incident for the post-incident/after action report.

EMS units and personnel should have a designated point of contact when arriving on scene, and be issued specific instructions on their re-sponsibility during the operation. This is particularly true during multiple-agency operations, where unit and personnel accountability are a potential problem.

The use of the incident command system for EMS operations at the in-cident facilitated communications and provided a more effective manage-ment structure for EMS group operations at this incident. The ICS also identified the lines of communication for the duration of the incident. It is imperative that documentation of EMS group activities take place either at the communications center and/or at the incident scene. This documenta-tion can prove to be vital in the event of worker's compensation investiga-tions or subsequent post-incident analysis of agency activities. In our situation, the EMS progress reports documented unit and personnel activ-ity throughout the operation. Additionally we were able to identify exactly when firefighters presented themselves to EMS personnel for care and the time they were subsequently transported to a hospital.

Incident in Westwood, California

By James P. Denney

In the evening, the day before the 1984 Olympics opened, Westwood, California was crowded with celebrants anticipating the Olympic opening. The small village borders the UCLA campus and consists of shops, restaurants, coffeehouses, and ice cream parlors. On warm nights like this one, it is not unusual for a thousand or more students and residents to stroll the sidewalk, meet at small cafes, or simply socialize while enjoying a walk through town.

On this particular evening a young man, under the influence of PCP, decided to drive his car at high speed down a sidewalk crowded with an estimated 700+ men, women, and children, including Olympic athletes.

Needless to say, we were presented with an immediate event of magnitude having several components. Not only were we faced with a multicasualty incident of unknown proportions, a crime scene, and a multi-cultural polyglot tourist population, but the international press would be present to observe our actions and to comment on how effective our system would be in mitigating this catastrophe.

The first calls received by the PSAP indicated that a motorist had crashed into a bus kiosk at the southern end of the block, injuring approximately eight people. This call resulted in the dispatch of two rescue ambulances, a fire task force (truck company and two-piece engine company with a total of ten personnel), a Battalion Chief (BC), EMS District Commander, and a police unit for traffic control.

Upon arrival the scene was bedlam. The task force and EMS personnel immediately began assessing the extent of the incident and the triage of victims. The Battalion Chief established a command post and implemented the multi-casualty incident plan. The EMS District Commander arrived within a few minutes, was briefed by the BC, and began the establishment of a Medical Division.

Three additional rescue ambulances and another task force established immediate, delayed, and minor care holding areas, and an ambulance control officer was assigned along with a patient transportation recorder. A separate radio frequency in addition to the med-net was allocated to the Medical Division.

As additional victims made themselves known and the incident began to expand, additional resources and personnel were requested. I arrived about 25 minutes into the incident and was immediately given the responsibility for incident site survey. (My initial assignment was to "360" the incident to ensure we had accurate information on the size and scope of the problem.)

By the time I had completed my survey, I had determined that the incident was linear and extended approximately 550 feet to the north in an eight-foot-wide corridor. I estimated that there were an additional 60 to 80 victims in various categories, extending the length of the incident. By now, the site was in pandemonium with convergent volunteers and spectators hampering rescue efforts and medical operations. I reported my findings to the Incident Commander, and additional resources were requested and dispatched to a staging area to the east of the incident. An ambulance staging area was established in the center of the incident, where a side street gave access and a traffic flow pattern was developed. A police command post was established adjacent to the Incident Commander and appropriate crowd control measures were taken.

The hospital system for the area was contacted by the local Medical Alert Center, and bed availability was obtained in addition to "blanket treatment orders." A medical cache was ordered and delivered to the Medical Division, where it was used to care for patients and to restock ambulances. (A medical cache provided BLS level supplies and equipment to treat 50 casualties.) An equipment recovery center was established adjacent to the Medical Division, where recovered backboards, traction splints, and other equipment were stored by returning ambulances.

Once the scope of the incident was determined and adequate resources were on scene, all patients requiring attention were processed (treated, packaged, and transported) within 48 minutes. The entire incident took less than two hours to complete. The Incident Command System provided a sequential, ordered, management tool that guaranteed a disciplined response to an otherwise chaotic event.

The AmTrak Sunset Limited Disaster in Mobile, Alabama

By Paul R. Smith, Fire Service Captain, REMTP, Mobile Fire-Rescue Department, Mobile, AL

September 22, 1993, a day that will never be forgotten by the members of the Mobile Fire-Rescue Department or the community as a whole. This was the day Mobile was indoctrinated into the world of Mass Casualty Disasters.

The AmTrak Sunset Limited, a coast-to-coast passenger train traveling from California to Florida, was carrying 206 passengers and crew members as she made her way south. While passing through New Orleans, LA, she was delayed for 33 minutes for AC and toilet repairs. There are many who say these 33 minutes doomed her. She arrived in Mobile, AL 30 minutes behind schedule. As she cleared the CSX railyard heading north out of Mobile, she gained speed to approximately 72 MPH, on her way to meet with destiny.

Meanwhile the tugboat MV Mauvilla was also moving north on the Mobile River. It was one of those foggy Mobile mornings along the river. The MV Mauvilla was piloted by Willie Odom, as testimony has shown, slowly making the trip north on the river.

Just north of Mobile in the middle of the river sits an island, Twelve Mile Island. At the north end of the island, the river forks. To the right you have the continuation of the Mobile River. To the left is big Bayou Canot, a navigable waterway, not for commercial use. For approximately one-half mile into the bayou, there is a railroad bridge, which, at that time, was not marked by lights and sits approximately six feet off the water. The MV

Mauvilla made the wrong turn! As the Mauvilla moved deeper into Bayou Canot, testimony has shown, Mr. Odom notes that the heal of his tow disappeared and he felt a bump. The rest of the story is a true tragedy.

The first call for help was received by an E-911 call taker at 0301 hours. Mr. Warren Carr from CSX railroad called and advised, "We have a passenger train derailed at the Bayou Sara drawbridge. People are in the water and cars are on fire." As you can imagine, the next 18 minutes in the E-911 communications center were very confusing. The operators were unfamiliar with the locations on the river and in the delta. They are used to taking street addresses or names. In a desperate attempt to locate the reported accident and to confirm its existence, the operators called all of the surrounding jurisdictions: Prichard, Chickasaw, Saraland, and the most northern jurisdiction to Mobile, Satsuma. To make matters even worse, the call-back number Mr. Carr gave was hooked up to a recording. This made the stress level in the E-911 center even greater for the operators. Now unable to even confirm the accident, the operators continued their frantic search for information on the accident. The company officer on duty at Fire Station 21 was called for information on the area. All he could assist with was advising the operators that they respond in the area when needed. After several more calls to the surrounding jurisdictions, the location was narrowed down to the Mobile River, then the northeast corner of the city limits.

The operator called the fire boat captain to ask if he had responded to Twelve Mile Island. At 0320 the initial dispatch was sent: "Attention Engine 21, Engine 14, Engine 1, Truck 4, District 1 Chief, and Fire Boat 2, for a possible train derailment at Bayou Sara drawbridge at the Mobile River." Eighteen minutes had elapsed from the receipt of the initial call.

I was the EMS Shift Commander that tragic morning. I responded prior to being dispatched along with Fire Rescue 14. While en route to the incident, Fire Boat 2 confirmed the accident via the marine radio. A Scott Paper Company (now Kimberly Clark) tug from the Scott fleet was on scene along with the MV Mauvilla. District 1 Chief Vernon Hall advised all units to stage at the Saraland Fire Department on HWY 43.

While I was en route, fire alarm called me and advised that we had 226 people on board the train. With this information I started notifying other agencies from which I felt we would need assistance. I first notified the University of South Alabama Medical Center, our regional level one trauma center, and the South Flite of the incident, to place the helicopter on standby to notify all area hospitals in Mobile and Baldwin Counties. Second, I notified Newmans Ambulance Service. Off-duty Firemedic Ed Wood was the supervisor on duty. I told him to start two ALS units, including himself, to Saraland, notify all private ambulance companies in the area, and to call in off-duty personnel. Next I contacted Dr. Ballard for Medical Control at Springhill Memorial Hospital, which the Mobile Fire-Rescue Department uses as our Medical Control Hospital. As the units started arriving in the staging area in Saraland, Chief Hall advised we would be unable to reach the scene through Saraland. He had been led approximately 1.5 miles into the area by a Saraland police officer, hoping to locate a land entrance to the incident scene. All units were ordered to relocate to the Cochran Bridge at Scott Paper Company on Bay Bridge Road, which sits on the Mobile River. En route to Scott, I called a fire alarm to notify the EMS chief and to call CSX to put together a rescue train, flat beds or box cars, and an engine—anything that could transport crews and equipment up and patients back.

Fire boat 2 arrived at the derailment scene at approximately 0400 hours, over one hour into the incident. South Flite advised just prior to the arrival of the fire boat: "They could see cars in the water, a large fire, and possible survivors in the water and on the tracks."

The command post was established by me at Scott Paper at 0410 hours. The Incident Command System was established, all Chief Officers were to be notified by fire alarm, EMA was notified, and all off-duty Firemedics were to be called into the staging area. Initially we used four sectors of the ICS: Operations, which included Task Force 1, two engine companies, one ladder company, and two fire rescues (for a total of twelve firefighters, three Firemedics, and one intermediate EMT); Planning; Logistics; and Medical. Finance was added later as staff personnel arrived in staging.

Task Force 1 loaded the rescue train to start toward the derailment. WKRG TV slipped a cameraman on board the train. He produced the only early photos and documentation of the scene and events. Ambulance staging, landing zones, and fire apparatus staging officers were appointed as additional resources arrived. When I was relieved of command by EMS Chief Byrd and then Deputy Chief Dean, I moved into my normal role as EMS Sector Officer. In this sector I had responsibility for extrication, triage, treatment, transport in, and rehab, both on site and, the remote areas. As additional personnel arrived at the staging area, I was able to assign people to start setting up the main triage area, rehab, and a possible, temporary morgue.

When the rescue train arrived on scene, "The people were waiting on the tracks," Fire Service Driver REMTP George Watson advised later in a debriefing session. "When the light came on, they got up and started walking towards us in silence," he said.

The fire boat activities included initial search and rescue, but all victims were removed from the water either by the tugs or by assistance from each other. No search of the cars was completed initially due to the lack of manpower on the fire boat which had responded with the usual three-man crew. The scene was described by Captain Greg Foster from the fire boat as "Something you would only see in a movie!" The fire consisted of three parts: (1) the train contents, three engines, the baggage car, and the crew coach; (2) a large area fuel fire caused by the ruptured fuel cell carrying 2500 to 3000 gallons of diesel fuel; and (3) the creosote bridge pilings and cross ties. All fires were allowed to burn, with only minimal suppression activities. This was because the fire was providing the only light in the bayou, except for three spotlights on the tugs and fire boat.

At day break, the reality of the incident set in. It was learned that we had one car half submerged, one car completely submerged, and dozens missing. The fire that was allowed to burn stubbornly persisted. The fire boat was unable to move around for fear of hitting a missing victim.

I was advised that the rescue train was departing the scene at 0530 hours, with 126 patients on board. It arrived at the main triage area, where the patients were retriaged, their names recorded, and then they were transported by ambulance or bus to local hospitals. I had made the decision that anyone off the train would be transported to the hospital for observation, regardless of a complaint of injury or not. I decided this because everyone who went into the water was contaminated with diesel fuel and I felt, emotionally they all needed to talk to someone.

A kink was thrown into my smooth-running EMS Sector when Task Force 1 advised that we had 28 victims coming in by tug to the east side of the river at Scott Fleet's Dock at 0615 hours. A second triage area was then established and these patients were triaged and transported accordingly. At this same time, I was advised by fire alarm of five patients at the United States Coast Guard Aviation Training Center Base at Bates Field, approximately 20 miles west of our location. They had been airlifted from the scene and flown there. These patients were removed from the north side of the accident. Four ambulances responding from the south part of the county were diverted to Bates and these patients were transported.

At 0640 hours the rescue train was loaded once again with personnel and extrication equipment for a second trip to the scene. Dr. John McMahon, our Fire Physician and Medical Control Physician, along with two additional physicians from the University of South Alabama Medical Center, went on the second trip. By approximately 0720 hours, Task Force 1 advised that we had no remaining treatable patients and that we needed eighty to one hundred body bags.

MFRD's activities continued on scene and at the command post. By 0730 hours, overhaul operations commenced. Divers from Lee Diving Company started searching the submerged cars. MFRD and Mobile Police Department photographers and Identification Sector arrived on the scene. At approximately 0750 hours the last patient was transported to the hospital from triage. That was the same time that the first patient was being discharged from the hospital.

When the first body was recovered, the need for a temporary morgue became apparent. A barge was used for an on-site, temporary morgue. The barge was used as an ID section and Alabama Department of Forensic Sciences could set up at the Port of Chickasaw. By 1130 hours national and international news media were at the Port of Chickasaw.

MFRD's three primary activities were: (1) to continue fire overhaul; (2) to retrieve and remove victims; and (3) to man the temporary morgue barge. Within the first 24 hours, most of the passengers and crew had been accounted for. The duration of body recovery lasted three days.

The three engineers in the lead engine were recovered on Friday, 48 hours after the accident, buried fifty-seven feet down in the north river bank. The final count of victims was 206. 159 patients were triaged, treated, and transported to local hospitals. Forty-two passengers and 5 crew members lost their lives that foggy Mobile morning. This became the worst Amtrak accident in U.S. history and the largest mass casualty disaster ever to occur in Mobile. Every agency involved should be commended on its performance.

I-10 Bayway Accident in Mobile, Alabama

By Paul Smith, Fire Service Captain, REMTP, Mobile Fire-Rescue Department, Mobile, AL

Monday, March 20, 1996, 0620 hours. My partner, Firemedic G. A. Tony Rutland, and I rolled out of bed, 40 minutes until shift change at Central Fire Station, Fire Rescue 3. The night went by with only one minor glitch, a run around 2100 hours. As we slept this morning, the fog rolled in over the bay and causeway, spilling slightly into downtown Mobile. Now as we prepared to be relieved of duty, the morning routine would soon be broken by yet another run.

At 0637 hours the alarm sounded for Fire Rescue 3 and Engine 2. There was a wreck with injuries on I-10 eastbound between the tunnel and the causeway. When I made it to the truck, Tony had checked en route already. I looked at Tony and told him, "This is probably going to be another minor accident which causes us to get off late." Oh, how wrong I was to be about that. Late yes, minor no. We respond to many calls on the Bayway, many of which I would say are minor. Yes, some are very bad accidents, but not at this time of the morning. The I-10 Bayway spans seven miles over the Mobile Bay and river delta connecting Mobile and Baldwin Counties.

En route we noticed some mild fog conditions in the downtown area, and as we entered the I-10 George Wallace Tunnel, I remember not thinking much about this at all. The area has fog on a regular basis. Going through the tunnel the procession of emergency vehicles was: Engine 2, Fire Rescue 3, and a single Mobile police car. We passed approximately

40 vehicles, including several tractor trailers, in the tunnel. Just as we exited the tunnel, Fire Rescue 3 signaled to Engine 2 that we were going to pass. As we passed, the MPD unit passed us all. This turned out to be one of the best things that could have happened.

Once out of the tunnel, there was some light fog. Again we did not pay it much attention because fog isn't out of the ordinary. Approximately a half mile east of the tunnel, the fog thickened. Visibility was approximately 50 to 60 feet, which happens on occasion. At one mile east of the tunnel visibility dropped from 50 to 60 feet to zero. The MPD unit was 12 feet in front of Fire Rescue 3, and Engine 2 was 30 feet behind us. Immediately Tony started slowing down fast. We had lost sight of the MPD unit and Engine 2. Within ten seconds we were on top of the MPD unit and the accident. Fire Rescue 3 stopped three feet from the rear bumper of the MPD unit, and Engine 2 stopped 20 feet from us.

Tony and I exited the unit at the same time Acting Captain Sam Downing and Firefighter Scott Johnson exited Engine 2. Visibility was near zero, but I could make out one jackknifed tractor trailer with three cars under it and approximately fifteen other vehicles piled into each other. Tony and I were standing approximately 10 to 15 feet in front of Engine 2, coming up with a quick game plan when a full-size pick-up truck slammed into the rear of Engine 2. As I reached for my speaker mike on my right shoulder, we heard a sound that we will never forget—the sound of air brakes locking up on a large truck. Suddenly, like out of a horror movie, we saw the tractor trailer come out of the heavy fog over behind Engine 2. Needless to say, everyone started running. The excitement level was off the scale and we were running for our lives. Tony dove over the hood of the rescue truck,

I dove over the first car I came to as Firefighter Johnson did the same. For those of you who have seen the movie *The Fugitive*, you can almost see what we did. Acting Captain Downing was just able to dive back into the cab of Engine 2 as it was hit, and Jay Atchison, the driver, was holding on for the ride of his life.

Once Engine 2, which was pushed down the interstate 20 feet by the tractor trailer which was traveling at 67 MPH, stopped and we came out of hiding, I started calling for assistance. As I made sure we were all OK, I continued calling for additional assistance. On the scene initially we had two Firemedics and three firefighter EMTDs. I established command within the first minute of the incident. The decision was made to work east on the Bayway ONLY since we could hear vehicles hitting each other behind us, or west of us. Triage was initiated by myself and Firefighter Johnson. I assigned Tony to treatment. Acting Captain Downing was assigned to extricate everyone he could, as Firefighter Driver Atchison pulled a 1 3/4 inch pre-connect line off the truck for a safety line.

Within the first five minutes of the incident, I had called for four additional ALS Fire Rescue trucks, three private BLS ambulances, two engine companies, extrication, and two wreckers. I was only off by 30 to 40 wreckers from what would finally be used. At this point, I was unaware of any additional patients or exactly how large the accident was. I could only see up to the jackknifed tractor trailer, approximately 50 feet.

At the ten-minute mark of on-scene activities, we had completely used all of the immobilization equipment and most of the bandaging supplies on Fire Rescue 2. Initially I thought the accident included only 20 vehicles. It was not until I climbed on top of the jackknifed tractor trailer's cab and several people ran to me saying that people were hurt and trapped further up that I determined this was a very large-scale accident. After it was all over, it was determined that the accident covered one and a half miles of the seven-mile bridge. There was one mile of accident east, or in front of us, and a half mile of accident west, or behind us. The 40 vehicles and tractor trailers we passed in the tunnel now made up the half mile of accident behind, or west of us. This totally isolated us from additional responding units and made it impossible to transport our injured.

I decided the only way to try to get a grasp of the incident was to find the east end of the accident. I started walking and climbing over and under vehicles, heading east. District Chief John Hicks, our Training Chief, was approximately a fourth of a mile behind our location when he called Fire Alarm to completely shut down the Bayway. He then became cut off from additional units as vehicles piled in behind him. Within the first 100 to 200 feet away from Fire Rescue 3, I had discovered six patients trapped in vehicles and several injuries. I made several stops along the way, treating and assisting patients, which allowed Chief Hicks to catch up with me.

I was relieved of command by District One Chief Mike Burnson, who responded to the tunnel control room and set up a command post. This placed me in an EMS triage officer position. Chief Hicks, after 45 minutes, found the east end of the accident. By this time several units had arrived at either end and were making their way toward the middle.

By 0717 hours the MFRD had committed 26 different units to the Bayway Incident. The triage and treatment areas were manned by 12 MFRD EMTDs and Firemedics, with approximately 200 other MFRD personnel assigned to extrication, transport, rehab, search and rescue, overhaul, public information, and command staff. There were approximately 10 private BLS and ALS Mobile County and Baldwin County ambulances used, along with two Mobile Metro Buses.

A second accident occurred at approximately 0700 hours in the westbound lanes of the Bayway. This accident was not as large as the eastbound accident the MFRD was working, but was a deadly accident. The Spanish Fort VRD in Baldwin County worked the accident which had 31 vehicles involved. There were 11 victims treated and transported to Thomas Hospital in Fairhope, Alabama. Sadly the only fatality occurred here. A woman was trapped in her car as uninjured victims attempted to remove her. The fire that she died in did not start at the time of the impact. A spark from somewhere ignited the fuel spilled on the Bayway, which claimed her life.

In all there were 193 vehicles involved in the eastbound I-10 Bayway accident and 64 confirmed patients. Twenty-nine of the patients were treated by the first arriving crews on Fire Rescue 3 and Engine 2. By 0900 hours command started releasing personnel from the incident. By 1400 hours some traffic was moving on the Bayway once again. By 1700 hours the Bayway was completely open and rush hour commuters sped, like nothing had happened just 12 hours earlier.

Lessons Learned in the AmTrak and the I-10 Bayway Incidents

1. The value of multi-agency mass casualty drills.
2. The Incident Command System or Incident Management System works.
   a. The need for a Unified Command at all large incidents with large numbers of players from different agencies.
3. The value of the Emergency Management Agency (The Human Yellow Pages).
4. Communications:
   a. Portable radios—Our VHF system was poor.
      1. Since the AmTrak incident the MFRD has gone to the 800 mhz.
      2. This did help us with the Bayway; much better communications.

    b. Cellular phone—great
      1. Bag phones
        a. They had about two hours on a battery,
        b. 12-volt outlets needed for charging and/or to use direct current.
      2. Pocket compacts
        a. Battery life short.
        b. No option for plug-in after battery is dead.
      3. Have extra batteries for both radios and phones.
5. Relieve personnel frequently.
    a. Assign them different duties.
    b. Limit total time at the incident if possible. (No such thing as Superman or Wonder Woman).
6. Rehab.
    a. Location
    b. Food, drink and rest
    c. Restroom facilities (Mother Nature doesn't stop calling at a disaster.)
7. Transport officer to get supplies moving to the scene.
    a. Acquire a mode of transportation for supplies if you are not in direct contact with the command post area.
      1. At the AmTrak we were 10 miles apart in the middle of a river delta.
8. Critical Incident Stress Debriefing (CISD) is needed for everyone involved.
9. Try not to overtax your initial personnel.
    a. I tried to be command and triage at the Bayway. You can't do two jobs at one time.
    b. I only had one treatment medic and he was definitely overloaded.
    c. But remember, we are trained to do what we have to do to get the job done.
10. Never let your guard down!!!!!!!!
    a. I'm guilty of it, as is everyone.
      1. I didn't think anything would hit us on the Bayway.
      2. The people in the westbound lane accident didn't think the vehicle would become a fireball.
      3. We are all taught to check for a secure scene, which can change in a flash. Always be prepared and ready for the unexpected.
11. Remember your safety.
    a. Wear your proper personal protective gear.
    b. If you become injured, you're not helping anyone and now you're part of the problem.

12. Pace yourself.
    a. If it is a large incident and you're alone or part of a small group, work at an easy pace. If you wear yourself out, again you are now part of the problem and can't help anyone.
13. Last, a personal favorite of mine NOW!
    a. Always place the largest or heaviest rescue vehicle between you and the accident or between you and any possible threat to you.

Remember, we are out there to help protect lives, and that starts with your life and those of your own personnel!!

Appendix II

Incident Management Forms

EMS Branch Checklist
EMS Incident Management Chart
Transport Checklist
Patient Disposition Data
Triage Checklist
Treatment Checklist
Staging Checklist
Communications Chart
Incident Objectives

All incident management forms that have an NFES number can be ordered from the NWCC, National Fire Equipment System Catalog Part 2: Publications (NFES# 3362) National Interagency Fire Center, Great Basin Cache Supply Office, 3833 S. Development Avenue, Boise, Idaho 83705.

Other forms can be expanded and duplicated for use in the EMS Incident Management System command cache. Forms should be inserted between sheets of one-eighth inch Plexiglass to ensure a "streetproof" checklist/command board for each IMS position. The sheets can be anchored with aluminum screwposts (office supplies). We recommend a Sanford Sharpe weatherproof marker.

EMS Branch Checklist

CHECKLIST: EMS BRANCH

RADIO CALL SIGN: "EMS BRANCH"

SUPPLIES

1. CMD BOX
2. RADIO – PAGER
3. CELL PHONE
4. VEST
5. MARKING PENS
6. LIGHTING
7. EMS IMS CHART

Check	Item
	ENSURE SAFETY
	COORDINATE WITH INCIDENT MANAGER (COMMANDER)
	TRIAGE OFFICER
	TREATMENT OFFICER
	TRANSPORT OFFICER
	ESTABLISH TACTICAL COMMUNICATIONS CHANNELS
	MED SUPPLIES — DISASTER CACHES
	RECON ALL POSSIBLE PATIENT AREAS
	PATIENT COUNT
	ADDITIONAL AMBULANCES/RESOURCES
	(IF REQUIRED) MUTUAL AID
	DIVISIONS IF MULTIPLE PATIENT AREAS
	COORDINATE WITH OTHER BRANCH
	CALL FOR ADDITIONAL EMS MANAGERS (OFFICERS)
	RECALL OFF-DUTY PERSONNEL
	MEDEVAC (GPS COORDINATOR)

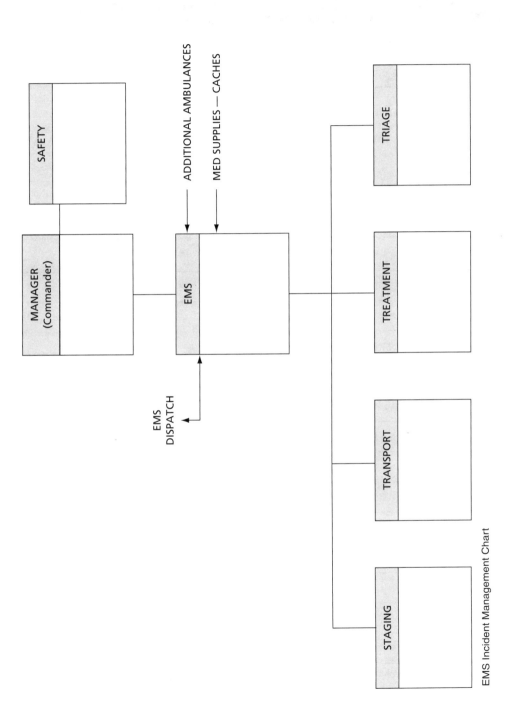

SAFETY

MANAGER
(Commander)

ADDITIONAL AMBULANCES

MED SUPPLIES — CACHES

EMS

EMS
DISPATCH

STAGING

TRANSPORT

TREATMENT

TRIAGE

EMS Incident Management Chart

Transport Checklist

CHECKLIST: **TRANSPORT**

RADIO CALL SIGN: **"TRANSPORT"**

SUPPLIES
1. VEST
2. RADIO
3. TRIAGE TAGS/RIBBONS
4. LIGHTING
5. MARKING PENS
6. GUIDESHEET
7. LZ IDENTIFICATION LIGHTING
8. SPRAYPAINT

Check	Item
	ENSURE SAFETY
	COORDINATE WITH EMS BRANCH
	TEST COMMUNICATIONS
	TRANSPORT GUIDESHEET (PATIENT DISPOSITION DATA)
	COORDINATE WITH MEDICAL COMMUNICATIONS
	ESTABLISH HELICOPTER LZ
	COORDINATE WITH TREATMENT OFFICER
	PATIENT TRACKING

INCIDENT _____   DATE _____

PATIENT DISPOSITION DATA

TIME	TAG #	SEX	NAME	HOSP	UNIT #	AGENCY	TRIAGE R-Y-G

Triage Checklist

CHECKLIST: | TRIAGE

SUPPLIES
1. VEST
2. RADIO
3. TRIAGE TAGS/
   RIBBONS
4. LIGHTING
5. MARKING PENS

Check	Item
	ENSURE SAFETY
	COORDINATE WITH EMS BRANCH DIRECTOR
	TEST COMMUNICATIONS
	TRIAGE ALL PATIENTS
	ESTABLISH ADDITIONAL TRIAGE AREAS IF NEEDED
	DIRECT PATIENT FLOW TO TREATMENT
	MARK PATIENT FLOW WITH SCENE TAPE (IF REQUIRED)
	COORDINATE PATIENT FLOW WITH OTHER AGENCIES/ BRANCHES
	COORDINATE WITH TREATMENT

Treatment Checklist

CHECKLIST: | TREATMENT

RADIO CALL SIGN: "TREATMENT"

SUPPLIES

1. VEST/RADIO
2. MED SUPPLIES
3. TREATMENT FLAGS
4. LIGHTING
5. MARKING PENS
6. SCENE RIBBON
7. PATIENT TRACKING DOCUMENTS

Check	Item
	ENSURE SAFETY
	COORDINATE WITH EMS BRANCH
	TEST COMMUNICATIONS
	MARK TREATMENT AREA
	COORDINATE PATIENT FLOW FROM TRIAGE
	DISASTER CACHES/RE-SUPPLY
	RED UNIT IF NEEDED
	YELLOW UNIT IF NEEDED
	GREEN UNIT IF NEEDED
	RECORD PATIENT TREATMENT
	ESTABLISH AND COORDINATE PATIENT FLOW TO TRANSPORT

Staging Checklist

CHECKLIST: **STAGING**

RADIO CALL SIGN: "STAGING"

SUPPLIES
1. VEST
2. RADIO
3. LIGHTING
4. UNIT TRACKING
   FORMS
5. MARKING PENS
6. VEHICLE KEY
   TAGS

Check	Item
	ENSURE SAFETY
	COORDINATE WITH EMS BRANCH
	COORDINATE WITH TRANSPORT
	TEST COMMUNICATIONS
	ESTABLISH ADEQUATE STAGING AREA
	REQUEST LAW ENFORCEMENT (IF REQUIRED)
	INVENTORY OF PERSONNEL/RESOURCES

COMMUNICATIONS CHART

AGENCY or POSITION	UNIT #	CHANNEL	FREQUENCY	CEL. PHONE	PAGER#	NOTES

INCIDENT OBJECTIVES	1. INCIDENT NAME	2. DATE PREPARED	3. TIME PREPARED

4. OPERATIONAL PERIOD (DATE/TIME)

5. GENERAL CONTROL OBJECTIVES FOR THE INCIDENT (INCLUDE ALTERNATIVES.)

6. WEATHER FORECAST FOR OPERATIONAL PERIOD

7. GENERAL/SAFETY MESSAGE

8. ATTACHMENTS (✓ IF ATTACHED)

- ☐ ORGANIZATION LIST (ICS 203)
- ☐ DIVISION ASSIGNMENT LISTS (ICS 204)
- ☐ COMMUNICATIONS PLAN (ICS 205)
- ☐ MEDICAL PLAN (ICS 206)
- ☐ INCIDENT MAP
- ☐ TRAFFIC PLAN
- ☐ _____
- ☐ _____
- ☐ _____

202 ICS 3/80	9. PREPARED BY (PLANNING SECTION CHIEF)	10. APPROVED BY (INCIDENT COMMANDER)

NFES 1326

6. SUMMARY OF CURRENT ACTIONS

ICS 201 (12/93) NFES 1325	PAGE 2	

8. RESOURCES SUMMARY				
RESOURCES ORDERED	RESOURCE IDENTIFICATION	ETA	ON SCENE ✓	LOCATION/ASSIGNMENT

ICS 201 (12/93)
NFES 1325

PAGE 4

Glossary

absorbed dose: The amount of energy deposited in any material by ionizing radiation. The unit of absorbed dose, the RAD, is a measure of energy absorbed per gram of material. The unit used in countries other than the United States is the Gray. One Gray equals 100 RAD.

absorption: The process of a substance being taken into the body through the skin (transdermal).

acetylcholine (ACh): The neurotransmitter substance widely distributed throughout the tissues of the body at cholenergic synapses, which causes cardiac inhibition, vasodilation, gastrointestinal peristalsis, and other parasympathetic effects.

acetylcholinesterase: An enzyme that hydrolizes the neurotransmitter acetylcholine. Nerve agents inhibit the action of this enzyme.

acute dose: A radiation dose received over a short periof of time.

adenopathy: Swelling or morbid enlargement of the lymph.

adrenergic: *See* **sympathomimetic.**

adsorption: The process of a substance becoming chemically attached to a surface.

aerosol: Fine liquid or solid particles suspended in air (e.g., smoke/fog).

aerosols: A suspension or dispersion of small particles in a gaseous medium.

agency representative: An individual assigned to an incident by a responding or cooperating agency, who is delegated complete authority to execute decisions for all dealings affecting that agency's incident participation. Representatives report to the incident liaison officer.

agent dosage: Concentration of a toxic vapor in the air multiplied by the time that the concentration was present.

agonist: A substance that causes a physiological response.

Air Operations Branch Director: An Organization position responsible for communicating and controlling all aircraft operating in the area. Acts as an air traffic controller.

air purification devices: Respirators or other filtration equipment that remove gases, particulate matter, or vapors from the atmosphere.

airborne pathogen: Pathological microorganisms spread by droplets expelled or dispersed in the air. While this occurs typically through productive sneezing and/or coughing, a deliberate release of pathogens can be accomplished via the use of a variety of aerosol delivery systems.

ALARA: The guiding principle behind radiation protection is that radiation exposures should be kept "as low as reasonably achievable (ALARA)," economic and social factors being taken into account. This common sense approach means that radiation doses for both workers and the public are typically kept lower than their regulatory limits.

alkali: Basic compound that possesses the ability to neutralize acids and form a salt.

all hazards planning: A fundamental planning approach that takes into account all hazards that a community may need to confront. This is the basic premise of planning and management presently being advocated by FEMA.

alpha particle: Alpha particles are composed of two protons and two neutrons. Alpha particles do not travel very far from their radioactive source. They cannot pass through a piece of paper, clothes, or even the layer of dead cells that normally protects the skin. Because alpha particles cannot penetrate human skin, they are not considered an "external exposure hazard." This means that if the alpha particles stay outside the human body, they cannot harm it. However, alpha particle sources located within the body may pose an "internal" health hazard if they are present in great enough quantities. The risk from indoor radon is due to inhaled alpha particle sources that irradiate lung tissue.

ALS (Advanced Life Support): Allowable procedures and techniques used by paramedics and EMT-Intermediate personnel to stabilize patients who exceed basic life support procedures.

ALS responder: Certified or licensed paramedic or EMT/Intermediate.

alveoli: Microscopic air sacs of the lungs where gas exchange occurs with the circulatory system.

ambulance: A ground vehicle providing patient care transportation capability, specified equipment capability, and qualified personnel (EMT, EMT/I, and Paramedic).

analgesic: A compound capable of producing pain relief by altering perception of nociceptive stimuli without producing anesthesia or loss of consciousness.

anaphylaxis: An acute, sometimes violent immunological (allergic) reaction characterized by contraction of smooth muscle and dilation of capillaries due to release of pharmacologically active substances (histamines, serotonin). Can be fatal.

anoxia: Absence of oxygen.

antagonist: A substance that inhibits (blocks) a physiological response or inhibits the response of another drug or substance.

antiadrenergic: *See* **sympatholytic.**

antibiotic: A drug that inhibits the growth of, or kills microorganisms.

antibody: A component of the immune system. A protein that eliminates or counteracts a foreign substance macromolecule or antigen in the body.

anticholinergic: *See* **parasympatholytic.**

anticholinestrase: A drug or substance that blocks the action of cholinesterase.

anticonvulsant: A substance that prevents or arrests seizures.

antidote: A drug or substance that neutralizes a poison or the effects of a poison.

antigen: Any substance that is capable of inducing an immune response.

antisera: A liquid component of blood that contains antibodies.

apnea: Not breathing.

APR: Acronym for air purifying respirators.

arsenical: Pertaining to or containing arsenic; a reference to the vesicant lewisite.

asphyxia: Condition in which cells experience oxygen deprivation.

assessment: (1) Patient assessment—evaluation of patient medical condition. (2) Scene assessment—evaluation of the emergency scene that occurs immediately upon arrival and periodically throughout the operation to ensure safety of members, status of activity, and to determine extent and implications of response operations.

assigned resources: Resources checked in and assigned work tasks on an incident.

assisting agency: An agency directly contributing emergency medical service, fire suppression, rescue, support, or service resources to another agency.

AST: Abbreviation for aspartate aminotransferase, a liver enzyme.

asthenia: Weakness or debility.

ataxia: Inability to coordinate muscle activity during voluntary movement so that smooth movements occur.

atelectasis: Absence of gas from part or all of the lungs due to failure of expansion or resorption of gas from the alveoli.

atom: Atoms are the smallest part of any material, which cannot be broken up by chemical means. Each atom has a center (the nucleus), which contains protons and neutrons. Electrons orbit around the nucleus. In an uncharged atom the number of electrons orbiting the nucleus equals the number of protons in the nucleus. The atom is primarily empty space. If the nucleus of an atom was the size of the button on a baseball pitcher's cap, the electrons would be like dust particles revolving around the outside of the baseball stadium at nearly the speed of light.

atropine: An anticholinergic medication used as an antidote for nerve agents to counteract excessive amounts of acetylcholine.

autoignition temperature: Lowest possible temperature at which a flammable gas or vapor/air mixture will ignite from its own heat source or a contacted heated surface without the necessity of flame or spark.

autonomic nervous system: Part of the nervous system controlling involuntary bodily functions; separated into the sympathetic and parasympathetic nervous systems.

bacillus: A genus of bacteria belonging to the family Bacillaceae. All specimens are rod shaped, sometimes occurring in chains. They are spore bearing, aerobic, motile or nonmotile, most are gram positive.

background radiation: Radiation is a part of our natural world. People have always been exposed to radiation that originates from within the Earth (terrestrial sources) and from outer space (cosmogenic or galactic sources).

bacteria: Single-celled organisms that multiply by cell division and that can cause disease in humans, animals, and plants.

base: (1) *See* **alkali.** (2) Location where primary logistics functions are coordinated and administered. (Incident name or other designator should be added to the term "base" to avoid confusion.) The incident command post may be located with the base, dependent upon incident type and scope.

beta particle: Beta particles are similar to electrons, except they come from the atomic nucleus and are not bound to any atom. Beta particles cannot travel very far from their radioactive source. For example, they can travel only about one-half inch in human tissue, and they may travel a few yards in air. They are not capable of penetrating something as thin as a book or a pad of paper.

binary munition: A chemical munition divided into two sections, each containing precursor chemicals, which, when combined, release a chemical agent.

bio: Abbreviation for biological.

bio-chemicals: Chemicals that make up or are produced by living things.

bio-regulators: Biochemicals that regulate bodily functions and are produced naturally in the body. Inappropriate levels can cause harmful effects.

bio-terrorism: The deliberate use of biological agents/substances as weapons to kill or harm humans, animals, or plants, or to incapacitate equipment.

bio-terrorism agent: Living organisms, or materials derived from them, that cause disease in or injury to humans, animals or plants or cause deterioration of material. Agents can be used in liquid droplets, aerosols, or dry powders.

biotechnology: Applied biological science (e.g., biofermentation processes or genetic engineering).

BL/P: There are four (4) biosafety levels (BLs) that conform to specified conditions. These conditions consist of a combination of laboratory practices and techniques, safety equipment, and laboratory facilities appropriate for the operations performed and the hazards posed by the infectious agents. Previously described as physical containment (P) levels.

blister agent: A chemical agent that produces local irritation and damage to the skin (vesicant) and mucous membranes, pain and injury to the eyes, reddening and blistering of the skin, and damage to the respiratory system when inhaled. Examples are lewisite, nitrogen mustard, and sulfur mustard.

blood agent: A chemical agent that is inhaled and absorbed into the blood, acting upon hemoglobin in blood cells. The blood carries the agent to all body tissues where it interferes with the tissue oxygenation process. Examples are cyanogen chloride and hydrogen cyanide.

blood-borne pathogen: Pathological microorganisms that are present in human blood and that can cause disease in humans (OSHA definition). Note: The term blood includes blood, blood components, and products developed from human blood.

BLS (basic life support): Basic noninvasive, pre-hospital care used by emergency medical technicians and the lesser trained certified first responders to stabilize critically sick and injured patients.

BLS responder: Certified or licensed emergency medical technician; basic or certified first responder.

B-NICE: An acronym for biological, nuclear, incendiary, chemical, or explosives.

body substance isolation (BSI): An infection control strategy that considers all body substances potentially infectious, requiring the use of universal precautions.

boiling point: Temperature at which a liquid changes its matter state to a gas/vapor. Also the temperature at which the pressure of the liquid equals atmospheric pressure.

branch: The organizational level having functional or geographic responsibility for major segments of incident operations. The branch level is organizationally between the section and the group/division sectors.

breakthrough time: The time required for a given chemical to permeate a protective barrier material. This is usually defined as the time elapsed between the application of a chemical to a protective materials exterior surface and its initial appearance on the inner surface.

briefing: An organized face-to-face meeting between IMS managers/officers during an MCI or disaster.

bronchi: The two large sets of branches that come off the trachea and enter the lungs. There are right and left bronchi.

bronchitis: Inflammation of the mucous membranes of the bronchial tubes.

bronchioles: The finer subdivisions of the bronchus.

bronchiolitis: Inflammation of the bronchioles, often associated with bronchopneumonia.

brucella: A genus of encapsulated, nonmotile bacteria (family Brucellaceae) containing short, rod-shaped to coccoid, gram-negative cells. These organisms do not produce gas from carbohydrates; are parasitic, invading all animal tissues and causing infection of the genital organs, mammary glands, and the respiratory and intestinal tracts; and are pathogenic for humans and various species of domestic animals.

bubo: Inflammatory swelling of one or more lymph nodes, usually in the groin; the confluent mass of nodes usually suppurates and drains pus.

carbuncle: Deep-seated pyogenic infection of the skin and subcutaneous tissues, usually arising in several contiguous hair follicles with formation of connecting sinuses; often preceded or accompanied by fever, malaise, and prostration.

CAS registry number: A number assigned to a material by the Chemical Abstract Service to provide a single unique identifier.

catecholamine: A hormone that acts on the autonomic nervous system including epinephrine (adrenaline), norepinephrine, and dopamine.

causative agent: The organism or toxin that is responsible for causing a specific disease or harmful effects.

caustic: A substance that strongly burns, corrodes, irritates, or destroys living tissue.

CBR: An acronym for chemical, biological, and radiological.

C-cubed I (C^3I): A military command term meaning command, control, communications, and intelligence.

ceiling exposure value: The maximum airborne concentration of a biological or chemical agent to which a worker may be exposed at a given time.

central nervous system (CNS): Pertaining to the body's central nervous system.

cerebrospinal: Relating to the brain and the spinal cord.

chain of command: The flow of orders/information from the command/management level to other levels in the IMS. In effective systems, information must flow upward as well as downward.

chemical agent symbol: A designation code assigned to a chemical agent, which is usually two letters. For example HD mustard, GB sarin, CX phosgene oxime.

chemical/biological (chem-bio) terrorism: The use of chemical or biological weapons to create a high-impact EMS incident (sometimes written as CW/BW).

chemical degradation: The altering of the chemical structure of a hazardous material usually accomplished during decontamination.

chemical protective ensemble (CPE): Garments specifically designed to protect the eyes and skin from direct chemical contact There are encapsulating and nonencapsulating versions available for use depending on the operation and the substance. Garments are usually worn with additional respiratory protection as required.

chemical resistance: Ability of the CPE to maintain its protective qualities when it has been contacted by a hazardous substance.

chemoprophylaxis: Prevention of disease through the use of chemicals or drugs.

chief: Title for individuals responsible for command of functional sections: Operations, Planning, Logistics and Finance/Administration.

choking agent: Substances that cause physical injury to the lungs. Exposure is through inhalation. In extreme cases, membranes swell, lungs fill with fluid (edema) and death results from lack of oxygen. The victim is choked. Examples are chlorine and phosgene.

cholinergic: *See* **parasympathomimetic.**

chronic dose: A radiation dose received over a long period of time.

chronic exposure: Repeated low dose exposures to a hazardous substance over an extended time frame.

clear text/clear speak: The use of plain English in radio communication transmissions. No "10" codes, agency-specific codes, or jargon is used when using clear speak/text communications.

CNS depressants: Compounds that have the predominate effect of depressing or obstructing activity of the central nervous system. The primary mental status effects yielded include the disruption of cognitive (thinking) ability, sedation, and lack of motivation (lethargy).

CNS stimulants: Compounds that have the predominant effect of flooding the brain with too much information (stimulus). The primary mental status effects yielded include loss of concentration, indecisiveness, and loss of the ability to act in a sustained, purposeful manner.

coagulated necrosis: Destructive process where acids cause proteins to precipitate as dense, coagulum (clotting) over an injured area.

coagulopathy: A disease affecting the coagulability of the blood.

coccus: A type of bacteria that is spherical or ovoid in form. Many are pathogenic, causing diseases such as septic sore throats, scarlet fever, rheumatic fever, pneumonia, and meningitis.

cocobacillus: A short, thick bacterial rod in the shape of an oval or slightly elongated coccus.

colorimetric tubes: Testing mediums that are used to identify the presence and approximate concentration of a substance in the atmosphere.

combustible gas indicator (CGI): Assessment equipment that measures the ambient concentration of flammable vapors or gases it has been set (calibrated) to monitor.

combustible liquid: Any liquid that has a flash point at or above 100°F (37.7°C) and below 200°F (93.3°C).

command: The act of directing, ordering, and/or controlling resources by virtue of explicit legal, agency, or delegated authority.

command cache: A kit of administrative materials and supplies necessary to operate the EMS incident management system; includes IMS forms, vests, checklists, and protocols.

command staff: The command staff consists of the safety officer, liaison officer, and public information officer, who all report directly to the incident commander.

communicable disease: A disease that can be transmitted from one person to another. Also know as contagious disease.

communications failure protocol: A protocol that dictates agency/unit operations when there is a failure of the telephone and/or EMS radio system.

communication order model: The process of briefly restating an order received to allow for verification and confirmation. This permits all involved to ensure that what was communicated and what was heard coincide, thus ensuring that the correct action is executed.

community disaster plan: A formal document that specifies who is in charge of various incidents, and what agencies/resources will be committed.

concentration: The amount of a chemical agent present in a unit volume of air, usually expressed in milligrams per cubic meter (mg/m^3).

concentration time: The amount of a chemical agent present in a unit volume of air, multiplied by the time an individual is exposed to that concentration.

conjunctiva: A fine mucous membrane that lines the eyelids and covers the exposed surface of the eyeball.

consequence management: The measures to alleviate the damage, loss, hardship, or suffering caused by emergencies. Consequence management includes measures to protect public health and safety, restore essential government services, and provide emergency relief to affected governments, businesses, and individuals. Consequence management is implemented under the primary jurisdiction of the affected state and local governments. As directed by PDD 39, FEMA is designated the lead federal agency for consequence management, and as such provides support to the state when required.

contagious: Capable of being transmitted from one person to another.

contaminant/contaminated: A substance or process that poses a threat to life, health, or the environment (definition from NFPA 472).

cooperating agency: An agency that provides indirect support or service functions such as the American Red Cross, Salvation Army, EPA, etc.

corrosives: Substances that destroy the texture or substance of a tissue.

crisis management: The measures to identify, acquire, and plan the use of resources needed to anticipate, prevent, and/or resolve a terrorist threat or incident. As directed by PDD 39, the FBI is designated the lead federal agency for crisis management, which is implemented under its direction.

cryogenics: Materials that exist at extremely low temperatures, such as nitrogen.

CSF: Abbreviation for cerebrospinal fluid.

culture: A population of microorganisms grown in a medium.

cumulative: Additional exposure rather than repeated exposure. The collective effect of having an HD exposure for 30 minutes and several hours later being exposed again for 60 minutes would yield the same effect as a single 90-minute exposure.

cutaneous: Pertaining to the skin.

cyanosis: A dark bluish or purplish coloration of the skin and mucous membranes due to deficient oxygen levels in the blood (hypoxia). Cyanosis is evident when reduced hemoglobin in the blood exceeds 5g per 100 ml.

decontamination (decon): The removal of chemical/biological/radiological contamination from responders, patients, vehicles, and equipment. Patients must be decontaminated before treatment/transport; usually accomplished through a physical or chemical process.

delayed patient: A patient that is stable, but will require medical care; could deteriorate to the immediate category; triage color is yellow.

dermal: Relating to the skin or derma.

dermis: The inner layer of the skin, beneath the epidermis, which contains blood vessels, nerves, and structures of the skin.

desiccation: Violent mechanical dehydration of the cells.

desorption: The reverse process of absorption. The agent is removed from the surface, outgassing.

dilution factor: Dilution of contaminated air with uncontaminated air in a general area, room, or building for the purpose of health hazard or nuisance control, and/or for heating and cooling.

diplopia: A condition in which a single object is perceived as two objects (double vision).

distal: Away from the center of the body or point of origin.

disaster cache: A store of predetermined supplies/equipment that is immediately transported to an MCI or disaster.

disaster-catastrophic incidents/events: An MCI that overwhelms both local and regional EMS response capabilities, typically involves multiple overlapping jurisdictional boundaries, and requires significant multi-jurisdictional response and coordination.

disaster committee: A formal committee of response agencies, planners, support agencies, and volunteer organizations that serves as a vehicle for threat assessment, emergency response planning, disaster exercises, and post-incident analysis.

disease: An alteration of health, with a characteristic set of symptoms, which may affect the entire body or specific organs. Diseases have a variety of causes and are known as infectious diseases when due to a pathogenic microorganism such as a bacteria, virus, or fungus.

disinfection: A procedure that inactivates virtually all recognized pathogenic microorganisms, but not necessarily all microbial forms (e.g., bacterial endospores) on inanimate objects (OSHA definition).

division: The organizational level having functional or geographic responsibility for major segments of incident operations.

DMAT: Disaster Medical Assistance Team—a deployable team (usually 35 people) of medical personnel and support units under the command of the Office of Emergency Preparedness, U.S. Public Health Service.

DNA: Deoxyribonucleic acid—the genetic material of all organisms and viruses (except for a small class of RNA-containing viruses), which code structures and materials used in normal metabolism.

domestic terrorism: The unlawful use of force or violence, committed by a group(s) of two (2) or more individuals against persons or property to intimidate or coerce a government, the civilian population, or any segment thereof, in furtherance of criminal, political, or social objectives.

dorsal: Toward the back.

dosage: (1) The proper therapeutic amount of a drug to be administered to a patient. (2) The concentration of a chemical agent in the atmosphere (C), multiplied by the time (t) the concentration remains, expressed as mgmin/m. The dosage (Ct) received by a person depends on how long they are exposed to the concentration. That is, the respiratory dosage in mgmin/m is equal to the time in minutes an individual is unmasked in an agent cloud, multiplied by the concentration of the cloud. The dosage is equal to the time of exposure in minutes of an individual's unprotected skin, multiplied by the concentration of the agent cloud.

DOT: *See* **U.S. DOT.**

DOT Hazard Classifications: *See* **U.S. DOT hazard classifications.**

downwind distance: The distance a toxic agent vapor cloud will travel from its point of origin, with the wind.

dysphagia: Difficulty swallowing.

dysphonia: Altered voice production.

dyspnea: Shortness of breath, breathing distress.

ecchymosis: A purplish patch caused by extravasation of blood into the skin, differing from petechiae only in size (larger than 3 mm).

edema: An accumulation of an excessive amount of watery fluid in cells, tissues or serous cavities.

electron: Electrons are very small particles with a single negative charge. They are a part of the atom and orbit around the nucleus. Electrons are much smaller than protons or neutrons. The mass of an electron is only about one two-thousandth of a proton or neutron.

emergency medical operations: Delivery of emergency medical care and transportation prior to the arrival at a hospital or other health care facility (according to NFPA 1581).

Emergency Operations Center (EOC): A central disaster management center staffed by representatives from response and support agencies.

emergency operations plan (EOP): An operational document that has resulted in the delineation of response plans for a community or organization. This plan is usually the result of issues that have been identified through a threat assessment survey.

emergency support functions (ESF): Support functions outlined in the Federal Response Plan. ESFs identify lead and secondary agencies, and are not a management system. The ESFs are grouped by 12 identified functional tasks. ESF 1 Transportation, 2 Communications, 3 Public Works and Engineering, 4 Firefighting, 5 Information and Planning, 6 Mass Care, 7 Resource Support (Logistics), 8 Health and medical services, 9 USAR, 10 Hazardous Materials, 11 Food, 12 Energy.

EMS: Emergency medical service generally referring to pre-hospital care resources.

EMS branch: The organization level having functional responsibility for conducting emergency medical operations at a multiple casualty incident.

EMT-Basic: An individual trained in basic life support according to the standards set forth by the authority having jurisdiction (local, regional, or state EMS authority).

EMT-Intermediate: An individual trained in basic life support having received additional training in advanced life support according to the standards set forth by the authority having jurisdiction (local, regional, or state EMS authority).

EMT-Paramedic: An individual trained in advanced life support according to the standards set forth by the authority having jurisdiction (local, regional, or state EMS authority).

endogenous: Originating or produced from within.

endotoxemia: Presence in the blood of endotoxins.

endotoxin: Endotoxin is composed of compounds called lipopolysaccharides found in bacteria such as *E. coli*. The presence of endotoxin from a blood-borne infection (sepsis) of a gram-negative bacteria can cause clotting, organ failure, and subsequent death.

endotracheal intubation: The introduction of a tube through the oral or nasal cavities into the trachea for maintenance of a patent airway.

enterotoxin: A cytotoxin specific for the cells of the intestinal mucosa.

enzyme: A protein-like substance that acts as an organic catalyst in chemical reactions.

enzyme poisons: Chemicals that inhibit (block) specific cellular reactions by competing with or modifying the enzymes needed to catalyze those reactions.

epidermis: The outer layer of skin.

epistasis: Profuse bleeding from the nose.

equivalent dose: The equivalent dose is a measure of the effect that radiation has on humans. The concept of equivalent dose involves the impact that different types of radiation have on humans. Not all types of radiation produce the same effects in humans. The equivalent dose takes into account the type of radiation and the absorbed dose. For example, when considering beta, x-ray, and gamma ray radiation, the equivalent dose (expressed in REMS) is equal to the absorbed dose (expressed in RADS). For alpha radiation, the equivalent dose is assumed to be 20 times the absorbed dose.

erythema: Redness of the skin due to capillary dilatation.

erythema multiforme: An acute eruption of macules, papules, or subdermal vesicles presenting multiform appearance, the characteristic lesion being the target or iris lesion over the dorsal aspect of the hands and forearms.

erythrocyte: A mature red blood cell.

erythropoiesis: The formation of red blood cells.

etiological agent: A living organism that may cause human disease (according to NFPA 472).

evaporation rate: The rate at which a liquid changes to vapor at normal room temperature.

exanthema: Skin eruption occurring as a symptom of an acute viral or coccal disease.

exogenous: Originating or produced externally.

exothermic reaction: A chemical reation that produces heat.

explosive range: *See* **flammable range.**

explosives: Compounds that are unstable and break down with the sudden release of large amounts of energy.

extraocular: Adjacent but exterior to the eyeball.

extrication: The action of disentangling and freeing a person from entrapment.

extrication sector: The EMS IMS organizational component responsible for freeing and disentangling victims from wreckage.

facilities unit: Responsible for support facilities, including shelter, rehabilitation, sanitation, and auxiliary power.

fasciculation: Involuntary contractions or twitching of groups (fasciculi) of muscle fibers; a coarser form of muscular contraction than fibrillation. Commonly described as movement resembling a "bag of worms."

febrile: Having or referring to a fever.

Federal Bureau of Investigation (FBI): The FBI is the principal investigative arm of the U.S. Department of Justice. It has the authority and responsibility to investigate specific crimes assigned to it. The FBI also is authorized to provide other law enforcement agencies with cooperative services, such as fingerprint identification, laboratory examinations, and police training. For the purposes of this textbook, the FBI is the lead federal agency for the crisis management of terrorism incidents as directed by PDD 39 and the FRP.

federal coordinating officer (FCO): Is the president of the United States' representative at a disaster incident. For the purposes of this textbook, the FCO is the individual responsible for coordinating the consequence management response, and will usually be a representative of FEMA.

Federal Emergency Management Agency (FEMA): Is the lead federal agency for the consequence management response to a terrorism incident as directed by PDD 39 and the FRP.

Federal Response Plan (FRP): The FRP provides the system for the overall delivery of federal assistance in a disaster. Twenty-seven federal departments and agencies and the American Red Cross provide resources. Resources are grouped into 12 emergency support functions (ESFs), each headed by a primary or lead agency. For the purposes of this textbook, the FRP presents the federal government's consequence management response to terrorism incidents.

feedback: A critical element in any form of communications whereby the receiver acknowledges the receipt of information to the sender.

finance/administration section: The section responsible for all costs and financial actions of the incident and administrative functions, which include the time unit, procurement unit, compensation/claims unit, and cost unit.

FIRESCOPE: Firefighting Resources of California Organized Against Potential Emergency; developed as a response to California wildfires and became the benchmark for the EMS incident management system.

first responder: The first trained personnel to arrive at the scene of an emergency.

flammability: The inherent capacity of a substance to ignite and burn rapidly.

flammable range: Range of a gas or vapor concentration that will burn or explode if an ignition source is present. Usually expressed as a percentage by volume of air. Depending on range there are lower explosive limits (LEL) and upper explosive limits (UEL). For an ignition to take place, the substance must be within the LEL and UEL. Any presences that do not meet or exceed these ranges should not ignite.

flash point: Minimum temperature at which a liquid gives off sufficient enough vapor to ignite and flashover, but not continue to burn without the availability of more heat.

fomite: Objects such as clothing, towels, utensils that possibly harbor agents of disease and are capable of spreading it.

formalin: A 37 percent aqueous solution of formaldehyde.

fulminant hepatitis: Severe rapidly progressive loss of hepatic function due to viral infection or other cause of inflammatory destruction of liver tissue.

fungus: A group of microorganisms including molds and yeasts, similar to the cellular structure of plants. Some fungi are pathogenic.

G series nerve agents: Chemical agents developed in the 1930s with moderate to high toxicity that act by inhibiting a key nervous system enzyme (GA, GB, GD).

gamma rays: Gamma rays are an example of electromagnetic radiation, as is visible light. Gamma rays originate from the nucleus of an atom. They are capable of traveling long distances through air and most other materials. Gamma rays require more shielding material, such as lead or steel, to reduce their numbers than is required for alpha and beta particles.

general staff: The individuals responsible for incident management. These individuals include the IM, operations section chief, logistics section chief, plans section chief, and administration chief. This level is above the branch/division/group/sector level.

genetic effects: Effects seen in the offspring of the individual who received the agent. The agent must be encountered before conception.

genetic engineering: The directed alteration or manipulation of genetic material.

Ground Support Unit: The unit within the Support Branch of the Logistics Section responsible for the fueling, maintaining, and repairing of vehicles, and the transportation of personnel and supplies.

group/sector: The organizational level having responsibility for a specified functional assignment at an incident (triage, treatment, extrication, etc.).

half-life: The time required for the level of a substance in the blood to be reduced by 50 percent of its initial level.

hazardous materials: Substances that can cause harm to people or the environment upon release.

helibase: A location within the general incident area for parking, fueling, maintaining, and loading helicopters.

helispot: A tactical location where a helicopter can take off and land.

hemagglutination: The agglutination of red blood cells; may be immune as a result of specific antibody either for red blood cell antigens per se, or other antigens that coat the red blood cells; or may be nonimmune as in hemagglutination caused by viruses or other microbes.

hemagglutinin: A substance, antibody, or other that causes hemagglutination.

hematemesis: Vomiting blood.

hematuria: Urination with blood or red blood cells.

hemodynamic: Referring to the physical aspects of the circulation of blood.

hemoglobin: The iron-containing pigment of the red blood cells. Its function is to carry oxygen from the lungs to the tissues.

hemolysis: The destruction of red blood cells with the liberation of hemoglobin that diffuses into the fluid surrounding them.

hemoptysis: Bloody or blood-tinged sputum.

hepatic: Pertaining to the liver.

high impact incident/event: Any emergency that requires mutual aid resources in order to effectively manage the incident or to maintain community 911 operations.

histamine: A chemical released by mast cells and basophils on stimulation. One of the most powerful vasodilators known and a major mediator of anaphylaxis.

hormone: A chemical substance released by a gland that controls or influences other glands or body systems.

hospital alert system: A communications system between EMS personnel on-site of an MCI and a medical facility that provides available hospital patient receiving capability and/or medical control.

Hospital Emergency Incident Command System (HEICS): A system for the management of internal/external hospital emergencies based on the IMS model.

host: A person that can harbor or nourish a disease-producing organism. The host is infected.

hydration: The combining of a substance with water.

hydrolysis: The reaction of any chemical substance with water by which decomposition of the substance occurs, and one or more new substances are produced.

hyperemia: Presence of an increased amount of blood in a part or organ.

hyperesthesia: Abnormal acuteness of sensitivity to touch, pain, or other sensory stimuli.

hypertension: Abnormally high blood pressure.

hypocalcemia: Reduction of blood calcium below normal levels.

hypotension: Abnormally low blood pressure.

hypovolemia: Abnormally low amount of blood in the body. Generally a result of trauma or internal bleeding.

hypoxemia: The reduction of oxygen content in the arterial blood.

hypoxia: A condition when insufficient oxygen is available to meet the oxygen demands of the cells.

idiopathic: Referring to a disease of unknown origin.

IDLH: Immediate danger to life and health.

immediate patient: A patient who is critical and in need of immediate care; triage color is red.

immunization: The process of rendering a person immune or highly resistant to a disease. Usually accomplished through vaccination.

immunoassay: Detection and assay of substances by serological (immuno-logical) methods; in most applications the substance in question serves as antigen, both in antibodies production and in measurement of antibodies by the test substance.

incapacitating agents: Substances that produce temporary physiological and/or mental effects via action on the central nervous system. Effects may persist for hours or days. Victims usually do not require medical treatment, but treatment will assist in speeding recovery.

incident action plan: A plan consisting of the strategic goals, tactical objectives and support requirements for the incident. All incidents require an action plan. For simple/smaller incidents, that action plan is not usually in written form. Larger or complex responses require the action plan be documented in writing.

incident command post (ICP): The location from which command functions are executed.

incident management system (IMS): Originally known as the incident command system, IMS has evolved into a systematic management approach with a common organizational structure responsible for the management of assigned resources to effectively accomplish stated objectives pertaining to an incident.

incident manager (IM): The designated person with overall authority for management of the incident (varies by jurisdiction).

incident objectives: Statements of guidance and direction necessary for the selection of appropriate strategy(s) and the tactical direction of resources to accomplish the same. Incident objectives are based on realistic expectations of operational accomplishments when all anticipated resources have been deployed. Incident objectives must be achievable and measurable, yet flexible enough to allow for strategic and tactical realignment.

incident termination/securement: The conclusion of emergency operations at the scene of an incident, usually the departure of the last resource from the incident scene.

incubation period: The time from exposure to the disease until the first appearance of symptoms.

industrial agents: Chemicals developed or produced for use in industrial operations or research by academia, government, or industry. These substances are not primarily produced for the specific purpose of harming humans or incapacitating equipment, but if utilized by rogue individuals as a weapon, will yield results similar to a chemical agent.

infection: Growth of pathogenic organisms in the tissues of a host, with or without detectable signs of injury.

infectious: Capable of causing infection in a suitable host.

infectious disease: An illness or disease resulting from invasion of a host by disease-producing organisms such as bacteria, viruses, fungi, or parasites.

infectivity: (1) The ability of an organism to spread. (2) The number of organisms required to cause an infection to secondary hosts. (3) The capabilities of an organism to spread out from site of infection and cause disease in the host organism. Infectivity can also be defined as the number of organisms required to cause an infection.

ingestion: Exposure to a substance through the gastrointestinal tract.

inhalation: Exposure to a substance through the respiratory tract.

initial response: The resources initially committed to an incident.

injection: Exposure to a substance through a break in the skin.

inoculation: *See* **vaccine.**

insecticide: Chemicals that are used to kill insects.

Integrated Emergency Management System (IEMS): A system of emergency planning and consequence response that integrates local response agencies, state agencies, and federal agencies into a comprehensive emergency management plan.

international terrorism: The unlawful use of force or violence, committed by a group(s) of two (2) or more individual(s) who is foreign based, and/or directed by countries or groups outside the continental United States (CONUS), or whose activities transcend national boundaries, against persons or property to intimidate or coerce a government, the civilian population, or any segment thereof, in furtherance of criminal, political, or social objectives.

ions, ionization: Atoms that have the same number of electrons and protons have zero charge since the number of positively charged protons equals the number of negatively charged electrons. If an atom has more electrons than protons, it has a negative charge, and is called a negative ion. Atoms that have fewer electrons than protons are positively charged, and are called positive ions. Some forms of radiation can strip electrons from atoms. This type of radiation is appropriately called "ionizing radiation."

ionizing radiation: Ionizing radiation is radiation that has enough energy to cause atoms to lose electrons and become ions. Alpha and beta particles, as well as gamma and x-rays, are all examples of ionizing radiation. Ultraviolet, infrared, and visible light are examples of non-ionizing radiation.

in vitro: An artificial environment, as in a test tube or culture media.

in vivo: In the living body, referring to a reaction or process therein.

ischemia: The lack of blood supply to a part of the body, leading to deficient oxygen levels and subsequent damage to anatomical structures.

ischemic necrosis: Death of cells subsequent to the lack of blood flow to affected tissues or organs.

Landing Zone (LZ): A designated area to land helicopters. The LZ must be secured and controlled by a helispot manager.

Law Enforcement Incident Command System (LEICS): A law enforcement incident management system based on the IMS model.

LD$_{50}$: Dose (LD is lethal dose) that will kill 50 percent of the exposed population.

Leader: The individual responsible for command of a task force, strike team, or unit.

LEL: Lower explosive limit. The minimum concentration of a substance (gas or vapor) required for a substance to burn.

Level A protection: The level of protective equipment required in situations where the substance is considered acutely vapor toxic to the skin and the hazards are unknown. Use of Level A is recommended when immediate identification of the substance is unavailable or unknown. Level A consists of a full encapsulating protective ensemble with SCBA or supplied air breathing apparatus (SABA).

Level B protection: The level of protective equipment in situations where the substance is considered acutely vapor toxic to the skin and the hazards may cause respiratory effects. Level B consists of a Level B encapsulating (non-airtight) protective ensemble or chemical splash suit with SCBA or SABA.

Level C protection: The level of protective equipment required to prevent respiratory exposure, but not to exclude possible skin contact. Chemical splash suits with cartridge respirators (APRs).

Level D protection: The level of protective equipment required when the atmosphere contains no known hazard, when splashes, immersions, inhalation, or contact with hazardous levels of any substance is precluded. Work uniform such as coveralls, boots, leather gloves, and hard hat.

liaison: The coordination of activities between agencies operating at the incident.

liaison officer: The point of contact (POC) for assisting or coordinating agencies and members of the management staff. The liaison officer is a member of the management staff.

liquid agent: Chemical agent that appears to be an oily film or droplet form, usually brownish in color.

liquifaction necrosis: The destructive process by which alkali causes cell death and turns solid tissue into a soapy liquid.

liver: The largest and one of the most complex internal organs of the body. The liver produces bile, secretes glucose, protein, vitamins, fat, and other compounds. It also processes hemoglobin to forage iron content, and is the body's primary detoxification center.

logistics section: The section responsible for providing facilities, services, and materials for the incident. Includes the communication unit, medical unit, and food unit within the service branch; and the supply unit, facilities unit, and ground support unit within the support branch.

low impact incident/event: An MCI that can be managed by local EMS resources and members without mutual aid resources from outside organizations.

lymph: A clear, transparent, colorless, alkaline fluid found in the lymphatic vessels.

lymph nodes: A rounded body consisting of lymphatic tissue found at intervals in the course of lymphatic vessels.

lymphadenopathy: Any disease process affecting a lymph node or lymph nodes.

macula: A small spot, perceptibly different in color from surrounding skin.

management staff: The incident manager's direct support staff, consisting of the public information officer, liaison officer, safety officer, and the stress management officer.

Mass Casualty Incident (MCI): An incident with several patients or an unusual event associated with minimal casualties (airplane crash, terrorism, HAZMAT, etc.); incident with negative impact on hospitals, EMS, and response resources.

mass decontamination: The decontamination of mass numbers of patients (pediatric, adult, and geriatric) from exposure to radiation or a chemical/biological agent.

mechanism of injury: A sudden and intense energy transmitted to the body that causes trauma, or exposure to a chemical or biological agent. A contaminated patient can transport a chem-bio mechanism of injury.

mediastinitis: Inflammation of the tissue of the mediastinum.

mediastinum: The median partition of the thoracic cavity, covered by the mediastinal pleura and containing all the thoracic viscera and structures except the lungs.

median incapacitating dosage (ID50): The amount of liquid chemical agent expected to incapacitate 50 percent of a group of exposed, unprotected individuals.

median lethal dosage (LCT50): The amount of liquid chemical agent expected to kill 50 percent of a group of exposed, unprotected individuals.

Medical Communications (EMS Com): A unit or individual that gathers on-scene patient information and transmits the information to medical control.

medical control: (1) Central focus of all medical treatment and direction being rendered at the scene of an emergency; usually an M.D. on site or via radio. (2) Unit responsible for monitoring and updating the patient receiving status of medical facilities in the area/region.

medical supply cache: A cache consisting of standardized medical supplies and equipment stored in a predesignated location for dispatch to MCI incidents.

medical unit: The unit within the service branch of the logistics section responsible for providing emergency medical treatment to emergency responders. This unit does not provide treatment to civilians. Rehab is often a function assigned to the medical unit.

medium: Substance used to provide nutrients for the growth and multiplication of microorganisms.

melena: Passage of dark-colored, tarry stools due to the presence of blood altered by the intestinal juices.

meninges: Membranous coverings of the brain and spinal cord.

meningococcemia: Presence of meningococci in the circulating blood.

Metropolitan Medical Strike Team (MMST): The Metro Medical Strike Team shall, at the request of local and/or regional jurisdictions, respond to and assist with the medical treatment/management and public health consequences of chemical, biological, and nuclear incidents resulting from deliberate or accidental acts.

METTAG: A four-color system of tagging patients during the triage process. Each color is demonstrative of a differing medical priority; red—critical, yellow—less serious and delayed transport, green—minor injuries (walking wounded), and black—deceased or unsalvageable.

microcyst: A tiny cyst, frequently of such dimensions that a magnifying lens or microscope is required to visualize it.

microorganism: Any organism, such as bacteria, viruses, and some fungi, that can be seen only with a microscope.

microscopy: Observation/investigation of minute objects by means of a microscope.

minor patient: A patient with minor injuries that requires minimal treatment; triage color is green.

miosis: A condition where the pupil of the eye significantly constricts (pinpoint) impairing vision, especially night vision.

mists: Liquid droplets dispersed in the air.

mitigation: Actions taken to prevent or reduce the likelihood of harm.

MMST: *See* **Metropolitan Medical Strike Team.**

morgue: A segregated area for deceased victims that is coordinated with the medical examiner and/or jurisdictional law enforcement authorities; triage color for deceased victims is black.

MSDS: Material Safety Data Sheets. A comprehensive document that delineates all pertinent information about a hazardous substance. This information sheet is provided by and available from the manufacturer of the product.

mucocutaneous: Referring to the mucous membrane and skin.

mustard agent: *See* **blister agent.**

myalgia: Muscular pain.

mycotoxin: A toxin produced by fungi.

mydriasis: Dilation of the pupil.

M8 chemical agent detector paper: A paper used to detect and identify liquid V and G class nerve agents and H class blister agents.

M256 Kit: A kit that detects and identifies vapor concentrations of nerve, blister, and blood agents.

nasopharynx: The part of pharynx that lies above the level of the soft palate and directly posterior to the nose.

National Interagency Incident Management System (NIIMS): An adaptation of fire ICS for interagency disaster operations.

naturally occurring radioactive materials (NORM): The term NORM is used to identify naturally occurring radioactive materials that may have been technologically enhanced in some way. The enhancement occurs when a naturally occurring radioactive material has its composition, concentration, availability, or proximity to people altered by human activity. The term is usually applied when the naturally occurring radionuclide is present in sufficient quantities or concentrations to require control for purposes of radiological protection of the public or the environment. NORM does not include source, by-product, or special nuclear material (terms defined by law and referring primarily to uranium, thorium, and nuclear fuel cycle products); or commercial products containing small quantities of natural radioactive materials (e.g., phosphate fertilizer, potassium chloride for road deicing) or natural radon in buildings.

NBC: A military acronym for nuclear, biological, and chemical weapons.

necrosis: Pathological death of one or more cells or a portion of tissue or organ resulting in irreversible damage.

nerve agent: Chemical agent that acts by disrupting the normal function of the nervous system.

neurotransmitter: A substance that is released from the axon terminal of a presynaptic neuron on excitation, and travels across the synaptic cleft to influence (excite or inhibit) the target cell, such as epinephrine, dopamine, or norepinephrine.

neutron: Neutrons are part of the nucleus of an atom. Neutrons are, as the name implies, neutral in their charge. That is, they have neither a positive nor a negative charge. Neutrons are about the same size as protons.

NIOSH: National Institutes for Occupational Safety and Health.

nonlethal agents: Chemical agents that can incapacitate but which, by themselves, are not intended to cause death. Examples are tear gases, vomiting agents, and psychochemicals such as BZ .

non-persistent agent: An agent that upon release loses its ability to cause casualties after 10 to 15 minutes. It possesses a high evaporation rate, is lighter than air, and will disperse quickly. This type of agent is considered to be a short-term hazard, however, in small and unventilated areas the agent will be more persistent than out in the open.

non-stochastic effect: Effects that can be related directly to the dose received. The effect is more severe with a higher dose, (i.e., the burn gets worse as dose increases). It typically has a threshold, below which the effect will not occur. A skin burn from radiation is a non-stochastic effect.

ocular: Pertaining to the eye.

oliguria: Markedly reduced urine output.

operations section: The section responsible for all tactical operations at the incident.

organism: Any individual living thing whether human, animal, or plant.

organophosphate: A compound with a specific phosphate group that inhibits acetycholinesterase. Used in chemical warfare agents, insecticides, and pesticides.

organophosphorous compound: A compound containing the elements phosphorous and carbon, whose physiological effects include inhibition of acetycholinesterase. Most pesticides and virtually all nerve agents are organophosphate compounds.

oropharynx: Portion of the pharynx that lies posterior to the mouth.

OSHA: Occupational Safety and Health Administration. A part of the U.S. Department of Labor.

osteomyelitis: Inflammation of the bone marrow and adjacent bone.

oxygen meters: Device that measures or monitors the concentration of oxygen in a specific area.

pandemic: Denoting a disease affecting or attacking the population of an extensive region, country, or continent; extensively epidemic.

papule: A small, circumscribed, solid elevation on the skin.

parasite: Any organism that lives in or on another organism without providing benefit in return.

parasympathetic nervous system: A division of the autonomic nervous system that is responsible for controlling the body's vegetative functions.

parasympatholytic: A drug or other substance that blocks or inhibits the actions of the parasympathetic nervous system. *See also* **anticholinergic.**

parasympathomimetic: A drug or other substance that causes effects like those of the parasympathetic nervous system.

pathogen: A microorganism that can cause disease. Pathogens can be bacteria, fungi, parasites, or viruses.

pathogenic: Capable of causing disease.

PEL: *See* **permissible exposure limits.**

penetration: The movement of a substance through a closure such as a flap, seam, zipper, or other vulnerable design feature of a chemical protective garment.

percutaneous: Referring to the passage of substances through intact skin (e.g., needle puncture, etc.).

percutaneous absorption: Substances absorbed through the skin.

percutaneous agent: A substance able to be absorbed through the body.

perivascular: Surrounding a blood or lymph vessel.

permeation: The process by which a chemical moves through protective clothing.

permeation rate: The rate at which the challenge chemical permeates the protective fabric.

permissible exposure limit (PEL): An occupational health term used to describe exposure limits for employees. Usually described in time-weighted averages (TWA) or short-term exposure limits (STEL). The maximum average concentration (over eight continuous hours, averaged), to which 95 percent of otherwise healthy adults can be repeatedly and safely exposed for period 8-hour days and 40-hour weeks.

persistance: Measure of the duration for which a chemical agent is effective. This property is relative and varies by agent, method of dissemination, and influencing environmental conditions such as weather and terrain.

persistent agent: A substance that remains in the target area for longer time frames. Hazards from both liquid and vapor may remain for hours, days, or in extreme cases weeks after distribution of an agent. As a rule of thumb, persistent agent duration will be greater than 12 hours.

personal protective equipment (PPE): Equipment for the protection of EMS personnel; includes gloves, masks, goggles, gowns, and biological disposal bags (red bags).

petechiae: Minute hemorrhagic spots in the skin, of pinpoint to pinhead size, that are not blanched by pressure.

pH: A scientific method of articulating the acid or base (alkali) content of a solution. pH is a logarithm of the hydrogen (H) ion concentration divided by 1. The higher the pH the greater the alkalinity, the lower the pH the greater the acidity.

pharyngeal: Relating to the pharynx.

phosgene: Carbonyl chloride; a colorless liquid below 8.2°C, but an extremely poisonous gas at ordinary temperatures. It is an insidious gas, and is not immediately irritating, even when fatal concentrations are inhaled.

photophobia: Significant dread and avoidance of light. Usually accompanied by severe pain with exposure to light.

physiological action: Most toxic chemical agents are used for their toxic effect. The effects are the production of harmful physiological reactions when the human body is exposed either through external, inhalation, or internal routes. The subsequent bodily response to the exposure is the physiological response.

planning meeting: Meetings, held as required throughout the duration of the incident, to select specific strategies and tactics for incident management and for service and support planning.

pleurisy: Inflammation of the pleura.

poison: Any substance which, taken into the body by absorption, ingestion, inhalation, or injection, interferes with normal physiological functions.

Poison Control Center: A toxicological information clearinghouse (usually staffed 24 hours a day/7 days a week) that serves as informational resource for toxic materials and the treatment of their exposures.

poisoning: The state of introduction of a poison into the body.

polyuria: Excessive urination.

post-incident analysis (PIA): A written review of major incidents for the purpose of implementing changes in operations, resources, logistics, and protocols, based on lessons learned.

ppm: Parts per million.

precursor: A chemical substance required for the manufacture of chemical agents.

Presidential Decision Directive (PDD): A presidential directive that establishes policy.

Presidential Decision Directive (PDD) 39: PDD 39 presents the United States policy on counterterrorism.

presynaptic: Pertaining to the area on the proximal side of a synaptic cleft.

Procurement Unit: A unit within the Finance Section responsible for financial matters involving vendors.

prophylaxis: Prevention of disease or of a process that can lead to a disease.

proton: Protons, along with neutrons, make up the nucleus of an atom. Protons have a single positive charge. While protons and neutrons are about 2,000 times heavier than electrons, they are still very small particles. A grain of sand weighs about one hundred million trillion (100,000,000,000,000,000,000) times more than a proton or a neutron.

pruritus: Itching.

psychochemical agent: Chemical agent that incapacitates by distorting the perceptions and cognitive processes of the victim.

ptosis: Drooping of the eyelids.

public information officer (PIO): The person responsible for interface with the media and others requiring information direct from the incident scene. Information is only disseminated with the authorization of the incident commander. The PIO is a member of the command/management staff.

pull logistics: A process of ordering supplies by field units, via communications, as they are needed at an MCI or disaster.

pulmonary edema: Edema of the lungs. Left unattended in severe cases can be fatal.

pupil: Opening at the center of the iris of the eye for transmission of light.

push logistics: A process of forwarding predetermined supplies, usually as a disaster cache, to an MCI or disaster.

pyrogenic: Causing fever.

radiation: Radiation is energy in the form of waves or particles (see types of radiation). Radiation comes from sources such as radioactive material or from equipment such as x-ray machines or accelerators.

radiation dose: The effect of radiation on any material is determined by the dose of radiation that material receives. Radiation dose is simply the quantity of radiation energy deposited in a material. There are several terms used in radiation protection to precisely describe the various aspects associated with the concept of dose, and how radiation energy deposited in tissue affects humans.

radiation exposure: Radiation exposure is a measure of the amount of ionization produced by x-rays or gamma rays as they travel through air. The unit of radiation exposure is the roentgen (R), named for Wilhelm Roentgen, the German scientist who, in 1895, discovered x-rays.

radiation half-life: The time required for a population of atoms of a given radionuclide to decrease, by radioactive decay, to exactly one-half of its original number. No operation, either chemical or physical, can change the decay rate of a radioactive substance. Half-lives range from much less than a microsecond to more than a billion years. The longer the half-life the more stable the nuclide. After one half-life, half the original atoms will remain; after two half-lives, one-fourth (or 1/2 of 1/2) will remain; after three half-lives one-eighth of the original number (1/2 of 1/2 of 1/2) will remain; and so on.

radiation meters: Monitoring devices that detect, measure, and monitor for the presence of radiation.

radioactive contamination: Radioactive contamination is radioactive material distributed over some area, equipment, or person. It tends to be unwanted in the location where it is, and has to be cleaned up or decontaminated.

radioactive decay: Radioactive decay describes the process where an energetically unstable atom transforms itself to a more energetically favorable, or stable state. The unstable atom can emit ionizing radiation in order to become more stable. This atom is said to be radioactive, and the process of change is called radioactive decay.

rate of action: Rate at which the body reacts to or is affected by a chemical substance.

rate of detoxification: Rate at which the body can counteract the effects of a toxic chemical substance.

rate of hydrolysis: Rate at which the various chemical substances or compounds are decomposed by water.

reactivity: Ability of a substance to interact with other substances and/or body tissues.

real world: A phrase transmitted to all units when there is an injury or actual emergency during a disaster exercise.

recombinant DNA (rDNA): DNA prepared in the laboratory by splitting and splicing DNA from different species, with the resulting recombinant DNA having different properties than the original.

recombinant vaccine: A vaccine produced by genetic manipulation (gene splicing) usually in yeast.

reconnaissance: The primary survey to gather information.

rehabilitation (rehab): The function and location that includes medical evaluation and treatment, food and fluid replenishment, and relief from extreme environmental conditions for emergency responders, according to the circumstances of the incident.

resource status unit (RESTAT): The unit within the planning section responsible for recording the status of, and accounting for, resources committed to the incident, and for evaluation of (1) resources currently committed to the incident, (2) the impact that additional responding units will have on an incident, and (3) anticipated resource requirements. Note: RESTAT is normally utilized at actual or escalating high impact or long-term operations.

respiratory dosage: Equal to the time in minutes an individual is unmasked in an agent cloud multiplied by the concentration of the cloud.

restriction enzyme: Enzyme that splits DNA at a specific sequence.

retrosternal: Posterior to the sternum.

rhinorrhea: Runny nose.

rickettsia: Generic name applied to a group of microorganisms, family Rickettsiaceae, order Rickettsiales, which occupy a position intermediate between viruses and bacteria. They differ from bacteria in that they are obligate parasites requiring living cells for growth and differ from viruses in that the Berkefeld filter retains them. They are the causative agents of many diseases and are usually transmitted by lice, fleas, ticks, and mites (anthropods).

riot control agents: Substances usually having short-term effects that are typically used by governmental authorities for law enforcement purposes.

Robert T. Stafford Disaster Relief and Emergency Assistance Act: A federal law that assigns disaster responsibilities to FEMA and defines federal support to local communities.

routes of exposure: The mechanism by which a contaminant enters the body.

SABA: Supplied air breathing apparatus.

safety officer: The command/management staff member responsible for monitoring and assessing safety hazards, unsafe situations, and developing measures for ensuring member safety on-site.

sarin: A nerve poison which is an extremely potent, irreversible cholinesterase inhibitor.

SCBA: Self-contained breathing apparatus.

scarification: The making of a number of superficial incisions in the skin.

sclera: Tough white supporting tunic of the eyeball.

secondary device: An explosive device designed and placed to kill emergency responders.

section: The organizational level having functional responsibility for primary segments of incident operations such as operations, planning, logistics, and finance/administration. The section level is organizationally between branch and incident commander.

section chief: Title referring to a member of the general staff (operations section chief, planning section chief, logistics section chief, and finance/ administration section chief).

sector/group officer: The individual responsible for supervising members who are performing a similar function or task (i.e., triage, treatment, transport, or extrication).

security unit: Responsible for personnel security, traffic control, and morgue security at an MCI or disaster.

seizure: A disorder of the nervous system owing to sudden, excessive, disorderly discharge of brain neurons.

sensitize: To become highly responsive (sensitive) or easily receptive to the effects of a toxic substance after initial exposure.

sequala (ae): A condition following as a consequence of a disease.

sequestration agents: Agents that bind specific salts and make them unavailable to the cells.

service branch: A branch within the logistics section responsible for service activities at an incident. Its components include the communications unit, medical unit, and food unit.

shigellosis: Bacillary dysentery caused by a bacteria of the genus Shigella, often occurring in epidemic patterns.

short-term exposure limits (STEL): A 15-minute, time weighted average (TWA) exposure that should not be exceeded at any time during a work day, even if the 8-hour TWA is within the threshold limit value (TLV). Exposures at the STEL should not be repeated more than four times a day and there should be at least 60 minutes between successive exposures at the STEL.

Single Point of Contact (POC): An individual in an assisting/ cooperating agency responsible for receiving and passing information and providing feedback.

single resource: An individual ambulance or piece of equipment used to complete a task.

Situation Status Unit (SITSTAT): The unit within the planning section responsible for analysis of the situation as it progresses, reporting to the planning section chief. Note: SITSTAT is normally utilized at actual or escalating high-impact or long-term operations.

skin dosage: Equal to the time of exposure in minutes of an individual's unprotected skin, multiplied by the concentration of the agent cloud.

sloughing: Process by which necrotic cells separate from the tissues to which they have been attached.

solubility: (1) Ability of a material (solid, liquid, gas, or vapor) to dissolve in a solvent. (2) Ability of one material to blend uniformly with another.

solvent: Material that is capable of dissolving another chemical.

soman: An extremely potent cholinesterase inhibitor.

somatic effects: Effects from some agent, like radiation, that are seen in the individual who receives the agent.

span of control: The number of subordinates supervised by a superior; ideal span varies from three to five people.

Special Agent in Charge (SAIC): The senior individual appointed by a federal law enforcement agency to manage and coordinate all activities. For the purposes of this textbook, the SAIC is the FBI representative at the terrorism incident in charge of crisis management response. The SAIC is usually the FBI's on-site commander.

specific gravity: Weight of a liquid compared to the weight of an equal volume of water.

spore: A reproductive form some microorganisms can take to become resistant to environmental conditions such as cold or heat. This is referred to as the "resting phase."

Stafford Act: *See* **Robert T. Stafford Disaster Relief and Emergency Assistance Act.**

staging: A specific status where resources are assembled in an area at or near the incident scene to await deployment or assignment.

staging area: The location where incident personnel and equipment are assigned on an immediately available status.

standard operating procedures (SOPs): An organizational directive that establishes a standard course of action.

standing orders: Medical treatment policies, protocols, and procedures approved by a local, regional, or state EMS authority for use by EMS personnel without having to first make direct medical control contact for authorization.

START: Acronym for "simple treatment and rapid triage." This is an initial triage system utilized for triaging large numbers of patients at an emergency incident. This system was developed in Newport Beach, California, in the early 1980s.

status epilepticus: Two or more seizures in succession without a lucid interval.

stochastic effects: Effects that occur on a random basis, and are independent of the size of dose. The effect typically has no threshold and is based on probabilities, with the chances of seeing the effect increasing with dose. Cancer is thought to be a stochastic effect.

strategic goals: The overall plan that will be used to control the incident. Strategic goals are broad in nature and are achieved by the completion of tactical objectives.

stridor: High pitched, noisy respirations. Usually indicative of an upper airway obstruction, either foreign or anatomical.

strike team: Up to five of the same kind or type of resource with common communications and an assigned leader.

subdermal: Below the skin.

superinfection: A new infection in addition to one already present.

supply unit: The unit within the support branch of the logistics section responsible for providing the personnel, equipment, and supplies to support incident operations.

sympathetic nervous system: A division of the autonomic nervous system that prepares the body for stressful stimuli (fight or flight).

sympatholytic: A substance that produces effects that inhibit (block) the actions of the sympathetic nervous system, also referred to as antiadrenergic.

sympathomimetic: A substance that produces effects that mimic those of the sympathetic nervous system, also referred to adrenergic.

syncope: A transient loss of consciousness caused by inadequate blood flow.

tactical objectives: The specific operations that must be accomplished to achieve strategic goals. Tactical objectives must be specific and measurable, and are usually accomplished at the division or group level.

tactical ultraviolence: Maximum violence used to accomplish a criminal goal or objective.

task force: A group of any type or kind of resource, with common communications and a leader, temporarily assembled for a specific mission (not to exceed five resources).

technical advisor: Any individual with specialized expertise useful to the management/general staff.

technical specialists: Personnel with special skills who are activated only when needed. Technical specialists may be needed in the areas of rescue, water resources, and training. Technical specialists report initially to the planning section, but may be assigned anywhere within the IMS organizational structure as needed.

teratogenic effects: Effects seen in the offspring of the individual who received the agent. The agent must be encountered during the gestation period.

teratogenicity: Capacity of a substance to produce fetal malformation.

threat assessment: An assessment of a community's vulnerability and potential for natural, technological, and terrorist risks.

time unit: A unit within the finance section. Responsible for record keeping of time for personnel working at incident.

time-weighted averages (TWA): Average concentration for a normal 8-hour work day and a 40-hour work week, to which nearly all workers may be repeatedly exposed without adversity.

toxicity: Property a substance possesses that enables it to injure the physiological mechanism of an organism by chemical means with the maximum effect being incapacitation or death. The relative toxicity of an agent can be articulated in milligrams of toxin needed per kilogram of body weight to kill experimental animals.

toxins: Poisonous substances produced by living organisms.

toxoid: A toxin that has been treated so as to destroy its toxic property, but retain its antigenicity. Its capability of stimulating the production of antitoxin antibodies is retained, thus producing an active immunity.

tracking officer: The EMS IMS organizational position, usually a subcomponent of the transportation sector/group, responsible for tracking all patients removed from the scene or treated and released.

transfer of command: A process of transferring command responsibilities from one individual to another. Commonly a formal procedure conducted in a face-to-face interaction with a event synopsis briefing and completed by a radio transmission announcing that a certain individual is now assuming command responsibility of an incident. A similar transition occurs when a sector/group or division/branch transfers responsibilities.

trauma intervention program (TIPS): A program to manage traumatic stress in emergency responders and disaster victims/families.

transportation sector/group: The EMS IMS organizational component responsible for acquisition and coordination of all patient transport resources. Most times this position is also responsible for coordinating the destination hospital for patients being removed from the scene.

treatment sector/group: The EMS IMS organizational component responsible for collecting and treating patients in a centralized location.

triage: The act of sorting patients by the severity of their medical conditions.

triage sector/group: The EMS IMS organizational component responsible for conducting triage of all patients at an MCI or high-impact incident.

UEL: Upper explosive limits.

unified command: A standard method to coordinate command of an incident when multiple agencies have either functional or geographical jurisdiction. This results in a command system with shared responsibility.

unit: The organizational element having functional responsibility for a specific incident planning, logistics, or finance activity.

unity of command: The concept of an individual being a supervisor at each level of the IMS, beginning at the unit level, and extending upward to the incident manager.

universal precautions: System of infectious disease control which assumes that direct contact with body fluids is infectious (OSHA definition).

Centers for Disease Control and Injury Prevention have published a series of procedures and precaution guidelines to assist the rescuer in fully understanding threat potential and protective measures required.

upwind: In or toward the direction from which the wind blows. Place yourself with the wind blowing toward the suspected release site.

urticaria: Skin condition characterized by intensely itching red, raised patches of skin.

USAR: Urban search and rescue.

U.S. DOT: The United States Department of Transportation. Federal agency responsible for regulating the transportation of hazardous materials.

U.S. DOT hazard classifications: Hazard class designations for specific hazardous materials as delineated in the U.S. DOT Regulations.

V series nerve agents: Generally persistent chemical agents of moderate to high toxicity developed in the 1950s that act by inhibiting a key nervous system enzyme. Examples are VX, VE, VG, VM, and VS.

vaccine: A preparation of a killed or weakened microorganism used to artificially induce immunity against a disease.

vapor agent: A gaseous form of a chemical agent. If heavier than air, the cloud will be down to the ground; if lighter than air, the cloud will rise and dissipate more quickly.

vapor density: A comparison of any gas or vapor to the weight of an equal amount of air.

vapors: Gaseous form of a substance that is normally in a liquid or a solid state at room temperature and pressure.

vesicant agent: *See* **blister agent.**

vesicles: Blisters on the skin.

vesiculation: Formation or presence of vesicles (blisters).

viremia: The presence of a virus in the blood.

virulence: The disease-evoking power of a microorganism in a given host.

virus: A microorganism usually only visible with an electron microscope. Viruses normally reside within other living (host) cells, and cannot reproduce outside of a living cell. It is an infectious microorganism that exists as a particle rather than as a complete cell. Particle sizes range from 200 to 400 nanometers (one-billionth of a meter).

viscosity: Degree to which a fluid resists flow.

volatility: Measure of how readily a substance will vaporize.

vomiting agent: Substance that produces nausea and vomiting effects; can also cause coughing, sneezing, pain in the nose and throat, nasal discharge and tears.

water reactive: Any substance that readily reacts with or decomposes in the presence of water with a significant energy release.

water solubility: Quantity of a chemical substance that will dissolve or mix with water.

weapons of mass destruction (WMD): Weaponization of nuclear, radiological, biological, or chemical substances.

weapons of mass effect (WME): Same definition as WMD, but reflects a more accurate description of the events surrounding use of these type weapons. Destruction is not guaranteed when utilized, but societal effects in many ways can be assured.

x-rays: X-rays are an example of electromagnetic radiation that arises as electrons are deflected from their original paths or inner orbital electrons change their orbital levels around the atomic nucleus. X-rays, like gamma rays, are capable of traveling long distances through air and most other materials. Like gamma rays, x-rays require more shielding to reduce their intensity than do beta or alpha particles. X-rays and gamma rays differ primarily in their origin: X-rays originate in the electronic shell; gamma rays originate in the nucleus.

Index